THE
BELIEVER'S
JOURNEY

God's Path of Transformation

CHRIS PALMER

WESTBOW
PRESS

A DIVISION OF THOMAS NELSON

WestBow Press books may be ordered through booksellers or by contacting:

WestBow Press
A Division of Thomas Nelson
1663 Liberty Drive
Bloomington, IN 47403
www.westbowpress.com
1-(866) 928-1240

ISBN: 978-1-4908-0476-7 (sc)
ISBN: 978-1-4908-0477-4 (hc)
ISBN: 978-1-4908-0475-0 (e)

Library of Congress Control Number: 2013914462

Printed in the United States of America.

WestBow Press rev. date: 8/22/2013

Rev. Palmer's *Believer's Journey* will make you want to rush headlong into an ever-deepening relationship with God—and he gives you the step-by-step Scriptural map of *how* to get there. The personal accounts of his own journey both hearten and enlighten, and dispel any fear about the path into the sacred Unknown. *Brilliant. Simply brilliant.*

—Doug Wead
New York Times best-selling author, historian, and presidential advisor

I proudly recommend *The Believer's Journey: God's Path of Transformation* by Chris Palmer, a greatly needed teaching and a book for today. Chris has done a tremendous job of presenting the Christian walk after the footsteps of Jesus Christ. I love the fact that it's loaded with scriptures and that it's for the everyday believer as well as the minister of the gospel. It covers especially well the Spirit-filled walk and the Spirit-filled life. It is obvious how much study and hard work he has put into this because of the immaculate way he has laid it out and how he has applied his thoughts with the thoughts of God. *May the entire body of Christ get their hands on it, may young preachers use it as a reference book, and may it change lives forever.* Job well done!

—Dr. Mark T. Barclay
Founder and Pastor of Living Word Church and Mark Barclay Ministries
Midland, Michigan

Chris Palmer takes you on an interesting and educational journey that, if read and applied, will transform your life! You will not be the same. *It's a must read for all.*

—Bishop Keith A. Butler
Founder of Word of Faith International Christian Center
Southfield, Michigan

Chris Palmer is a young man with a heart for God. *He preaches the Gospel of Jesus Christ and demonstrates the supernatural power of God through healing and miracles.* We pray God continues to use Chris in a mighty way to reach lost souls for Christ and to raise up many others who also manifest the presence and power of God to this generation.

—Apostle Guillermo Maldonado
Founder and Pastor of King Jesus International Ministry
Miami, FL

Chris Palmer has taken a fresh look at a timeless revelation. This book is a cry for the Body of Christ to return praying in tongues to its proper place of significance in our lives and to reestablish a genuine expectation that the 'God of miracles' is still confirming His word with signs following today. *A much needed insight for ministers and laity alike.*

—Bishop George Davis
Pastor of Faith Christian Center
Jacksonville, FL

Table of Contents

To my Dad—my best friend and hero.

Foreword

It is always an honor to write forewords and comments for friends and sons and daughters of El Rey Jesus. In this case, it is also a privilege to do so for Chris Palmer, a very special son of the house.

The Believer's Journey: God's Path of Transformation deals with the transformation of the believer in order to live the abundant life Jesus promised us and to walk in the fullness of our inheritance. The Word of God teaches that the renewal of our mind is necessary for this transformation, but this can only be done through our reborn spirit, by the power of God's love, and by the leading of His Holy Spirit.

By learning to depend on God, Chris overcame many obstacles that stood in his way of fully enjoying God's inheritance—which is rightfully yours as a child of God—and he has chosen this book to share his personal insight and first-hand experiences to inspire you to overcome your own obstacles, as you trust God to lead you in your personal journey to living a victorious life in Christ.

Reading and understanding God's Word will inspire, restore, transform, and highly bless you. So get ready to "go" and get what is rightfully yours, in Christ.

Apostle Guillermo Maldonado
Founder and Pastor of King Jesus International Ministry
Miami, FL

Acknowledgments

When I first began writing *The Believer's Journey: God's Path of Transformation*, little did I realize that completing this work would be a journey of its own. Countless hours of writing, study, and prayer were placed into pushing this book across the finish line. Fittingly, the content of this book wasn't just developed in my office in Michigan. Rather, it was developed in my journeys to Africa and Europe, and in numerous cities across the United States.

I remember the first week of actual writing, I thought, *I wonder what the final book will look like?* I had no idea at that point that *The Believer's Journey* would end up being such a thorough and comprehensive guide to the Born-Again experience and the Spirit-empowered life that will follow. It can be read for personal use, studied like a textbook, or used as a resource to teach and preach from. Be as it may, hold this revelation close, start mastering it for yourself, and your transformation will be sure.

Like any true journey, I needed others to come alongside me and help assist me along the way. Faithful as He always is, *The Lord* handpicked each and every person who accompanied me. And that is why I give Him the first acknowledgment and make Him The Lord of this work.

Next, are *my parents*, whom I love dearly. Their devotion to me and my ministry, encouragement, and unwavering support kept me confident and steady the whole way. I honor them here.

After the first draft was complete, The Lord brought *Stephanie Carter* to me. I am not sure how she got so involved with the work, other than by the divine providence of God. Her steadfast support never let this book fall short of what it was intended to be. If that weren't difficult enough, putting up with me certainly was. Next to her are *Sharrah Cooley and Della Cooley-Fields*. Their meticulous personalities, sense of humor and straightforwardness, even during the tough times, helped scoot this work along the way.

As the journey went on, The Lord brought forth the brilliant and loving *Mary Achor* to serve as Chief Editor. Mary's exceptional intelligence and heart for the Kingdom served this book in ways that are known only to her and the Father. She made sacrifices for this writing and cared for this work as much as I and at times, I felt, more than myself. Needless to say her role was invaluable.

This journey would never have begun if it had not been for my two big brothers in the Lord, *Rev. Marlin Reid and Pastor Larry Mack*. Much of what they have known for years and have selflessly taught me reverberates through this work. For them I am grateful.

Last, and certainly not least by any means, is *the Romero family— Pacho, Mama Mia, and Carolina*. While standing in the American Airlines Center in Miami, Florida, in October 2011, Mama Mia first envisioned the book you now hold in your hands, and she prophesied that it would be written. Because of their rare love and humility, the Romero's unceasingly held this work up in prayer and never allowed me to tire before I finished. Their love and support brought the book forth from beginning to end. And, when writing got the better of me, the Romero's always found a way to cheer me up—usually with *paella*.

Special thanks, as well, goes to *Apostle Guillermo Maldonado (KJM), Bishop Keith A. Butler (WOFICC), Dr. Mark T. Barclay (MBM), Bishop George Davis (FCC),* and *Doug Wead* for their confidence in this work and for being a part of *The Believer's Journey*.

Although only the author's name is listed on the cover, all of those listed above are just as valuable and responsible for what you are soon to read. I imagine that whatever lives are changed through the words on these pages, we shall all share the same reward for it in the age to come.

Maranatha.
Chris Palmer
Novi, Michigan
June 2013

Introduction

The Lake House was our family's cottage in western Michigan near Muskegon. Year after year, we packed up the car and headed out for fun-filled weekends of swimming, barbecuing, and go-carts. Typically, we started the day at the beach on Lake Michigan. The common way to the beach was to walk the shaded, rocky road where most of the cottages sat. The lane was always crowded, full of people carrying their coolers and inflatable rafts. I can't remember how many years I endured that road, especially since the rocks always made my feet ache.

One day, my uncle said to us kids, "I want to show you something." He took us a few feet from our house to a little path. He asked, "In all your time here, have you kids ever gone down this path?"

All of us looked at each other. "No, we never even noticed it." That wasn't surprising. The path was difficult to see, especially if you were in a hurry to get to the beach, which was always the case. It was a tiny track covered by brush and pine needles.

"Follow me!" he laughed. As we walked down this narrow strip of sand it felt as though we were headed through a time zone into another dimension.

Finally, after climbing over, under, and through snags, we reached a place where the path opened onto a splendid stream. Our eyes got as big as saucers. It was like discovering a new world. This stream became our favorite place to hang out, and it gave us some of our greatest memories over the years. Amazingly, we would have missed out had we not slowed down to notice, then to detour down this tiny, unbidden path.

If you think about it, life is full of paths. As soon as we get into high school we immediately begin to ponder the path of education that we should take. Once we get into college, the academic counselor asks, "Have you begun thinking about your career path?" You nod, and begin making concrete steps toward pursuing your dreams and goals.

Soon you graduate, get a job, and begin to make money. If you are using wisdom and common sense, you will choose to invest. Your financial advisor pulls out a colorful folder full of pamphlets and charts from under his desk and says, "Tell me. Have you decided about what kind of financial path you want to select? Aggressive? Non-aggressive?" At this point in your life, you are single, and you say, "Aggressive!" as the dollar signs begin to roll in your eyes.

When you tire of toys and realize that companionship is now more important, you begin thinking about pursuing a family path. "What kind of mate am I looking for?" Whomever you choose to marry will be a path in and of itself. Talk to married people: it is not uncommon for them to admit that they have wondered where they would be had they married the "other person." Eventually, however, you choose, and the two of you begin planning what kind of family you want. Two kids? Five?

In the fullness of time, you will weary of working, and stroll down the path of retirement, getting joy in seeing your kids go through the same journey you did (and golf, of course).

All this is often called "The Rat Race." In all your busyness, have you ever once stopped to consider that perhaps there is another path besides the rat race? As the world hurries down the road to riches or worldly power or fame, could it be that God has hidden a side path for those who slow down enough to recognize it?

In Mark 10:17-27, a powerful story is told about a nameless individual who has been labeled "the rich young ruler." Here was a young guy with lots of money and power, (and, no doubt, women). His ambitions were fulfilled, his life was a success, he had mastered his course, and he was scrupulous in following the Ten Commandments. However, he was still unhappy at his core. One day, he noticed another Way, named Jesus. When the young man asked Jesus about this path, Jesus didn't attempt to sugarcoat it, or glamorize it, or make it anything that it was not. This disappointed the young guy, who was still attached to the rat race and could not let go, and he turned away, grieved.

If I have learned one thing over the years, it is that God will do nothing to make the path more appealing to us. He doesn't make it extravagant like the Las Vegas strip. (Glitz and glamour is how Satan usually entices us into entrapment.) Instead, God's path will never look anything other than simple and modest. At most, Jesus simply says, "Come." It is like that unassuming path to the lake that was virtually hidden.

God's Word is not a guide to the rat race. It is your guide to His path of power. The Old Testament Prophets speak of it, the Old Testament Books of Wisdom tell of it, Jesus declares it, and the Great Apostle brings it to light. This book, *The Believer's Journey*, has been written to echo them once more. You will discover the sacred path that is woven into the fabric of the New Testament teachings of Jesus Christ and the letters of the Apostle Paul. Through careful consideration and illumination from our Great Teacher, the Holy Ghost, (or Holy Spirit), you will see this path become clearer and richer, purer and deeper, as you prayerfully consider what has been written. Just as my uncle had to show us the hidden path, I have sought to do the same in this book.

Using a careful breakdown of Scripture, I have endeavored to make plain to you the path of Sonship, first blazed for us by the One who loves us and gave Himself for us, Jesus Christ. As all paths lead somewhere, the path of Sonship leads us to the marvelous inheritance that has been laid up for us as sons and daughters of God. By the time you have completed this reading, you will be familiar with this inheritance, and you will have a greater handle on how to walk in that inheritance in this life.

As with every adventure, many trials and difficulties will arise to try and block our progress. In the coming chapters, I have shed light on some of these obstacles. Fortunately, God has given us great and mighty weapons of the Spirit to overcome anything that would thwart our headway. This book reveals many of those spiritual weapons and shines light on how they work and what you can do to utilize them.

I have decided to be transparent in this book in sharing my own life's hurdles. I am certain that much of what I have encountered is quite similar to what you may be facing. Peter said, ***"Knowing that the same afflictions are accomplished in your brethren that are in the world"*** (1 Peter 5:9 KJV). The goal is to show you how I overcame, perhaps cutting down the time you waste trying to figure out how to do the same.

There was once a difficult point in my life where I had grown so weary that I was no longer walking forward down my path. It took some time before I even noticed. But I had reached an impasse that lasted *three long years*. It was not until I turned myself over to my faithful Friend, the Holy Spirit, that I began to come into the truth that I share with you now. This journey marched me out of the misery that stared at me face to face, and it walked me into tremendous power and understanding, resulting in the forces responsible for the miracles and deliverances that follow my ministry.

Remember this vital point: The life we live in Christ is done through our reborn spirit by the power of the Holy Spirit (Romans 8:13-16). It took me a while to learn this, and even more time to live it. Much of the book discloses the truths I picked up absorbing this crucial truth. Get a firm grasp on this, and your life will be a walk of power. You will step into the armor of God, something that is accessible only by revelation knowledge from the Spirit of God.

Be patient as you walk through the Scriptures that we explore. Turn them over and ask the Holy Spirit to form the image within your heart. This is not a race to see how fast you can get through the Scriptures, but a contemplative path meant to change your heart and mind.

You can do it, I assure you. A large portion of this book is dedicated to showing you how to employ the Spirit of God once you are born again. These truths will revolutionize your identity in Christ, accelerate your understanding of the Word of God, fasten you closer to the Holy Ghost, and launch you down a dynamic journey. This will place you on a path that transforms and empowers you to follow it all the way into God, allowing nothing to stop you from what Jesus said that you could be *in* Him. The path will be plain, and you will have what you need to go for it.

We cannot follow two paths; we must decide. Do we keep plodding the rat race, pursuing the desires of our ambitions? Or do we take the Way, the Truth, and the Life? Though the path invites, it does not always look inviting. Though it promises life, it asks us for one thing in return, *our life*. The path has existed since the fall of Adam, and it awaits any pilgrim who desires to take the journey. Henry Ward Beecher wrote, "God asks no man whether he will accept life. That is not the choice. You must take it. The only choice is how."

Before we go any further I want you to pause and pray this prayer:

Father, I am Your child. You have laid a path before me, a path that will walk me out of all the torments, fears, insecurities, and anxieties that this life has brought.

It doesn't matter where I am in life; I can set sail today. Spirit of God, breathe Your wind into my sails and launch me forward. Give unto me the Spirit of wisdom and revelation in the knowledge of You, and let the eyes of my heart be enlightened to know the authority I now have in Christ.

Teach me, Holy Ghost. I have entered the classroom of the Spirit, and my spirit is pliable. Empower me and fill me. May I catch the revelation and spirit that is embedded and entwined into this book.

In Jesus name, Amen.

You are now ready. Let us begin the Journey.

Part I

Who We Become On the Journey

CHAPTER ONE

The Ultimate Blessing of God

**"I soon realized that I am this man.
But it is not only I."**

I dreamed a dream.

There is an ordinary man standing at the beginning of a bright and glorious path. I could say that the path looked like the yellow-brick road in *The Wizard of Oz*, except that I always thought that particular path was a bit bizarre. This new bright road, however, seemed to be saying, "Come along. Take the Journey." Whoever this man in the dream is, poised at the start of the path, I somehow knew that if he had enough guts to go for it, each step forward would equate to another step into transformation and splendor.

I soon realized that I am this man. But it is not only I. It is every human being who wants to go forward into God. The path is unending, as far as the eye can see, with no limits and no barriers. It leads straight into glory.

Too frequently, Christians believe that once we are born again, all that is left is to strive to live a Christian life. But there is more, there is *so* much more. *I have discovered that when you are walking with the Lord in the fullness of fellowship, even achieving the call of God upon your life cannot bring the satisfaction that knowing Him intimately and personally does.* Of course, I desire to fulfill the call of God, but even that is not the highest achievement. *No, the greatest attainment is fellowship and companionship with God.* This happens along a path that shines ever brighter unto the perfect day.

There is a journey right in the Word of God, laid out for those who will come to Him, that leads right *into* Him. I soon realized that this is the walk of fellowship; this is the journey of faith.

Solomon wrote a brilliant metaphor in Proverbs 4:18 (NKJV): ***"But the path of the just is like the shining sun, that shines ever brighter unto the perfect day."*** When Solomon was inspired to write this portion of Proverbs, he was uncovering a great truth: there is a literal path of power that anyone, anywhere, can take as far into God as he or she want to go. In the Amplified Bible, this verse reads:

> *[18]But the path of the [uncompromisingly] just and righteous is like the light of dawn, that shines more and more (brighter and clearer) until [it reaches its full strength and glory in] the perfect day [to be prepared.]* (Proverbs 4:18 AMP)

I first saw this path early in my ministry. I had reached a point where no seminar, book, or conference could satisfy my true inward longings to know the Lord more deeply. Late nights would turn into mornings as I tossed and turned in my bed, hearing my heart crying out for a way to know Him the way I hoped was possible. Days turned into months and months into a couple of years. Yet, my heart wouldn't let me give up the search. Like a treasure hunter in search of gold, using the Bible as my map and the Spirit of God as my guide, I began to uncover this path. The path spans the length of the Bible from Genesis to Revelation and beyond, into the age to come. I noticed it is a path that leads humanity into deeper and deeper fellowship with God, all the while leading us out of every damnable thing that causes us misery. This path was the answer my heart had been searching for and led me to the treasure that had been laid up in store for me: an unlimited fellowship with the Lord. He quickly showed me ways to advance down this path, and with every step, I discovered myself knowing Him deeper.

It wasn't long before I thought, *My God, this is so incredible. The Lord has laid out a path so that every member of humanity can have the ultimate blessing of fellowshipping with the One who created us and gave Himself for us. Any individual can elect to take this path and truly find what their heart is reaching for.*

It soon wasn't enough to take this journey alone. I had to show others how to come along.

CHAPTER TWO

The First Birth

"What is one of the most interesting facts about conception and birth is that, although God knew about it and my parents orchestrated it, I had absolutely nothing to do with it. When I looked the world in the face on that sunny June day, I had no say so whatsoever."

I was born in 1984, June 2, at 10:50 a.m., to be exact. My parents conceived me in September of 1983 in Niagara Falls, Ontario, Canada. When I was a young child, they drove me by the hotel where it happened. Dad said, "To our knowledge, son, this is where it all began for you." The thought of that now is not as welcoming as when my innocence guarded my understanding of what they were actually saying.

God knew that my parents would meet at the Bendix Corporation in 1980, fall in love, get married in 1981, conceive me in 1983, and give birth to me as a healthy, nine pound eight ounce baby boy at Beaumont Hospital in Royal Oak, Michigan.

What is one of the most interesting facts about conception and birth is that, although God knew about it and my parents orchestrated it, I had absolutely nothing to do with it. When I looked the world in the face on that sunny June day, I had no say so whatsoever. I was brought into this world against my will. The path of human life had begun for me and, whether I wanted to or not, I was to be raised to walk the journey of life. I didn't choose the country I was born in (the United States), the parents I was born to (Michael and Susan), the sibling I inherited (Mikey), the religion of my parents (Christian-Pentecostal), the financial tier of my parents (middle class), nor the environment of my home (nurturing and well balanced).

According to the United States Census Bureau in 2010, there are estimated to be around 361,000 births each day all over the world, equaling roughly 251 new, innocent lives born each minute. Take into consideration that there are now 196 countries in the world, each of them having thousands of cities and territories. These countries, cities, and territories are dominated by: culture, history, war or peace, abundance or poverty, health or disease, technology or the lack thereof, political conditions, art and music, and, at the foundation of them all, religion. A worldview is established in time by the fragments that make up society mentioned above, and provides the lenses through which life will be filtered.

Today, one baby's human course began in Iran. He was put into the arms of Shiite parents and will soon become a student of the Quran. Without wasting any time he will begin to say the Takbir ("Allahu Akbar" meaning "God is the greatest"). He will say it when he is happy, and in distress. He will repeat it in formal and informal prayer, during celebrations, and in moments of resolve. If all goes according to plan, he will marry, conceive his own children, and teach them the same. The way of life in which he has been trained is intended to be handed down from generation to generation, endlessly. Any deviation from the route of Islam, as explained very clearly while he is young, would mean his life.

Traveling southeast from Iran, another young boy's course just began in Cambodia. His path of life will be dissimilar from the baby born just minutes before in Iran. Like 95% of other infants born in Cambodia, he will be trained to walk in Theravada Buddhism. As he matures and grows, this young man will not be found in a mosque or fasting during Ramadan. Rather, he will be found in one of Cambodia's 4,000 Buddhist temples, observing the Tipitaka and practicing Samatha meditation, trying to reach enlightenment and realize Nirvana.

Heading northwest to Belgium, another child is born to a family that practices atheism. Since walking away from the Catholic Church as a young man, the father of this new child is convinced that all religions are self-deluded political organizations used to keep the masses under control. He will teach his child to appreciate the liberal thinkers of the Age of Enlightenment that broke the molds of religious orthodoxy, and placed intelligence, philosophy, and reason in eminence. If the parents have anything to do with it, the young man will mature and grow, never seeking anything beyond what his five senses and brain capacity provide him.

If we continue assessing the circumstances into which people begin their course of life, we will eventually have to contend with troubling aspects of the human condition: poverty, starvation, homelessness, pandemics. This would lead us to acknowledge the plethora of children who are born with the AIDS virus each year in Africa. Going beyond AIDS, consider the kids who are born with cleft lips, deformities, excess limbs, or who are conjoined twins attached at the head.

Though some of these horrors are not as common in the United States as they are in developing countries, children all over America are born into their own nightmares and potential hells. In many cities it is common to find fatherless homes offering no positive male influence, gang-run neighborhoods, and bankrupt education systems, leaving those children with little hope of ever getting out. They also share the same risk as suburban homes for child molestation, incest, sexual and verbal abuse, and domestic violence. Having served in pastoral care at a large church that provided ministry to the Detroit, Michigan area, I witnessed everything listed above, and more.

A combination of these experiences, plus my trips overseas, made me aware just how rare it is in this world to be born without some kind of major setback at the start of your life. Indeed, reading this should have caused you to take a subconscious inventory of your own upbringing, pondering the positive and the negative things you were born into. If you can say with certainty that you were born against your will into something that impaired your ability to sprint from the shot of the starting pistol, then you are among the great majority. Physical disabilities, emotional pain caused by tormenting memories of the past, sexual abuse done at the expense of peaceful sleep, and personality disorders resulting from relational imbalances in the home are just a few that scratch the surface. Needless for me to tell you what you already know, these major setbacks could not be prevented, at least not by you.

CHAPTER THREE

The Indictment on God

"People get caught up in accusing God directly for all of the good and bad that happens, without having the understanding that there is a particular order to the universe, and that order is responsible for much of what we have been given, fair or unfair, equal or unequal as it is."

In popular belief, God takes little spirits and sends them into infant bodies as they are born. I have never seen a scripture supporting this idea, any more than any other concerning the how's of procreation. But it just doesn't make sense to believe that God would take an innocent spirit that He made in heaven and send it randomly into a body to grow up and run the risk of going to hell.

Thinking this way would be like believing that spirits come off a heavenly assembly line. Once they are hot and ready to go, God takes these blank slates and sends them down into an earth suit. He sends the first one to an Ethiopian body, where the society is entrenched in Islam. The chances of this child hearing the Gospel and believing are, say, 1/100,000. He sends the second one to an American body in a Christian family in Texas. There is no chance that this child will not hear the Gospel. The chances of her believing are, perhaps, 9/10. He sends the next child to a body in Malawi where the expecting parents intend to have the baby delivered by the local witchdoctor. As soon as its eyes see light, the witchdoctor will hoist the baby up and invite a legion of demonic spirits to fill him. The odds of hearing and believing the Gospel are, say, 1/15,000,000.

If this were the case, I would have to wonder what God was up to. He certainly would be a candidate for injustice. But God is not a respecter of persons (Romans 2:11; Ephesians 6:9). So I hope you aren't

8

too disappointed to find out that there is no spirit-making factory in heaven.

If we asked the six billion people on earth what they were born into, we would be shocked by the answers. I imagine there would be a whole bevy of questions—including a mass indictment—directed at God.

Paul dealt with indictments on God; he was accustomed to hearing believers blame God for misfortune. In Romans 3:1-4 (NLT), Paul was answering a question that he had encountered previously in his apostolic ministry.

> *First of all, the Jews were entrusted with the whole revelation of God. True, some of them were unfaithful; but just because they were unfaithful, does that mean God will be unfaithful? Of course not. Even if everyone else is a liar, God is true.*

Paul is saying that just because Jews were unfaithful, this does not make God unfaithful or ultimately responsible for the consequences of their disobedience.

Paul then makes a case in God's defense: *"As the Scriptures say about Him, "You will be proved right in what you say, and you will win your case in court."* If ever taken to court and put on trial by His creation, God will always be proven just.

Then, in verses 5-6, Paul proves that he understands fully the human thought processes that want to lay off responsibility on someone or something else.

> *5'But,' some might say, 'our sinfulness serves a good purpose, for it helps people see how righteous God is. Isn't it unfair, then, for Him to punish us?' (This is merely a human point of view.)*
> *6Of course not! If God were not entirely fair, how would he be qualified to judge the world? (Romans 3:5-6 KJV)*

One thing the Apostle Paul makes very clear in the third chapter of Romans is this: God is entirely fair. He is just, even within the bounds of

His sovereignty. "But how could that be," you are asking, "when you just pointed out that billions of people are born against their own will into a path of life with a major impairment or disability that will cause them to limp dreadfully through?"

Not too long ago, God was placed on trial by one of my kin, a nurse whom I'll call Natalie. Stationed on the oncology floor, she deals with many cancer patients. She sees that the disease eventually defeats many of them. Nurses tell me they do their best to accommodate the patients with love and care, all the while not getting too close emotionally. Becoming too personally attached could affect their job performance, their private lives, and their emotional health when they punch the clock at the end of the day.

Having the big heart that she has, Natalie courageously made an exception for Renee, who would become her most haunting patient. Renee was a thirty-seven-year-old single mother of two, and a proclaimed believer in Christ, and she was fighting malignant ovarian cancer. I was able to visit her on three or four occasions before she lost her battle.

Renee's death was a devastating blow. Before Natalie met Renee, she had been tirelessly reading books on the authority of the believer, faith, healing, and the supernatural power of God. When the healing principles that these authors were speaking of did not manifest in Renee's life, anger and confusion lodged in Natalie's tender, compassionate heart.

God, Jehovah, Adonai—the sovereign God of Creation—was now going to be prosecuted by the offended. I accompanied Natalie to the funeral and, on the way home, she put God on the hot seat. The accusation came forth in a sweeping statement that reminded me of the verses in Romans. With bitter, salty tears choking her words, she asked: "Chris, how could you say that God is fair? How was He fair to Renee? How is He fair to anyone like Renee, in pain and suffering? How could He be fair in sending anyone to hell? How? How!" I bowed my head in sadness, knowing I couldn't manufacture an answer. This was one of those questions, I felt, comparable to asking me, "Why is the sky blue?" or "Why is a cat called a cat?" I just didn't know what to say.

She continued, "I was talking to my sister and she raised a good point. Nobody ever asked to be born. So, we are just supposed to come into a world against our own will, maybe get lucky and do good, maybe get sick and die, then risk being sent into the endless inferno of hell if we don't subscribe to Christian doctrine? This is the plan of the fair and just God?"

And with that, I began searching for an answer from the Spirit of God. I knew there was a major revelation in this that I had not uncovered at the time. Little did I realize, it had everything to do with the path of the just, which shines more and more unto the perfect day (Proverbs 4:18).

The Psalmist says in Psalms 51:5 (NKJV), ***"Behold, I was brought forth in iniquity, and in sin my mother conceived me."*** This Psalm gives the idea that sin was part of the building material used to construct mankind since the fall (Genesis 3:15-19).

Walk the street in any town or city today and you will observe all kinds of genetic differences. Height, weight, hair color, gender, voice, personality, temperament, race, *ad infinitum*, are results of the genetic code that every individual inherits against his or her own will. I will call this the path of life. The road that you have inherited is by and large determined from the genetics that you have been given.

A famous athlete may attribute practice and time spent in the gym for his or her success, but don't be completely fooled, genetics played a great part in it. How many 5'8" NBA players have ever made any significant contribution to their basketball team? Definitely not as many as those who are 6'8". Fortunes are wrapped up in inherited DNA. A person's voice, mind, talents, and strengths are all building material given through genetics. With the right amount of practice and networking, the person could step into fame and success in an instant. Go to a concert today and I am sure you will hear someone say, "Wow. That voice sure is a gift from God." That could very well be.

However, what do we say about the individual who inherited Down syndrome? Or what about the mentally impaired person, who, with three to four times the effort and assistance, may be able to graduate from high school by the time they are twenty-six? Can anyone say with any confidence that this is an inherited gift of God? No, rather, God goes back onto the hot seat. Indictments are then made again against God, challenging His fairness.

Unfortunately, people get caught up in accusing God directly for all of the good and bad that happens, without having the understanding that there is a particular order to the universe, and that order is responsible for much of what we have been given, fair or unfair, equal or unequal as it is.

The process of procreation is very different. Procreation happens as the result of the observance of order and law. God established the law of procreation, and it has become the order of how human life begins. Procreation is what gave you the path of life. In John 1:13 (NKJV), it says, **"Who were born, not of <u>blood,</u> nor of the <u>will of the flesh,</u> nor of the <u>will of man,</u> but of God."** Before you understand to whom John is referring in the first part of this verse, it is important to know that he lays out the three ways that every person who has been born into this world came about.

1.) Blood: As stated above, the blood of an individual is their testimony of origin. A person's blood speaks of who they are. Through tracing the strands of DNA within, an offspring's parents and ancestry can be determined. This sets the parameters and gives the individual his or her definition.

2.) The Will of the Flesh: People are born today because both or one parent has directly or indirectly willed it. Sexual intercourse is the will of the flesh and results in childbirth. When a man and a woman have sex, they have triggered the potential for an innocent life to enter into the world. Even in the reprehensible case of rape, the law of procreation is still being observed. Every person who passes you as you drive along the freeway has been born through the will of the flesh. At least one of their parents, through a fleshly impulse, made it possible.

3.) The Will of Man: This means having a child for the purpose of extending the family line. Should a father want to keep his wealth and property in the family and place it in hands he can trust, he would will to have an heir to pass it to.

John makes it known through the order of procreation: parents are responsible for the children that they have produced. You didn't ask to be born. I didn't ask to be born. We were born of our parents' blood and brought into this world because of the will of the flesh or the will of man. There are no exceptions to this rule. Everyone has a set of parents. Everyone came about the same way. Everyone inherited his or her parents' DNA. And no child had a say in it.

When God commissioned Adam to be fruitful and multiply (Genesis 1:28), He was giving man the highest responsibility he would ever receive. This was not just telling man to produce physical beings who would till the ground. Instead, He was placing within human stewardship the awesome privilege of bringing eternal creations into the earth at will. Should man, at any point, will to have a child, he can try to have one (the grand purpose of marriage). He doesn't need to ask God for the power to bring about an eternal being. God designated that power to him. What does this mean? It means that God is not making spirits in heaven and sending them down to the earth, but rather, man, by observing the law of genesis, is producing eternal beings every single day. As the population has increased, so has the rate.

There have been only two official "begotten" children of God since Genesis 1:2 and the creation story. The only two individuals named as children of God in the section popularly called "the begats" are Adam and Jesus. Aside from them (and Eve), everyone else is begotten of parents. The difference is that Adam and Jesus were not born by the will of the blood of their parents, nor by the will of the flesh, nor by the will of man. God directly willed it and had His way. From reading Luke 3:23-38, we can see that God had no direct involvement in our first birth to our parents.

Everyone in between Adam and Jesus had a different story. If we read this chronology backwards it would say, "God was the father of Adam, who was the father of Seth, who was the father of Enos, who was the father of Cainan." Adam could claim God as his father because God willed for him to be begotten and created him with dirt and spirit to create the race of human beings (Genesis 2:7). The dust of the earth represents the flesh of our bodies, and the breath of God represents our spirit. Even to think that God creates our spirits in heaven through His breath would mean that He would have to use dirt down here to create our bodies.

Instead, He gave Adam that ability, should he will it. Adam's sperm carried in it the ingredients of body and spirit, and the result was Seth. Seth's sperm carried in it the ingredients of body and spirit, and the result was Enos. Enos's sperm carried in it the result of body and spirit, and the result was Cainan.

In the master blueprint of things, this was a great plan. God placed a perfect law in place and had a perfect creation to carry out that law. Perfect pecple, with eternal, God-like natures, would become fruitful and begin to multiply upon the face of the earth. Intelligence would increase, and God would be able to reveal more and more of Himself to humankind. I am not sure how long Adam and Eve walked the earth perfectly with the potential of this plan in motion. However, something dreadful happened before the first child was even produced. Mankind fell.

CHAPTER FOUR

The Fall of Mankind

"How is a child who was born bright equal in his birth to the child who was born impaired? It was never designed by God to be this way. Sin crept in and began to call the shots."

Through Adam's disobedience, humanity destroyed its perfection. Sin and rebellion embedded itself into Adam's DNA. From Adam, the father, a rebellious and wayward spirit would be passed into every spirit and body entity known as a living human being. Paul gives us a description of this wayward spirit in Romans 3:9-18:

> *⁹They are all under sin;*
> *¹⁰As it is written: "There is none righteous, no, not one;*
> *¹¹There is none who understands; There is none who seeks after God.*
> *¹²They have all turned aside; They have together become unprofitable; There is none who does good, no, not one.*
> *¹³Their throat is an open tomb; With their tongues they have practiced deceit; The poison of asps is under their lips;*
> *¹⁴Whose mouth is full of cursing and bitterness.*
> *¹⁵Their feet are swift to shed blood;*
> *¹⁶Destruction and misery are in their ways;*
> *¹⁷And the way of peace they have not known.*
> *¹⁸There is no fear of God before their eyes."* (Romans 3:9-18 NKJV)

These verses include the symptoms of sin. When Adam willfully rebelled against God, he opened the door and allowed sin to enter into the human race. Sin immediately disoriented everything, and threw off the order in which everything was intended to function. By one man's transgression (Adam), death began to rule and reign. Death and corruption sat on the throne of mankind and lorded over the human race. Sin is a slave master that holds the world hostage (Romans 6:23), and each member of humanity inherits its wayward spirit (Romans 5:14). Sin causes moral transgressions against the law of God. Worse, sin is a moral crime against God's holiness.

What did not get obliterated, however, was the law of procreation. That law stayed the same, but the order of it grew distorted. Instead of everyone being born the same, equal and fair, sin and death saw to it that corruption had its way.

Thomas Jefferson wrote in the Declaration of Independence, "We hold these truths to be self-evident, that all men are created equal." What he meant was that each human has equal rights and should be treated equally in the eyes of government because we are equal in the sight of God. This is true. There is no apex race of people.

However, is this statement true in light of what is said above concerning the conditions people are born into? How is the child born with genetics of a skier equal in his birth to the child born without a leg? How is a child who was born bright equal in his birth to the child who was born mentally impaired? It was never designed by God to be this way. Sin crept in and began to call the shots. Unless the order in which sin ruled was interrupted, every child born would be dependent upon the randomness of chance, in hopes he or she wouldn't receive a major disadvantage. In human birth, nobody would ever be born equal again. God's order had been replaced by sin. Sin is the reason things are no longer fair. The law of procreation is what brought you into this world against your own will, and the law of sin and death is what is responsible for the corruption seen in innocent babies.

Since Adam was responsible for inviting sin and rearranging the order, God (however illogically) could be successfully indicted by the masses and masses of people who have been affected by sin, and even more severely, for the masses of those who have gone to hell. Yet, the prophets spoke of the goodness of God that lay in the promise of a divine hope (1 Peter 1:10-12).

John, two thousand years later, answered the prophets by echoing back with his writings. The *Logos* had come. If anyone ever had a revelation of the Son of Man, it was the Apostle John. His Gospel and epistles shed more light on who Christ is in His humanity and in His divinity than any of the other books of the Bible.

The following two portions of Scripture were written after John had become a spectator of Jesus Christ's death, burial, and resurrection. John, writing of his encounters with Jesus, says:

> *¹That which was from the beginning, which we have heard, which we have seen with our eyes, which we have looked upon, and our hands have handled, concerning the Word of life—*
> *²the life was manifested, and we have seen, and bear witness, and declare to you that eternal life which was with the Father and was manifested to us—*
> *³that which we have seen and heard we declare to you.*
> (1 John 1:1-3 NKJV)

Similar to this account, John writes in his Gospel:

> *¹In the beginning was the Word, and the Word was with God, and the Word was God.*
> *²He was in the beginning with God.*
> *³All things were made through Him, and without Him nothing was made that was made.*
> *⁴In Him was life, and the life was the light of men.*
> (John 1:1-4 NKJV)

In this eyewitness account, both in his Gospel and first epistle, John begins with the origin of Jesus Christ. In John there is no birth account, as in Matthew and Luke. And unlike Mark, John doesn't begin with an account of John the Baptist. Instead, John passionately begins his testimony by letting his audience know that this Man is the embodied source of life. This Jesus is responsible for creating everything seen and unseen, known and unknown.

The greatest part of John's revelation was in his understanding that Jesus Christ is the epicenter and source of all life. If you were to wander through his writings, you would notice that the theme of "light" and "life" dominate every other major theme that you can find. The Spirit of God made sure that John captured this vital revelation about the Son of God and passed it on to us.

Often people get hung up in John 1:1 when Jesus is called "The Word". I have heard people go as far as saying that this is a reference to the Bible. Obviously that is not what John had in mind, since: 1.) The canon had not yet been formed, and 2.) This was intended to be an eyewitness account of what John had seen in the person of Jesus. Rather, the "Word" comes from the Greek word: *Logos*. John selected this term well, perhaps knowing that it was first used in 600 BC by a Greek philosopher, Heraclitus, to describe the divine plan, which is responsible for the always-changing events of universal affairs.

So, if it weren't enough to *be* the Creator, the Logos interrupted the course of history and the earthly condition of mankind by shredding the dimension of invisibility and *becoming* embodied as God-Man. The prophets foretold of this event (Romans 1:2; 16:25-26 KJV), and Paul agreed that it had occurred exactly as John had witnessed, ***"But when the fullness of the time had come, God sent forth his Son, born of a woman, born under the law"*** (Galatians 4:4 NKJV). What follows in John's account are vivid descriptions of the humble unknown from Galilee, the stem of Jesse, (Isaiah 11:1-2), who came to change the destiny of every man, woman, and child.

The Divine Plan of God, seen in a human body, had arrived to interrupt the order of sin and corruption and realign God's plan for mankind. Although the first birth (John 1:13) inevitably promised to be unfair and unequal, the *Logos* came to provide a second birth that would enable anyone, irrespective of circumstance, situation, or condition, to get off the path of what they had been born into, and get onto the path that would shine brighter and brighter unto the perfect day.

You didn't have a say in your first birth. So, my cousin was right; it isn't fair. We didn't ask to be born. We didn't will our lives or the circumstances that we have inherited. We aren't all born equals.

But, friend, I have Good News. There is a *second* birth. And this second birth provides you with everything that you need to walk right into God, without any limitation. God interrupted all of that unfairness and sent to us the Son of Man, the Logos. Through Him, we can begin getting back what sin took from us. Have you heard of the second birth?

CHAPTER FIVE

The Second Birth

"Jesus was the *people's* champion."

Sitting on the mountainside, people are waiting with abated breath to hear what the Son of God has come all the way from heaven to say. The writings of the Old Testament have set the stage, and the people are ready. Everything grows quiet as the Messiah begins to speak. It is, at last, time for the heart-tingling Sermon on the Mount that will touch billions of lives in the centuries to follow. He serenely sets the standards for our hearts and minds.

Yet, in the last part of His sermon, Jesus warns:

> *¹³Enter by the narrow gate; for wide is the gate and broad is the way that leads to destruction, and there are many who go in by it.*
> *¹⁴Because narrow is the gate and difficult is the way which leads to life, and there are few who find it.*
> (Matthew 7:13-14 NKJV)

I used to love to preach this verse when I was in high school. I preached my first sermon to over 150 high school students when I was a freshman. From that point, my preaching career began to blossom. Coming from a church that emphasized toiling to do that which was upright, I tried to find a way to belt out this verse, usually around the altar call. It was effective, and people gave their hearts to Christ. For that I am thankful. If God puts His approval on it, it becomes anointed, and He can use it. However, the further the Holy Ghost brought me, the more light He began to shed on this verse. As we pray and learn, we are always growing into more and more light of God's Word (1 John 1:7). The more revelation that we receive, the fuller our understanding of Christ becomes, resulting in more liberty and freedom from the damnable things that Christ delivered us from.

I soon realized that I was preaching it backwards. I had been beating people over the head with it and warning them of the hell that waited them if they stayed along the wide path. "Brothers and sisters, hear me! Many people tonight will wind up in hell! Many people have chosen the path of destruction! Don't make the same choice! You might walk out of here, crash your car into a tree, and if the paramedics can't glue you back together, you'll find yourself regretting not coming down to this altar as you burn in the fires of Hades!"

I was a tough preacher. I was so tough, I can remember seeing the same people responding to this altar call over and over again, crying the same tears they shed the week before. This was because I had had years and years of church where the pastors beat into me a sin-consciousness. All I had heard were the follies of sin, and the need to do right.

I am not saying that we shouldn't ever preach hell under the anointing of the Holy Ghost. We must never deviate from warning people of eternal punishment. If there is any preacher who believes in the reality of hell, it is I. Promiscuous grace and the "gospel of inclusion" are heresies. Hell exists, and people are going there every day.

Yet, Jesus knew that the Father is the source of goodness, forbearance, and patience. ***"The goodness of God leads you to repentance"*** (Romans 2:4 NKJV). The whole reason He came was to shine forth God's love for humankind. ***"For God did not send His Son into the world to condemn the world, but that the world through Him might be saved"*** (John 3:17 NKJV).

Jesus did not have a message of condemnation. The only places we see Him condemning anything are when He is contesting with the religious hypocrites of His day (Matthew 23:13-23). Jesus was the *people's* champion. The religious leaders hated Him because He was freeing the people from the bondage that the High Priests had put them in, with centuries of hypocritical Judaism and their insistence on people observing masses of impossible, entangling laws.

Because of sin, we are all born on the path that leads to destruction. We come into the world, are sinners against our own will, and experience

21

misery and death. Despite the short periods of temporary happiness and delight, there is always the inevitable sickness, tragedy, and suffering. The further we walk down the wide path, the more wretchedness we stumble into, until finally, we have to pay the price of our sins through eternal separation from God. Another name for the path that leads to destruction is the *first birth*.

But, in a sudden stroke of divine providence, Jesus reveals the hope of the prophets, and the people's hearts leap. Jesus tenderly tells them: "There is another path. I am that path. I am the way, the truth, and the life. Through me, you can get off the path of the first birth. You can have a second birth. You can be born—again. The reason why I have come is to offer you another path to walk on. In time, my work will make it all possible. Follow me." The intent of Jesus' teachings about the broad and narrow ways was to illustrate the revelation of a great truth. He was revealing the reason why He had come. If there was ever a verse that pointed toward His goodness, it is John 14:6 (KJV), ***"I am the way, the truth, and the life."***

The next thing Jesus does in the context of the Sermon on the Mount is to warn the people of false prophets that will destroy their souls (Matthew 7:15-20). These are hypocrites and religious leaders that Jesus called "whited sepulchers," painted beautifully on the outside, but full of dead men's bones. They are products of the first birth, and nothing they promise can change that, even though they believe that they are upright before God.

Jesus then addresses people who hold onto the deceits of religion and refuse to follow Him into His work, ***"And I will profess unto them, I never knew you: depart from me, ye that work iniquity"*** (Matthew 7:23 KJV). Because these religious leaders had refused the path that Christ had blazed, they were eventually lost in their sins. They were lost because *they* were born into the first birth. However, they remained lost because *they* had refused the second birth. Jesus ends His sermon by saying:

> ***²⁴Therefore whoever hears these sayings of Mine, and does them, I will liken him to a wise man who built his house on the rock;***

> *²⁵and the rain descended, the floods came, and the winds blew and beat upon that house; and it did not fall, for it was founded upon the rock.*
> *²⁶"But every one who hears these sayings of Mine, and does not do them, will be like a foolish man who built his house on the sand:*
> *²⁷and the rain descended, and the floods came, and the winds blew and beat on that house; and it fell. And great was its fall.* (Matthew 7:24-27 NKJV)

This Scripture obviously illustrates wisdom in all kinds of things in our own lives, not the least of which is building our lives on the bedrock that is Christ. But, in the truest form of context, this is referring to a judgment. Floods were always a final and last judgment that sealed the fate of the guilty. The most notorious example we have of a flood is the deluge of Noah's day (Genesis 6-9). Because Noah followed God's instruction, even though the waves and winds beat against his ark, he was saved. Yet for the rest of the world, those who refused the voice of the prophet Noah, the winds and waters collapsed society, and they were lost.

In due time, God's wrath must come down on sin (Romans 1:18). But Jesus came to place the world on a path that would steer them *around* that judgment. Jesus, out of love and compassion, warned that any one who kept people from getting on this path was a hindrance to the work of God, and was a false prophet. The end of these people would be harsh judgment, indeed.

Jesus was teaching that it was this second birth that would change the heart of a person, putting him or her along a different path, keeping them from the judgment that awaits the world. So we don't need to be anxious or apprehensive in any way. We are free to get on the path that Christ laid for us and walk as far into God as we want.

compare Noahs flood with Jesus

CHAPTER SIX

True Christianity:
The Blessed Gift of Sonship

"God didn't send Jesus into the world so that He could just have Christians. He sent Jesus so that He could make sons (and daughters)."

But as many as received Him, to them He gave the right to become children of God, to those who believe in His name. (John 1:12 NKJV)

And because you are sons, God has sent forth the Spirit of His Son into your hearts, crying out, "Abba, Father!" (Galatians 4:6 NKJV)

If you have spent more than two years sitting in pews of a church, take a moment to inventory all the sermons and teachings you have heard. If you were to make a list of the top three things you have been taught, what would they be? I have done this mental arithmetic on numerous occasions and can identify a number of wonderful things. So I am not criticizing or demanding any kind of change in what should be taught at your church.

What I am trying to do is to emphasize what the Gospel of the Lord Jesus Christ really boils down to: It is Sonship. The Holy Ghost sparked me to begin a greater study on the area of Sonship when I heard Him whisper to my heart: "God didn't send Jesus into the world so that He could just have Christians. He sent Jesus so that He could make sons (and daughters)."

I realize how this statement could be a bit shocking for some. Allow me to explain.

It wasn't until Acts 11:26, during Barnabas and Saul's (the Apostle Paul) time in Antioch that the name "Christian" was first used. The word is used two other times in Scripture (Acts 26:28; 1 Peter 4:16) and simply means "a follower of Christ."

There have been countless Christians whose loyalty in following Christ led to their deaths. Many early followers of Christ lost their life in the process of holding onto that which they believed. Peter walked the walk and was eventually hung on an X-shaped cross, upside down. Mark was dragged through the streets by horses until he died. Luke was hung in Greece. Bartholomew was flayed to death with a whip. Paul answered persecution by exhorting believers to embrace it as if it is unavoidable in 2 Timothy 3:12 (KJV): ***"Yea, and all that will live godly in life shall suffer persecution."***

Now, of course, this didn't mean a Christian was *supposed* to go looking for persecution. It just meant they were to embrace it if it came, as a legitimate follower. Could there be anything greater than a bona fide follower, who glories in tribulation (Romans 5:3)?

Let's think about this. What makes a Christian different, in the purest definition of the word, from a follower of Mohammed? Millions of Mohammed's followers have followed their faith to the death. Probably the most horrific instance, fresh in our minds, is the group of hijackers who organized and carried out the 9/11 attacks. They were genuine followers of Mohammed.

Google the phrase, "Buddhist monk sets himself on fire," and you will see the world famous picture of a bona fide follower of Buddhism, losing his life to propagate his faith.

Is following our Master to the death what separates the Christian? Does this give us our significance as followers, that we are capable of loyalty unto death, the paramount trait of any follower? Obviously not. The term "Christian" as a *follower* of Christ should not be denigrated in any way, but being a follower is not the pinnacle of Christ's work. There is more to the Christian faith, and it is this that gives Christianity its uniqueness. *It is the blessed gift of Sonship.*

The New Testament's major emphasis is man's *transformation to becoming a child of God*. The Gospels are the testimony of Jesus Christ who made all of this possible. The letters that Paul wrote to the Churches (the Pauline Revelation) are a divine explanation of what has become of those who have accepted the sacrifice of Christ.

Too often the saints of God get caught up in "trying": trying to witness, trying to have church, trying to pray, trying to cast out devils, trying to heal the sick, trying to live for Jesus. When a believer is *taught* the revelation of Paul and it begins to sink into the confines of their spirit, their whole life will begin to change. When we *catch* the revelation of Paul, no longer will we have to *try* to live for Christ. Instead, Christ will live through us. Our walk with God will become a delight. All of the aspects of that walk will simply fall into place, and we will be free from any self-condemnation. This begins when we understand the *second* birth, the dawning of our Sonship with God, the putting forth of our lives onto a brand new path that leads unto life.

CHAPTER SEVEN

The Light and Life of Christ

"What occurs when two opposing forces come speeding at one another with momentous force? Something has got to give. Darkness always gives way to the light."

¹³And leaving Nazareth, He came and dwelt in Capernaum, which is by the sea, in the regions of Zebulun and Nephthali,
¹⁴That it might be fulfilled which was spoken by Isaiah the prophet, saying:
¹⁵"The land of Zebulun and the land of Naphtali, By the way of the sea, beyond the Jordan, Galilee of the Gentiles:
¹⁶The people who sat in darkness have seen a great light, and upon those who sat in the region and shadow of death, Light has dawned." (Matthew 4:13-16 NKJV)

Jesus, the *Logos*, is described here as "light." When He entered into Zebulun and Nephthali, the darkness that covered those areas disappeared just as it does when you flick the lights on in a dark basement. This verse has always been one of my personal favorites because it gives us a picture of the triumphant Christ. The picture ultimately becomes more triumphant and will lead us to the meaning of the Beatitudes, if we can put our finger on what is meant by "light" and "darkness." The better job we do at defining what these two terms refer to, the greater our understanding becomes.

¹In the beginning was the Word, and the Word was with God, and the Word was God.

Jesus was from the start in genesis

> *²He was in the beginning with God.*
> *³All things were made through Him, and without Him nothing was made that was made.*
> *⁴In Him was life, and the life was the light of men.*
> *⁵And the light shines in the darkness, and the darkness did not comprehend it.*
>
> *⁹That was the true Light which gives light to every man coming into the world.*
> *¹⁰He was in the world, and the world was made through Him, and the world did not know Him.*
> *¹¹He came to His own, and His own did not receive Him.*
> *¹²But as many as received Him, to them He gave the right to become children of God, to those who believe in His name.* (John 1:1-5, 9-12 NKJV)

In the first two verses of John 1, the Logos is seen existing in the eternal past, an equal counterpart with the Father. These verses reinforce Genesis 1:1-2. The Logos is the second person of the Godhead and is the source of everything, seen and unseen.

In the next verse, we see the Logos' role in creation. Whereas the Father *upholds* the drafted plan of creation designed by the Godhead (1 Corinthians 3:23; 11:3) and the Holy Spirit *furthers* the plan (Luke 1:35), the Logos is the agent of the Godhead who *created* everything and brought it into existence. He is the head of everything seen and unseen. Through Him everything that contains life has its origin (Colossians 1:16-17).

Many times we hear the terms, "God's wisdom," "God's love," "God's power," or "God's life." Mistakenly, we think, "God *has* wisdom," "God *has* love," and "God *has* life." If that were the case, then from whom did He obtain them? Where did He acquire them?

No. God doesn't *possess* wisdom, love, power, life; He *is* wisdom, power, love, life. They exist *because* of Him (Proverbs 8:22-36). They are the essence of what springs forth out of Him.

Paul tells us in 1 Timothy 6:16 (KJV) that God dwells **"in a light which no man can approach unto."** This light of glory is composed of all that God is. The ingredients of God's glory include the purest forms of love, wisdom, joy, peace, gentleness, faith, forbearance, virtue—the list goes on.

By the time we get to the fourth verse of John 1, a significant event takes place. In verse 3, the life and light is seen in an eternal state, in the heavenlies. In verse four, the Essence of Life goes from an eternal state and wraps Himself in human flesh: ***"But made himself of no reputation, and took upon him the form of a servant, and was made in the likeness of men"*** (Philippians 2:7 KJV). When the majesty and splendor of the Godhead takes the form of a body, in the person of Jesus Christ, it gets called life. The last time that the earth had witnessed this kind of life was in the Garden of Eden, before Adam had sinned (Genesis 2:7). Since that time, mankind had been living spiritually dead, corrupted by sin. But with Jesus, such was not the case; He was the first man since Adam to be born spiritually alive.

The Scripture tells us that Christ had a different origin than Adam's descendants. Anyone who is a child of Adam through birth has inherited physical life, but also spiritual death. First, Thessalonians 5:23 informs us that we are made up of body, soul, and spirit. Our body is the shell that houses who we really are, a spirit. The spirit of man possesses a mind, a will, emotions, and a conscience, which are the components of the soul. At birth, sin is embedded into our spirits and separates us from God.

As we've said before, this rebellious gene came from our fathers, and our fathers got it from our grandfathers, and our grandfathers from our great-grandfathers, all the way back to Adam. Have you ever noticed that although Eve was technically the first to rebel, we are punished because of Adam's sin (Romans 5:12-21)? The reason is because it is the father who passes down sin.

Humanity, being driven by the whips of sin, was walking a road that got darker and darker as every minute passed. Christ, composed of the life and nature of God, was walking the altogether different path that shone more and more unto the perfect day (Proverbs 4:18). Not being born of Adam, the Logos interrupted what Paul refers to as the **"course of this world"** (Ephesians 2:2 KJV). Since He wasn't born of Adam, Jesus didn't inherit Adam's sinful DNA, therefore He walked the earth, blazing another trail. With every step, Christ was building a road that differed from the one that the multitudes had been on for over 4,000 years. Man's spirit was

We are a body, soul and spirit

But Adam chose to disobeyed God so Jesus had the same option but he obeyed God dead, not having any fellowship with God, but Christ's spirit was alive, in perfect union with the Father. The difference was their genesis.

By the time Jesus Christ had reached the age of thirty He had grown in wisdom and stature (Luke 2:52), and had begun His ministry. This ministry was quite simple in its essence: Proclaim to the world the new path that the world could get on, made possible through a new birth, compliments of His death, resurrection, and ascension into heaven. More than just preaching this great truth, the Son of God would demonstrate His path by healing the sick, raising the dead, casting out devils, and restoring sight to the blind. Whatever was in the clutches of bondage because of the disorder of sin, Christ would put it back into order, demonstrating the life God originally designed humanity to have.

When we get to Matthew 4:16, we see the crossing of two paths. When Jesus entered Capernaum, light came into contact with darkness. Before the Holy Ghost opened up my understanding, I used to think that "the people which sat in darkness" was referring to those involved in deeply grotesque sins. I imagined Capernaum to be a place full of rapists, murderers, child molesters, raging demoniacs, and insane people.

Though it may have included those, "those that sat in darkness" is referring to everyone born of the *first* birth. These are the people born into sin against their own will, headed down the grievous path of darkness that leads to destruction. It included husbands, wives, mothers, fathers, brothers, sisters, teachers, rabbis, lawyers, tax collectors, fishermen, Jews, Samaritans, Romans. Not one person was excluded (Romans 3:23).

What happens when light meets darkness? What occurs when two opposing forces come speeding at one another with momentous force? Something has got to give. Darkness always gives way to the light.

> *[24]Then His fame went throughout all Syria; and they brought to Him all sick people who were afflicted with various diseases and torments, and those who were demon-possessed, epileptics, and paralytics; and He healed them.*
> *[25]Great multitudes followed Him--from Galilee, and from Decapolis, Jerusalem, Judea, and beyond Jordan.* (Matthew 4:24-25 NKJV)

This is a marvelous verse. Where Matthew 4:16 introduced the light, this verse *demonstrates* the light. The life of God began to replace the death, sin, and corruption of the first birth. These ill people in Matthew 4:24-25 weren't nobodies. They were people with names, personalities, temperaments, families, personal lives, and vivacity behind their eyes. They were all unfairly and unjustly affected by the first birth. Included in this mix could have been Renee from the hospital, my grandmother Lucia who died of lung cancer, and any person that you know to be suffering. It may even include you.

After Jesus Christ makes a mockery of corruption's power through the life that is in Him, the Word says, ***"Great multitudes followed Him."*** Down in hell, the eyebrows of the devil had to be cringing in confusion above his beady eyes. The Savior had arrived, and He was pulling people off the path of darkness and leading them to the foot of the new path of life.

Now, with a multitude of followers, the Light that illuminates every human sits down on the mountain to explain the life that humanity can now enter through this new path.

Enter the Beatitudes.

The Beatitudes were always a source of intimidation for me. I memorized almost two hundred Scriptures while I was in college. The Beatitudes were not any of them. As a young boy attending Sunday school, I remember beautifully illustrated coloring books that tried to illuminate the mystique contained within these lessons of Jesus. I went years thinking, "Gosh, how come I can't be impressed with these teachings?" I, at least, had enough sense to know that there was some kind of revelation to be gained within the Beatitudes. Still, sermons here and there would contain the Beatitudes, and I'd have to force my drifting mind back to the sermon.

One night, I took a seat in a back room of my friend Larry's church, and began praying in the Holy Ghost while reading the Word of God. It wasn't long until I noticed that the Holy Spirit had gotten into that room with me. I went into meditation, which is a word describing the process that occurs when the Holy Spirit starts opening up His Word to your understanding.

When the Holy Spirit was through with me that chilly fall night, I couldn't wait to preach the Beatitudes. I realized that they were more than nine simple nuggets of truth. They are all separate strokes of color that, when combined, form one great picture. The Beatitudes had finally come alive, and I took them to California and preached them at the first conference I ever hosted out there.

> *³Blessed are the poor in spirit: for theirs is the kingdom of heaven.*
> *⁴Blessed are they that mourn: for they shall be comforted.*
> *⁵Blessed are the meek: for they shall inherit the earth.*
> *⁶Blessed are they which do hunger and thirst after righteousness: for they shall be filled.*
> *⁷Blessed are the merciful: for they shall obtain mercy.*
> *⁸Blessed are the pure in heart: for they shall see God.*
> *⁹Blessed are the peacemakers: for they shall be called the children of God.*
> *¹⁰Blessed are they which are persecuted for righteousness' sake: for theirs is the kingdom of heaven.*
> *¹¹Blessed are ye, when men shall revile you, and persecute you, and shall say all manner of evil against you falsely, for my sake.*
> *¹²Rejoice, and be exceeding glad: for great is your reward in heaven: for so persecuted they the prophets which were before you.* (Matthew 5:3-12 KJV)

When I had meditated this thoroughly, I could see Jesus as the master artist, sitting at His easel, using words instead of paint, to draw a picture upon the canvas of His followers' hearts. What was Jesus describing? Look at the qualities:

1.) A poor spirit gains access to the Kingdom of Heaven—having been made rich with the opulent resources of heaven.
2.) A sorrowful and mourning spirit receives encouragement and strength.

3.) Meek, in Scripture, doesn't mean some flabby, gutless soul. It refers to those who, knowing that they have no strength in and of themselves, humbly and obediently accept God's will and plan, and thus receive all.

4.) Those who have constantly desired and sought for righteousness as much as a starving man desires food are filled, and placed into right standing with God.

5.) Those who have forgiven and who have not repaid wrong with wrong are forgiven and shown that same mercy.

6.) Those whose pure intentions have been to reach God eventually reach Him.

7.) Those who work for peace with God eventually become the children of God.

8.) Those who desire to enter into righteousness eventually receive this free gift, and receive a massive amount of persecution. Despite the tribulation, they enter into the Kingdom of Heaven.

9.) Those individuals who follow Jesus to the path that leads to life, despite the persecution and false accusations made against them, enter into eternal life, receiving the reward that comes from God.

Are you beginning to see what Jesus was referring to? The Master Teacher began His teaching ministry by describing the *second birth*! In the Beatitudes, Jesus is outlining the life of a reborn human spirit, illuminated by the Light that came to light every human who would believe on Him. Jesus was talking extensively about the new creation reality that is possible in Him. How marvelous it must have been to see the ministry of Jesus in action, to witness the Light of the world and His powerful acts. If that weren't already enough, Jesus goes on to say:

> *14You are the light of the world. A city that is set on a hill cannot be hidden.*
> *15Nor do they light a lamp and put it under a basket, but on a lampstand, and it gives light to all who are in the house.*

> **¹⁶*Let your light so shine before men, that they may see your good works and glorify your Father in heaven.*** (Matthew 5:14-16 NKJV)

Jesus was announcing that the life of God would light the spirit of each man and woman who followed Him. Each person who encountered Him *and believed* would be pulled out of darkness and enter into the Light of life. Notice that good works are *not* the great emphasis of this verse. The good works are the *result* of being lit by the Light of the world. Hence, the Beatitudes are about becoming before doing. They are about being before working. I realized that the Beatitudes had frustrated me in time past because I did not understand this crucial principle. *The Beatitudes are not something you do; they are something you become.*

I have met countless people in my life and ministry who have been brought out of radical darkness into light. These people have legitimately encountered the Light of the world. When they walk into any room where other people are present, the atmosphere changes, sadness halts, and gloom pauses. Can you identify what I am talking about? Even the look and the expression on their faces appear angelic and radiant with life.

Often, in one way or another, people tell me: "I see life behind your eyes. When I look at you, I can see something pure and radiant." These people usually don't know it, but through my eyes, they are looking directly at my spirit. They are encountering a reborn human spirit that has come out through the second birth. What they will eventually notice is that every time they see me, my radiance will grow brighter, and the life will grow deeper. I have been placed upon the path of the righteous, and I shine brighter and brighter with every step I take, all thanks to Jesus.

CHAPTER EIGHT

The Purpose of an Unkeepable Law

"A flawless God gave the Law to Israel, *knowing* they would be unable to keep it. "'Why would He ever do such a thing, Chris? It sounds indictable.'"

Unless someone is sick and twisted, he believes in doing good, more or less. It's easy to find people who give to charities, donate their time to good causes, and serve their communities in a positive way. These things can be accomplished without ever having experienced spiritual life and right standing with God. There is, however, something lacking. There is a vast difference in good works done for reward, and those that are the byproduct of a spirit that has been lit with the life of God.

Things were much the same in Jesus' day as we see today. Vain words had pushed people towards religiosity and the idea that we must *work* to get God to extend His hand toward us. Certainly Jesus' teaching about this freedom of the second birth was a doctrine that the people had never heard before. Paul said, regarding what Christ taught (and which he later expounded in his letters):

> *17But God be thanked that though you were slaves of sin, yet you obeyed from the heart that form of doctrine to which you were delivered.*
> *18And having been set free from sin.* (Romans 6:17-18 NKJV)

When Jesus started teaching these things, accusations arose in people's hearts: "Is He saying we don't need the Law of Moses anymore? Can we throw the Law away? Who does He think He is that He is above the works of the Law?"

What is the Law, and why was it so important to the people of Israel? The Law contains the Ten Commandments and the endless convoluted dietary and other laws of Leviticus. The sum total of the Law made up the moral and religious rules that were to guide the nation of Israel *until the coming of the Messiah.* Among these include the observance of Sabbath days, the offering of sacrifices, the feasts of Jehovah, and the countless commands that make up the scores of regulations and rules that Israel possessed.

When Jesus started teaching a new dispensation, the people condemned Him, or at least looked at Him askance, fearfully. They thought they were protecting what God had given.

Knowing the fears of the people's hearts, Jesus replied:

> [17]***Do not think that I came to destroy the Law or the Prophets. I did not come to destroy but to fulfill.*** [18]***For assuredly, I say to you till earth and heaven pass away, one jot or one tittle will by no means pass from the law till all is fulfilled.*** (Matthew 5:17-18 NKJV)

At this point, the whole world had only experienced the first birth. The Law had been delivered to a world of people who were spiritually dead; it was actually a step up from what had been in ancient days. An "eye for an eye" replaced "death for an eye," for example. Paul later shed a massive amount of light on this truth in his great masterpiece, the book of Romans.

In giving the Law, God knew that the world was never going to be able to maintain it consistently. Though the Law was good and holy (Romans 7:12), the Children of Israel did not have the ability to keep it in its fullness. This is why Israel had to have a High Priest go into the Holy of Holies once a year to make atonement for them. Had people been able to keep the Ten Commandments, this would have been unnecessary. Oh, the people desired to keep the Ten Commandments. Having been born in bondage to sin, however, this was not ever possible; *sin always wins the battle over human will power.*

because human will power is powerless without God.

> *²²For I delight in the law of God after the inward man:*
> *²³But I see another law in my members, warring against the law of my mind, and bringing me into captivity to the law of sin which is in my members.*
> (Romans 7:22-23 KJV)

A flawless God gave the Law to Israel, *knowing* they would be unable to keep it. "Why would He ever do such a thing, Chris? It sounds indictable."

The Law was given as a schoolmaster, to teach everyone the truth concerning their nature and the course of the world (Galatians 3:24). It was to make people realize their need to be regenerated and to give them a way, through the keeping of ordinances, to nurture a faith in the Messiah who was to come. The Law, however, could not change the heart of a man. It was never given to create a clean heart (Psalms 51:10). It lacked regenerating power.

God first had to prove the need for a Redeemer, legally. The Law revealed to Israel the sinful nature that was in them, from Adam. Up to this point, they had been unable to see that nature. This would be the preparation necessary to bring the Messiah into the world, to redeem the world from sin and death.

Before the time of the Law, God winked (turned His head) at sin (Acts 17:30), allowing mankind to be led by its conscience. It did not work. God's Word says, *"Then the Lord saw that the wickedness of man was great in the earth, and that every intent of the thoughts of his heart was only evil continually"* (Genesis 6:5 NKJV). Without God, neither conscience nor the Law could do away with the problem of sin.

With an imposed Law that Israel (and ultimately the whole world) was unable to keep, there was nothing left but to conclude that the world was cursed. This curse is known as the *"curse of the law"* (Galatians 3:13 KJV). It is the inability to keep the Law *because* of the deadness of nature inherited in the first birth.

Religiosity became the stumbling block as Israel began to ignore the hope given to the prophets concerning the Messiah, and started believing they could have a relationship with God, solely through the Law. The idea that simply observing the Law was adequate corrupted the religious order of Judaism and zapped it of the power and purpose it once held.

By Jesus' day, Judaism had become a political organization, and a corrupt one. The High Priest was a tyrant, and the sects of Judaism (Pharisees, Sadducees, Essenes, and Zealots) were hypocrites full of guile, having no understanding of God and twisting the Law to serve their own purposes. They became Christ's greatest challenge on the earth, and eventually were ruined in their blindness by putting Jesus on the cross.

In Matthew 5:17-18, Jesus—with the nature of God in mind—is saying that He is the first man born in 4,000 years with a nature that can keep the Law of God. Because He had not been corrupted by sin in the first birth, the glory and nature of God that was in the Law was also inside of His spirit (2 Corinthians 3:3). The universal struggle, described by Paul in Romans 7:15-24, is a result of being born in sin by the first birth. It never affected Jesus. Jesus had no struggle in keeping the righteousness of the Law. The Law was simply *a description of the nature He had received from God.*

The new nature was always the emphasis of Jesus. Pulpits today oftentimes emphasize the fight against sin, ungodliness, unrighteousness, and a whole lot of other iniquities. Though this has its place, beating people over the head with evils has never helped anyone. If an unrighteous person comes into a church, *only* telling him that he is unrighteous is not going to help him much, and may preclude his ever coming back to hear the Good News.

Because of the Law, Israel was already aware of the fact that they didn't measure up to God's standards. God had no need to send the Messiah to condemn Israel; the Law of Moses had already served this purpose. Instead, God sent the Logos, the original blueprint by which all mankind was originally designed, to give man the glorious possibility of a nature change. In Matthew 5:17-18, the original blueprint speaks about how one can come out of darkness (Matthew 4:17, 23), receive a new nature, and be able, by that nature, to keep the Law.

> ¹⁹ ***Whosoever therefore shall break one of these least commandments, and shall teach men so, he shall be called the least in the kingdom of heaven: but whosoever***

shall do and teach them, the same shall be called great
in the kingdom of heaven.
²⁰For I say unto you, That except your righteousness
shall exceed the righteousness of the scribes and
Pharisees, ye shall in no case enter the kingdom of
heaven. (Matthew 5:19-20 KJV)

Pharisees and Sadducees were the religious teachers of the day. Jesus knew that these men were not as holy as they tried to make themselves publicly. Breaking laws and teaching others to do so, according to Jesus, would make you the *"least in the kingdom of heaven."* This was common among the religious leaders. Because they realized their own inability to measure up to the prescribed laws of Judaism, they would twist the Law through interpretation. A crafty and deceptive interpretation beguiled the people. Instead of looking foolish for sinning against the Commandments, the leaders would look brilliant for uncovering a supposed truth regarding the Law that would allow them to sneak through a loophole.

The religious leaders were in the same predicament the Apostle Paul found himself when he was a Pharisee.

¹⁵For that which I do I allow not: for what I would,
that do I not; but what I hate, that do I.
¹⁶If then I do that which I would not, I consent unto
the law that it is good.
¹⁷Now then it is no more I that do it, but sin that
dwelleth in me.
¹⁸For I know that in me (that is, in my flesh,) dwelleth
no good thing: for to will is present with me; but how
to perform that which is good I find not.
¹⁹For the good that I would I do not: but the evil which
I would not, that I do.
²⁰Now if I do that I would not, it is no more I that do
it, but sin that dwelleth in me. (Romans 7:15-20 KJV)

Twisting the Law was a Pharisee's way to soothe his conscience and spare himself humiliation. But the people knew that the interpretations were based on the agendas of the interpreters. Then, suddenly, this new rabbi was teaching the unheard-of idea that it was not only possible, but essential, both to *do* and to *teach* the whole Law, without corrupting it. They must really have perked up their ears at this point. Jesus was telling them that in order to be great in the Kingdom of Heaven, they must do and teach men to do *all* the Law. How could that be possible?

Jesus told His followers that the answer lay far beyond anything the Pharisees and Sadducees were pontificating. He makes it very clear: it is a change in righteousness.

CHAPTER NINE

Righteousness:
The Grand Finale of the Gospel

"Instead of telling people that they should 'turn or burn,' we should preach the reality of righteousness under the anointing and demonstration of the Holy Ghost. It is such a subtle change, yet it means everything."

When I was a teenager, I received my first official leather Bible from my father. I went straight to the book of Romans and started underlining stuff that sounded good. Eventually, I came back and cruised these chapters and regretted my markings. "Now, why in the world did I do that?" The point is that I, like so many others, knew there was something extra special about these chapters. Cracking them, I knew, would be pivotal. If only I knew how, though.

One day, the Lord spoke to me and told me to read the book of Romans fifty times. "*Fifty* times? What? How can I manage that? Doesn't God know that Romans is sixteen chapters long? Why, that is eight hundred chapters, (21,650 verses), total." You can probably imagine what it must have been like when I finished reading it for the first time. "All right. One down, forty-nine to go."

In Bible school, I had Romans class in my junior year. We spent a semester going through the whole book, verse by verse. Those who approach God's Word strictly to pick it apart and scrutinize it, verse by verse, will never catch the spirit behind it. (That is essentially what the Pharisees did with the Law, and look where that got them.) I did my best to follow along the first couple of weeks and maybe even the first month.

As time went by, I found my mind drifting and disengaged from the lectures.

Frustrated, I would comment to friends in the cafeteria, "It is wrong for a class like this to be so boring. This is the great revelation of the Apostle Paul. We should be excited. We should be changed from the inside!"

"Well, Chris," the professor would tell me, "the Word of God is not an emotional experience."

Yes, it is. If we have never had an experience like that with the Word of God, we are doing something wrong. Listen, any time the veil upon my eyes has been lowered one more notch, I have found that I can't contain myself. My emotions kick in and I just want to worship God. I am glad the Spirit of God mercifully suggested I read it fifty times, with His help. Later on I had moments while reading Romans when I would almost throw off my blankets and jump out of bed to start dancing.

As I was reading Romans fifty times, I was learning things here and there, but, I must admit, nothing appeared life-changing until somewhere around my twentieth time through. I was sitting on an airplane coming back from Miami, Florida, when God unlocked my understanding of righteousness.

Righteousness is what I refer to as "The Grand Finale of the Gospel." No greater chapter than Romans 8, in my opinion, helps us understand righteousness more. Let me define it for you the way that God gave it to me when I was traveling home from Miami. *Righteousness in its purest definition is when a person moves from calling God "God," and, through faith in Jesus Christ, legally becomes re-created and reborn in Him, and can now call Him "Father."* The difference between the righteous and the unrighteous is that the unrighteous only know Him as "God," but not as "Father." This transformation is a complete shift of mind, heart, relationship, and nature.

Do this for me: Close your eyes and, for a few seconds, think: God. Then, immediately think: Father. See how the feeling in your heart changes? It is frequently quite dramatic. This is a taste of the relationship we seek to deepen in our walk with our Father.

Ever since I got hold of the word of faith as a 14-year-old boy, I've heard lots on righteousness. Truthfully, I didn't enjoy hearing sermons on it. Nothing against those preaching and teaching it, I just felt there was a missing element. I would ask, "Well, what exactly is righteousness? I mean, *what* is it?"

I'd be told, "It is right standing with God."

I would accept this rudimentary definition and think, "Hmmm, so be it, but why doesn't that make me excited?" In worship, I'd confess, "I am righteous," and quote the scriptures that "I am righteous in Christ," always hoping I would discover more beyond "It is right standing with God."

Pushing the book of Romans through my spirit over twenty times gave me enough understanding for the Holy Ghost to come and make sense out of it for me. When the Spirit of God showed me that day on the plane, I nearly spit my soda out onto the seat in front of me.

Understanding righteousness connected the teachings of Jesus and Paul in a way that I never knew existed before. *The things that Jesus proclaimed, Paul came along after Him and explained.* This included righteousness.

> *¹⁶For I am not ashamed of the gospel of Christ, for it is the power of God to salvation for everyone who believes, for the Jew first and also for the Greek. ¹⁷For in the gospel the righteousness of God is revealed.*
> (Romans 1:16-17 NKJV)

Righteousness is critical; in fact, if we don't understand it and walk in it, much of the benefits that Christ provided for us in the second birth will go unrealized in our lives. Paul introduces the Gospel as the power of God to bring salvation to all those who will believe and receive it, universally, whether Jew or otherwise. The finished work of Christ made new life in Him possible for *all* humanity. In verse 17 (KJV) he gives the reason as to why the gospel is so powerful, *"For therein is the righteousness of God revealed."*

The way the Apostle Paul sets up the book of Romans is literally a progressive, ongoing legal argument that contains perfect logic. Yet, it is much more than just logic. Logic is combined with divine revelation, and unfolds a mystery that was previously unknown. The book of Romans begins and ends the same way. It begins with Paul preparing his audience to hear the Gospel of righteousness, and it ends with him telling them that what they just read was the revelation of all that was a mystery to the prophets concerning Jesus:

> *²⁵Now to Him who is able to establish you according to my gospel and the preaching of Jesus Christ, according to the revelation of the mystery kept secret since the world began*
> *²⁶but now made manifest, and by the prophetic Scriptures made known to all nations, according to the commandment of the everlasting God, for obedience to the faith.* (Romans 16:25-26 NKJV)

In the first chapter of Romans, Paul explained why he was trying to get to Rome. "Jesus Christ crucified" was the revelation that the Roman Church began on, but it wasn't enough. Had the revelation that Christ was crucified been enough, Paul would not have been pressed to go. He was not the one who started the Church at Rome, yet he believed he had something powerful they needed to hear (Romans 1:11 KJV). The cross was the means to a greater end: righteousness. The power of the Gospel is fully experienced in our lives when we clothe ourselves in righteousness (Ephesians 6:14 KJV), a reality that can only occur through revelation from the Spirit of God.

First, after vaguely introducing Romans, Paul jumps right in to discuss the wrath of God, from Romans 1:18 through Romans 3:21. When it comes to preaching on the wrath of God, there must be a balance. While it is not supposed to be the main concentration of our preaching, it should not be ignored, either. Paul wants to show that unrighteous people who *"suppress the truth in unrighteousness"* (Romans 1:18 NKJV) are *"treasuring up for [themselves] wrath in the day of wrath and revelation of the righteous judgment of God"* (Romans 2:5 NKJV). This final judgment is one day coming.

Then, abruptly, Paul interrupts his discourse on sin, wrath, and judgment by saying, *"But now the righteousness of God <u>apart from the law is revealed</u>"* (Romans 3:21 NKJV). Despite all of the sin mentioned in previous chapters, righteousness came upon all those of faith in Jesus Christ, and they were justified. In Romans 3:21-26, righteousness is

righteousness

mentioned *four times* as a way of emphasizing that it inoculates people against the wrath of God.

Instead of telling people that they should "turn or burn," we should preach the reality of righteousness under the anointing and demonstration of the Holy Ghost. It is such a subtle change, yet it means everything.

This is why Paul was so adamant about getting to Rome. Paul fully intended to labor among the Romans from the time he arrived until he began to see the fruits of his Gospel work there (Romans 1:13). The Church at Rome was key. If he could teach these people the revelation that he received from Christ concerning righteousness (Galatians 1:12), they would spread it all over the world, for after all, "all roads lead to Rome." Rome was the epicenter of human civilization, and every nation and tribe of people trafficked in and out of Rome, bringing back what they found, and taking all things new to the far reaches of the Roman world.

As believers, what often prevents our forward progress in God is that we think the simple message of the cross is enough to sustain us in a walk of righteousness. While Christ's work on the cross was enough to save mankind, God expects our understanding of that work to deepen into a solid awareness of our righteousness—recognizing God as our *Father*, giving us boldness to approach Him. This is what awaited the Church beyond the cross. Paul knew that, all too well.

I have never been an advocate of trying to create a simpler Gospel for Christians. I believe that trying to create a simpler Gospel is another way of saying that the Church of Jesus Christ should begin decelerating. Instead of making the Gospel "simpler" for believers, we should be exhorting the Body of Christ to grow deeper and more profoundly in their understanding (Ephesians 1:17-23). Simplicity is not the answer. A revelation concerning who we are in Christ, is.

CHAPTER TEN

No Longer Sinners

"The leak that sprang, allowing sin into the world, came through Adam. Christ dealt with the source of sin, and delivered mankind from its captivity."

I once was talking with a young lady from church when we began discussing the Word of God, the Bible. My ministry had just experienced a successful campaign, and she felt the need to pry into my theology. She had been to my event, she said, and in just ten minutes of my preaching she could tell I had a different way of teaching things. "You said we are no longer sinners. I felt led to pray for you after that. That is heresy, Mr. Palmer. I told my pastor about you."

"Really?" I said. "So did you make sure to pray for the Apostle Paul, as well? Did you ask God to use you to rewrite the book of Romans? Did you warn your pastor not to use the book of Romans on Sunday mornings anymore? If my theology is 'dangerous', then so is Paul's."

She was shocked that I would speak to her that way. "What are you talking about?" she muttered in a shocked, victimized tone. I explained to her exactly what I am attempting to explain in this chapter. For whatever reason, people do not want to accept that we are no longer sinners if we are in Christ. Even saying that throws people off.

If you want to find out where a person is in his or her understanding of sin, redemption, and righteousness, ask what they think Romans 7 means. Sadly, most people think it is Paul talking about his weaknesses with sin. "Yes, Chris, I know that Jesus set us free from sin," they'll say, followed by the classic, "but even the Apostle Paul said, *'For that which I do I allow not: for what I would, that do I not; but what I hate, that do I... Now then it is no more I that do it, but sin that dwelleth in me'* (Romans

7:15, 17 KJV). So, you see, we are all sinners." They will then look at you with pursed lips, "Are you saying you are better than Paul?"

I think I am going to do Bible checks from now on. The next time someone says that to me, I am going to ask to see his or her Bible. Likely Romans 7:15-20 will be highlighted, along with Romans 5:20, *"Where sin abounded, grace did much more abound."* These verses are the artillery used by people who are having problems with their flesh. Pulled out of their context, they can be used to assist one into thinking that they are just like a supposedly struggling Paul.

After I check Romans 5:20, I will go back two verses to see about Romans 5:19 (NKJV): *"For as by **one man's** disobedience many were **made sinners**, so also by **one Man's** obedience many will be **made righteous**."* Goodness, why is *that* verse awaiting yellow ink? They don't know that one man's [Adam's] disobedience made us *sinners*, but that Christ's obedience made us *righteous*. Romans 5 concluded that if we accept Jesus Christ (the last Adam) by faith, we could no longer be called sinners.

> *¹⁵For if by the one man's offense many died, much more the grace of God and the gift by the grace of the one Man, Jesus Christ, abounded to many.*
> *¹⁷For if by the one man's offense death reigned through the one, much more those who receive abundance of grace and of the gift of righteousness will reign in life through the One, Jesus Christ.* (Romans 5:15, 17 NKJV)

Adam messed up the original blueprint. Instead of being born with the life of God, Adam's posterity was born with a genome of sin. John introduced Christ as "the Logos" because He was the divine sperm, containing the original, pre-Adam blueprint of life that would interrupt the course of sin and undo what Adam had caused through his rebellion. It is popular to teach that Jesus died for the sins of humankind. This is, of course, true. He did.

Yet, what is interesting is that Paul mentions the word "one" twelve times in nine verses of Scripture (Romans 5:12-21 KJV).

1.) "By *one* man sin entered into the world, and death by sin" (v. 12 KJV).

2.) "Through the offence of *one* many be dead" (v. 15 KJV).

3.) "Much more the grace of God, and the gift by grace, which is by *one* man, Jesus Christ, hath abounded unto many" (v. 15 KJV).

4.) "And the result of God's gracious gift is very different from the result of that *one* man's sin" (v. 16 NLT).

5.) "That *one* sin led to punishment" (v. 16 CEV).

6.) "For if by *one* man's offense" (v.17 KJV).

7.) "Death reigned by *one*" (v. 17 KJV).

8.) "Much more they which receive abundance of grace and the gift of righteousness shall reign in life by *one*, Jesus Christ" (v. 17 KJV).

9.) "Therefore as by the offence of *one* judgment came upon all men to condemnation" (v. 18 KJV).

10.) "Even so by the righteousness of *one* the free gift came upon all men unto justification of life" (v. 18 KJV).

11.) "For as by *one* man's disobedience many were made sinners" (v. 19 KJV).

12.) "So by the obedience of *one* shall many be made righteous" (v. 19 KJV).

It is evident from Romans 5 that the contest of sin and righteousness was between two individuals, Adam and Jesus, with the world in the middle. The leak that sprang, allowing sin into the world, came through Adam. Christ dealt with the source of sin, and delivered mankind from its captivity. In examining Christ's work, one can see that He did two specific things: 1.) He paid the price that Adam and humanity were to pay because of sin. 2.) He gave humanity the option to leave the slavery of sin and become children of God. In doing this, Christ laid out another blueprint that humanity could enter into by faith. This was the blueprint of the divine nature, the life that was originally in Adam, which came a second time in Jesus.

When Jesus went to the cross, He took on the world's onus as an innocent but willing substitute. This is *why* we can become righteous:

the substitutionary work of Jesus Christ as mankind's representative. Through this substitutionary act, Jesus paid the price of sin and offered righteousness and life to the whole world through the blueprint in His blood (Romans 3:25).

When we observe communion, we are acknowledging that our faith in the shed blood of Christ is a spiritual blood transfusion. It becomes our observation during the ordinance of communion that not only did Christ shed His innocent blood, but also through our faith in it, we have received the genome of life that proceeded out from the Logos.

> *53 Then Jesus said to them, "Most assuredly, I say to you, unless you eat the flesh of the Son of Man and drink His blood, you have no life in you.*
> *54 Whoever eats My flesh and drinks My blood has eternal life, and I will raise him up at the last day."*
> (John 6:53-54 NKJV)

After this presentation in Romans 5, look at how Paul introduces the believer in Romans 6. This chapter opens, oddly, with a concluding statement, "What shall we say then?" In other words, "In light of what Romans 5 just stated, where does that bring us?"

> *How shall we who died to sin live any longer in it?*
> (Romans 6:2 NKJV)

> *Our old man was crucified with Him, that the body of sin might be done away with, that we should no longer be slaves of sin.* (Romans 6:6 NKJV)

> *Likewise you also, reckon yourselves to be dead indeed to sin, but alive to God in Christ Jesus our Lord.*
> (Romans 6:11 NKJV)

> *For sin shall not have dominion over you.* (Romans 6:14 NKJV)

> ¹⁷***But God be thanked that though you were slaves of sin, yet you obeyed from the heart that form of doctrine to which you were delivered.***
> ¹⁸***And having been <u>set free from sin</u>, you became <u>slaves of righteousness.</u>*** (Romans 6:17-18 NKJV)

Let me ask then:

- Can we be dead to sin and still consider ourselves sinners? *NO*
- If the sinful agent that controlled us is dead when we come to Christ, can we still say we are sinners? *NO*
- Is it possible *not* to serve sin, yet still call ourselves sinners? *NO*
- If sin doesn't have dominion over us, is it right for one to say that he or she is still under the control of sin? *NO*
- If we *were* the servants of sin, are we *still* the servants of sin? *NO*
- If we *are* the servants of righteousness, then *are* we sinners? *NO*

No! No! No! How could anyone say that they are in Christ, yet still suggest that they are a sinner? I imagine it stems from false humility, which is really gross pride mixed with lack of knowledge. Sadly, many congregations and denominations are more driven by false humility than by the Word of God. Fearful lest they become proud, they suppress the Word of God and keep it from saying what it actually says. This is why so many people are afraid of God, and work so hard trying to please Him. They have been blinded from understanding true righteousness and how it came to be.

If Romans 5 answers *why we become righteous*, Romans 6 answers *what this means for us now*. It means that we are no longer sinners. Romans 5 discusses *why* we can partake of the righteousness that has come from God, while Romans 6 puts into perspective *what* it means for those who choose to accept the Logos. The purpose of Romans 6 is to explain that Christ Jesus has made us free from sin—and now we have eternal life. We owe this to the Divine blood transfusion: Adam's blood being replaced by Christ's.

As they say in old time church, "There is something about the Blood!"

CHAPTER ELEVEN

How We Are Made Righteous

"When Jesus came, humanity was in this dreaded state, dragging around the carcass of sin. Far be it to think that the work of Christ would leave *anyone* in this putrid state of existence."

When a magician does a card trick, bystanders ask, "How did you do that?" When you stare at some youngster's smart phone, it is common to wonder, "Gosh, how did they make this thing?" Kids disconcert their parents when they ask, "Dad, how are babies made?"

"How" is one of the most thought provoking of all the words used for information gathering and exploration. God understands this, so He gave us the seventh chapter of Romans to show us *how* we became righteous. Even so, Romans 7 has been known to confuse believers. I certainly can understand this. The illustration given by Paul concerning a man and a woman involved in marriage is complex. It takes some careful consideration to catch what he is attempting to say.

> *¹Or do you not know, brethren, (for I speak to those who know the law), that the law has dominion over a man as long as he lives?*
> *²For the woman who has a husband is bound by the law to her husband as long as he lives. But if the husband dies, she is released from the law of her husband.*
> *³So then if, while her husband lives, she marries another man, she will be called an adulteress; but if her husband dies, she is free from that law, so that she is no adulteress, though she has married another man.*

> *⁴Therefore, my brethren, you also have become <u>dead to the law through the body of Christ</u>, that you may be married to another--to Him who was raised from the dead, that we should bear fruit to God.* (Romans 7:1-4 NKJV)

The first three verses do not illustrate anything other than the fact that death dissolves the bonds of marriage. When Paul wrote this, he chose a custom of the day to show that death cancels out any bond (law) that marriage brings. The tricky part of understanding these verses is to figure out what/who is dying.

It would not have solved any problems at all if the Law had died. Notice what Paul said, *"Is the law sin? Certainly not. Therefore the law is holy, and the commandment holy, and just and good"* (Romans 7: 7, 12 KJV). The Law was not humankind's problem.

Paul states the real problem in Romans 7:8 (KJV), *"But <u>sin</u>, taking opportunity by the commandment, produced in me all manner of evil desire."* Sin was what needed to die, and it did die when we identified with Christ.

Paul gives the three major occurrences that brought our righteousness:

1.) Death took place: *"Therefore, my brethren, you also have become dead to the law through the body of Christ"* (v.4 NKJV). The "you that died" refers to the sinful you that is alive before your journey begins. It is this man that drives you against your will to do sin and lands you into trouble, eventually culminating into a day of great wrath from the Supreme Judge of the Universe (God). When this "you" dies, there is nothing more that the Law has a right to.

2.) A new man was born: *"Having died to what we were held by, so that we should serve in the newness of the Spirit"* (Romans 7:6 NKJV). This new man is the literal rebirth of our spirit that occurs when it is reconciled to God. The new man is the man born in the second birth. This man has been given authority, power, understanding of God, and is in cooperation with the Holy Ghost. More than just that, it is born without any obligation to the Law.

3.) A marriage occurred: *"That you may be married to another—to Him who was raised from the dead, that we should bear fruit to God"* (v.4 NKJV). Having been born apart from the Law, this new man is free to enter into Union with another, who is Christ. From out of this Union is produced the fruit that earmarks us as a child of God, something that a Union with the Law could never give birth to: *"But the fruit of the spirit is love, joy, peace longsuffering, gentleness, goodness, faith, meekness, temperance, against such there is no law"* (Galatians 5:22-23 KJV).

The idea behind Romans 7 is to take Romans 6 to the next level by showing us that if we are free from sin, then we are also free from the Law: *"Having died to what we were held by, so that we should serve in the newness of the spirit and not in the oldness of the letter"* (Romans 7:6 NKJV). This verse is explaining *how*: There has been a transformation of our nature.

In understanding *how* we became righteous in Romans 7, we must pay close attention to this shift of natures. This change of nature is also seen in Ezekiel 36:26-28:

> *26I will give you a new heart and put a new spirit within you; I will take the heart of stone out of your flesh and give you a heart of flesh.*
> *27I will put My Spirit within you and cause you to walk in My statutes, and you will keep My judgments and do them.*
> *28Then you shall dwell in the land that I gave to your fathers; you shall be My people, and I will be your God.*
> (Ezekiel 36:26-28 NKJV)

Though this was being spoken by the prophet Ezekiel to the nation of Israel and still has its victorious fulfillment in the future, the change of nature and the principle of it are available today and forever through Christ Jesus. Gentiles and Jews have been experiencing this since the New Testament began.

Often we think sin is only a moral transgression of God's code. It includes that, but there is something far more sinister behind the transgression. It is a living, working spirit that is alive in every person born in the first birth—the sinful nature. The sinful nature teaches people how to lie, steal, cheat, and miss God's mark without ever having to be literally taught. It is natural. This nature entered through Adam (Romans 5:12), not the Law. All the Law did was aggravate this nature, so that those under the Law could recognize it. What the Law lacked was the ability to free man from this nature, recreate a *new* nature within man, and place him on a supernatural path of life that could develop him further and further unto the perfect day.

To illustrate that the sinful nature, not the Law, is the problem, Paul gives the famous inflammatory statement of Romans 7:14-24 that causes many Christians to believe they are still sinners. Paul is not writing this as a believer struggling with the sinful nature. He is writing this as a believer attempting to explain to other believers that the Law could not deliver him from the power of this nature, but the work of Jesus Christ *did*.

Paul is referring to his old life. *"For we know that the law is spiritual, but I am carnal, sold under sin"* (Romans 7:14 NKJV). Well, obviously Paul, at this point in his life, wasn't carnal and sold under sin. "Being sold under sin" means to belong to the Kingdom of Darkness, with Satan still presiding as father (John 8:44). If Paul were, it would conflict with everything he stated in the fifth and sixth chapters. Rather, Romans 7:15-24 paints the calamitous picture of what the sinful nature does to a person bound by its power. It refers to the *time* Paul was sold under sin, married to a Law that agitated the sin inside him.

Writing from the point of view of a sinner and product of the first birth, Paul exclaims, *"O wretched man that I am! Who shall deliver me from the body of this death?"* (Romans 7:24 KJV). There are commentators who tell us that "the body of this death" refers to a torture method in which the dead corpse of a murder victim was chained to its offender. For the rest of life, the murderer had to drag the stinking, decaying body around everywhere he tried to go. The rot of the corpse would eventually infect the criminal, destroying him with the same decay.

When Jesus came, humanity was in this dreaded state, dragging around the carcass of sin. This is the darkness that He came to set the world free from. Far be it to think that the work of Christ would leave *anyone* in this putrid state of existence.

In summing up our understanding as to *how* we are made righteous, we can already fathom a few things:

1.) *The first birth made us unrighteous:* Adam, as mankind's representative, opened the door to sin and allowed it to corrupt the human race.

2.) *The Law was not given to make us righteous*: The Law only condemned our nature and gave us overwhelming evidence that we had come short of God's glory and blueprint.

3.) *Our identifying with the death, burial, and resurrection of Jesus makes it possible for us to be righteous:* Just as Adam represented mankind when he sinned, Jesus represented mankind when He paid the price and laid out another genetic code of life for mankind to inherit through our faith in His work. This contains the necessary equation we need to stand as righteous. Consider it spiritual science!

CHAPTER TWELVE

The Work of Christ

"Christ died our death, received life back from the Father, and looked upon the world as candidates for reconciliation with God because the penalty had been paid."

It is popular to believe that we are all children of God, whether Muslim, Buddhist, agnostic, atheist, gay, straight. "Everyone is a child of God," so they say. This may be a human theory, but this is not what the Bible says (John 8:44; Ephesians 2:1-3). Those who are children of God are those who have had a change in nature through the second birth.

To gain an understanding of *how* we went from being a sinner and having no ability to stand confidently before God, to being an actual, literal child of God by nature, having the freedom to approach Him boldly (Hebrews 4:16), it is important we understand what is happening in John 5.

In John 5, Jesus went up to Jerusalem on the Sabbath and entered a place where there was a great horde of sick people: blind, lame, and paralyzed. Jesus singled out one man from the bunch who had been paralyzed for thirty-eight years. With just a word, Jesus made the man whole and told him to rise and walk. Believe it or not, the chapter becomes most interesting *after* the miracle.

Just about everything Jesus did had a deeper meaning involved with it. To our benefit, Jesus never sought to hide things *from* people. Anything He hid, He hid *for* people. He nearly always left an explanation. Such is the case here.

The Pharisees did not like that Jesus had performed this miracle on the Sabbath. They went to extreme lengths of plotting to kill Jesus, because He was a repeat offender in healing people on the Sabbath. When Jesus opened His mouth to give them a rebuke, He said something that I have always thought was humorous. I don't think Jesus was trying to be funny. What makes me laugh is how sharp and quick Jesus was. His precision and accuracy of speech made hypocrites wish they had never messed with Him.

"But Jesus answered them, My Father worketh hitherto, and I work" (John 5:17 KJV). Jesus was telling them, in another way, "My Father, who is God, is doing the work through Me. If He works on the Sabbath, I can be working on the Sabbath." The Jews got even more upset, *"because He not only broke the Sabbath, but also said that God was His Father, making Himself equal with God"* (v. 18 NKJV). The problem with the Jews is that they were too blinded by pious religion to recognize the Logos right in front of them.

Obviously, they disparaged what they may have heard about His birth, and thought the way those in Nazareth thought, as seen in Luke 4:22 (NKJV), "Is this not Joseph's son?" Jesus was never the son of Joseph. He was Joseph's stepson. God was the Father of Jesus. Because Jesus was the Son of God, He was not subject to the same laws, and that included the ones dealing with the Sabbath. Jesus was not like others. His blueprint was not the same.

This is where it gets really interesting. Jesus explains the work of the Logos in coming to restore man back into right standing with God:

> *19Verily, verily, I say unto you, The Son can do nothing of himself, but what he seeth the Father do: for what things soever he doeth, these also doeth the Son likewise.*
> *20For the Father loveth the Son, and sheweth him all things that himself doeth: and he will shew him greater works than these, that ye may marvel.*
> *21For as the Father raiseth up the dead, and quickeneth (them;) even so the Son quickeneth whom he will.*
> *22For the Father judgeth no man, but hath committed all judgment unto the Son:*
> *23That all men should honour the Son, even as they honour the Father. He that honoureth not the Son honoureth not the Father which hath sent him.* (John 5:19-23 KJV)

Astoundingly, Jesus says that *"The Father loveth the Son…and he will shew him greater works than these, that ye may marvel."* What work could possibly be greater than the instant healing of a man who was paralyzed for thirty-eight years? In order for this miracle to occur, bones would have to have been reshaped, muscles would have to have been strengthened, and the brain would have to have been energized.

In John 5:21 Jesus gives the answer. Often, verse 21 is understood to mean that the Father is going to quicken the human race because the word *"them"* is used in the King James Version. The word, however, is in parenthesis and was added by translators. It is beneficial to attempt to understand a verse without the italicized word. It isn't rare for an italicized word to create confusion and lock out the chapter to understanding.

Instead of "quickeneth them", the verse should simply say "quickeneth." *Quicken* means to restore life and vigor. A body can only be resurrected when the spirit that animates the body is quickened. The quickening that Jesus is referring to is also mentioned in Romans 4:16-17 (KJV):

> *[16] But to that also which is of the faith of Abraham; who is the father of us all,*
> *[17] (As it is written, I have made thee a father of many nations,) before him whom he believed, even God, who quickeneth the dead, and <u>calleth those things which be not as though they were.</u>*

Clergymen who regularly preach on faith use this verse to prove that our words have power—and they do. However, Paul did not pause his meticulous argument on law, sin, and the reborn nature just to tell everyone that we should start speaking positively. *More than that, these verses portray the kind of faith that Abraham had in the work of the coming Messiah and the result of that faith.*

To understand further, we have to figure out who "the dead" is that is being quickened. Some think it is the resurrection of the saints. Others just brush past it as insignificant. Yet, the faith of Abraham depends on *who* he believed that God could raise from the dead. The answer is revealed a few verses down: *"Now it was not written for his sake alone, that it was* *imputed to him; But for us also, to whom it shall be imputed, if we believe on him that <u>raised up Jesus Christ from the dead</u>"* (v. 22, 23).

The dead is referring to Jesus Christ. Abraham believed that God could raise the coming Messiah from the dead. He believed that in his son's loins was a Redeemer that would pay the price of spiritual death, only to later be quickened back to life. Because of this faith, God called Abraham righteous even though the work of Christ had not yet been accomplished. Long before the Messiah came, God credited righteousness to Abraham because he believed.

In view of this, Christ was telling the Jews who were present that the greater work that they would witness would be when He would bear the sins of humanity, die spiritually, be quickened again by His Father, and spread life to all who would believe in Him. The Messiah, now having accomplished the necessary work, awaits those who will demonstrate the faith of Abraham and believe on Him.

Not only did Christ die physically, He died spiritually. Some don't like to believe this. They think that suggesting that Christ died spiritually is some sort of blasphemy. When the sins of humanity were placed upon Christ, His nature was separated from God, which equates to spiritual death. If His nature weren't separated, ours would have had to be. The heaviness of sin extinguished the light *"which lighteth every man that cometh into the world"* (John 1:9 KJV). Being our substitute, the light of life in Christ was put out *temporarily* as He tasted our spiritual death.

When this happened, the sins of mankind were paid for, in full, through His sacrifice. Notice what Jesus says concerning this, *"For the Father judgeth no man, but hath committed all judgment unto the Son"* (John 5:22 KJV). Judgment is now in the hands of Christ because the judgment of God on a sinful world was laden upon Him. Jesus was given the responsibility of judging the world, because in Christ all men were judged.

Whether we accept Him or not, Jesus still stood in our place. As a substitute, Christ died without any guarantee that we would accept Him. And yet, if any man accepts the work of Christ, Jesus says that they are whole, and they are whole. If any one accepts that His stripes have healed us, Jesus says we are healed, and we are healed. He judged it as so.

The life that was in Christ was extinguished by sin. Innocently and willingly, Christ allowed this to happen so that He could stand in the place of every man and woman. Now, notice what Jesus says:

> *24 Verily, verily, I say unto you, he that heareth my word, and believeth on Him that sent me, hath everlasting life, and shall not come into condemnation; but is passed from death unto life.*
> *25 Verily, verily, I say unto you, The hour is coming, and now is, when the dead shall hear the voice of the Son of God: and they that hear shall live.* (John 5:24, 25 KJV)

What Jesus was saying is awe-inspiring. Jesus is clearly defining the second birth. Here Jesus takes a microscopic look at how we move from the broad road of destruction into the narrow road that leads to life. Jesus was saying that anyone who believes on Him and follows His Word is allowing Him to stand as his sacrifice. That being the case, Christ and those of us who believe all legally died together.

Notice that John 5:25 (KJV) says, *"The dead shall hear the voice of the Son of God: and they that hear shall live."* Not a reference to the resurrection of dead bodies, this is specifying the spiritually dead. Once Christ's work is finished, anyone who hears and believes receives the same life that Christ received when God raised Him from the dead. The life that God gave to Jesus while He was spiritually dead now becomes our possession, as Christ gives it to us because of our faith. *"For as the Father hath life in himself; so hath he given to the Son to have life in himself"* (John 5:26 KJV).

Just as Adam stood in for us when he rebelled and we all awoke to sin, so Christ stood in for us when He died, and we all died to sin. When we awoke to sin in the first birth, we found that our spirits had died because death had wormed its way in. Yet, in this second birth that leads to everlasting life, when we died to sin, through faith, we found that our spirits had been made to live. Do you know why? *When the Father gave Jesus new life, Jesus turned around and gave it to us.*

This is what John was saying in John 1:9 (KJV), ***"That was the true Light, which lighteth every man that cometh into the world."*** This life is a *new nature* with eternal life embedded into its makeup. Christ died our death, received life back from the Father, and looked upon the world as candidates for reconciliation with God because the penalty had been paid. Christ took the life that He had been given and said that anyone could partake of this life through faith in Him. This is the bread of life, spoken of in John 6:35 (KJV), ***"I am the bread of life: he that cometh to me shall never hunger; and he that believeth on me shall never thirst."***

Power and Authority

John goes on to talk about "power." ***"But as many as received him, to them gave he power to become the sons of God, even to them that believe on his name"*** (John 1:12 KJV). This is making mention of our reborn human spirits, not the Baptism in the Holy Spirit. That comes a bit later.

However, when I was a young minister on staff at my first church, I used to throw out this verse as a reference to the Baptism in the Spirit as seen in Acts 2. Something in me would say, "Now, Christopher, you know this isn't referring to that." I would try to ignore it because I didn't want to take the time to really delve into what "power" He was referring to.

One day I couldn't take it anymore. The "still, small voice" would not let me alone. I sat down and began to study. Understanding didn't come right away, but when it did, wow. The first chapter of John is a preface of what to expect in the rest of the book. Everything that Jesus said or did in front of this great apostle was taken into account when John wrote the first chapter. In those first few verses, John outlines all that Jesus did and taught. The rest of the book is John winding it back up, giving reason behind all that he spoke in the first chapter.

What does this mean in its totality? It means, gloriously, that we have become the sons and daughters of God. The "power" in John 1:12 is the same "power" Paul spoke of in Romans 1:16-17 (KJV): ***"For I am not ashamed of the gospel of Christ: for it is the <u>power</u> of God unto salvation to everyone that believeth…For <u>therein is the righteousness of God revealed.</u>"***

The power that John was referring to is *righteousness*. This gives us tremendous authority and power. How was this made possible? By a nature change. The moment we accepted Jesus and His finished work on the cross, our natures switched and we became part of the family of God. The proof of that work is in our nature or, as my mom would say, "The proof is in the pudding."

CHAPTER THIRTEEN

Sonship is What Christ Came to Bring

**"Chris, you don't have to pay the bill to honor me.
You honor me enough by being my son."**

Whenever I am given the option to dress casually or to wear a suit during a service, I always go with the suit. Maybe it's psychologically linked to watching my Dad leave the house every day in an immaculate two-piece suit, dressed to impress.

My dad is a businessman. Ever since I was a kid I've marveled at what he does. Always a busy man, Dad got busier as he continued to be promoted. Toward the end of my high school years, he was traveling around the country as a top executive in an S&P 500 company.

For thirty-five years my dad put on his tie, stomped around the kitchen in his dress shoes hurrying to get out the door, started his car, and headed to work where he began to make things happen. According to him, he has hundreds of emails, dozens of problems to solve, and enough meetings to keep his brain in perpetual motion. Should anyone show up at his office unannounced, without an appointment, there is no chance they'll get in. Even if someone is qualified to get his time, they know they must make an appointment. And this appointment is not going to be made through my dad. Rather, they have to reach a receptionist who may, in turn, put them through to one of my dad's two administrative assistants. There isn't much access to my dad's presence unless you have the right relationship with him.

The thing that constituted a special relationship between my father and me was that I knew he was always busy, yet he always had time for me. The same guy I'd see coming home late on Monday night and clomping around in the kitchen a few hours later on Tuesday morning would somehow always be early for my basketball game, in time to see me warm-up. Home games and away games, my dad never missed a single one that I can remember. There were times when snowstorms nearly canceled the game and the stands would be virtually empty. But when I ran onto the court from the locker room, I'd look into the stands, and there he'd be, wearing his grey trench coat and munching on a bag of popcorn.

I never had to ask my dad to come, and I never had to talk to his secretary about getting an appointment. He always seemed to know where my games were, and he always arrived early. Even when I had stepped into some mischief at school or disobeyed his parental authority, he still came to see me play. I don't think you need to ask why. But I will go ahead and tell you anyway: I am his son, and he is my father. The only way that my dad would fight the snow, pull the plug early on his work, exhaust himself by driving across town, and delight in doing so is through a relationship called "sonship." I can't recall ever seeing or hearing that my dad went to any other kid's game. Just mine.

Although my father and I are two separate entities, he is in me because I came forth from him. His genetics compose my constitution and my physique. I was aghast when I first heard about that in junior high science class. I was at that awkward phase where parents are "uncool." I am not sure how long my denial lasted, but I finally had to accept it when I moved out on my own and got a swift kick of reality.

In the family, my dad is known as "Monk," the television detective with obsessive-compulsive disorder. By now, I am sure he is accustomed to being the brunt of so many jokes. My dad has this predilection to check, over and over again, to see if the front door is locked at night. The door may be anchored but he insists on tugging on it to see how strong the deadbolt is. My mom just grins and rolls her eyes.

So, while living in my first place on my own, truth crept in. At first, I didn't even notice, until I suddenly realized that I was checking and re-checking the locks before going to bed. Horror oozed down my head and onto my feet. "I used to make fun, but I am just like him." You know what they say: "Like father, like son," or, "The apple doesn't fall far from the tree." For years, I didn't stop to think how that fit the description between God and me, or what a blessing it is.

I once had lunch with my dad at a Mediterranean restaurant. It has the most phenomenal food, and the ambiance makes it a popular place.

Even though we were both busy, we decided to stop for an hour to eat and catch up. When the bill came, I went to grab it.

All of a sudden I felt a hand grab my wrist. It was too big to be the waitress's. I looked up. My dad didn't have to say a word. His face said it all. "You are not paying this bill. No compromise." Responding to the look he gave me, I said, "Come on, Dad. Let me honor you and pay this bill." I will never forget what my dad said after that. It brought about a great revelation that genuinely helped me understand my heavenly Father.

"Chris, you don't have to pay the bill to honor me. You honor me enough by being my son."

If only the world could see this today. God has become our Father. He delights in fellowshipping with us for that one, solitary reason. This must have been a very tough reality for people in Jesus' time to understand, because for thousands of years they had been accustomed to rituals, customs, laws, and ordinances. As a result of Christ's work, fellowship with God for the rest of eternity would be through Sonship and right of family, as opposed to works and labor. Being the master teacher that He was, Jesus sought to explain these deep truths in a simple manner.

The story of the Prodigal Son is probably the most popular parable that Jesus taught, because we can all relate, in one way or another. So many truths are illustrated in this one simple story. Everything Jesus taught was three-dimensional. A simple truth can be seen at different angles, without changing the integrity of the meaning, and something fresh can be grasped every time that adds to the overall meaning of what is being conveyed.

There is a very important element that Jesus was sending in this story. I believe it is foundational truth and motivation for why Jesus spoke this parable: *fellowship with God is by Sonship and not by works.*

> *11 Then He said: "A certain man had two sons.*
> *12 "And the younger of them said to his father, 'Father, give me the portion of goods that falls to me.' So he divided to them his livelihood.*
> *13 "And not many days after, the younger son gathered all together, journeyed to a far country, and there wasted his possessions with prodigal living.*

¹⁴But when he had spent all, there arose a severe famine in that land, and he began to be in want.

¹⁵"Then he went and joined himself to a citizen of that country, and he sent him into his fields to feed swine.

¹⁶And he would gladly have filled his stomach with the pods that the swine ate, and no one gave him anything.

¹⁷"But when he came to himself, he said, 'How many of my father's hired servants have bread enough and to spare, and I perish with hunger!

¹⁸I will arise and go to my father, and will say to him, "Father, I have sinned against heaven and before you,

¹⁹and I am no more worthy to be called your son. Make me like one of your hired servants."'

²⁰"And he arose, and came to his father. But when he was still a great way off, his father saw him and had compassion, and ran and fell on his neck and kissed him.

²¹"And the son said unto him, 'Father, I have sinned against heaven and in your sight, and am no longer worthy to be called your son.'

²²"But the father said to his servants, 'Bring out the best robe and put it on him, and put a ring on his hand and sandals on his feet.

²³And bring the fatted calf here and kill it, and let us eat and be merry;

²⁴for this my son was dead and is alive again; he was lost and is found. And they began to be merry.

²⁵"Now his older son was in the field. And as he came and drew near to the house, he heard music and dancing.

²⁶"So he called one of the servants and asked what these things meant.

²⁷And he said to him, 'Your brother has come, and because he has received him safe and sound, your father has killed the fatted calf.'

²⁸"But he was angry and would not go in. Therefore his father came out and pleaded with him.
²⁹"So he answered and said to his father, 'Lo, these many years I have been serving you; I never transgressed your commandment at any time; and yet you never gave me a young goat, that I might make merry with my friends.
³⁰But as soon as this son of yours came, who has devoured your livelihood with harlots, you killed the fatted calf for him.'
³¹"And he said to him, 'Son, you are always with me, and all that I have is yours.
³²It was right that we should make merry and be glad, for your brother was dead and is alive again, and was lost and is found.'" (Luke 15:11-32 NKJV)

In just twenty-one verses, the word "son" is used nine times and the word "father" is used twelve times. This emphasis hints at the true intent of the parable. Sadly, not all sons have fellowship with their fathers because, like the elder son, they think that *works* is the way to bring it about. Jesus tells us that it is not. The only thing that brings that fellowship is our position as sons. All we have to do is embrace it and use our position to continually become closer to our Father.

Notice:

1.) *Both brothers were* sons *of the same father (v. 11):* The story begins with a father/son relationship already in effect.

2.) *Both sons had an inheritance as sons of their father (v. 12):* Every good father leaves an inheritance for his children (Proverbs 13:22). God expects *us* to do this because that is how *He* is as a Father. As many good *servants* as the father had, *none* of them had an inheritance. This should, in itself, prove that *inheritance does not come by service* (Galatians 4:1-7 KJV).

3.) *Poverty came when the younger son stepped away from fellowship with his father (v. 14):* Before then, he had everything that he needed, and an inheritance on top of that. Breaking fellowship with God to fulfill youthful lusts and worldly ambitions has never gotten anyone anywhere in the long run. When temporary pleasure is sated, misery always sets in. I always wonder what a good Jewish boy thought about having to feed the pigs, those unclean animals of his faith. It would certainly have brought double misery to the shamed, starving boy.

4.) *As unworthy as the younger brother was, the heart of his father never changed towards him (v. 18-20):* The young man was unworthy in *deed*. However, *deeds* are not what make up a father/son relationship. *Genetic nature* constitutes this relationship. It was the *nature* of the son that made him worthy, not his *actions*.

5.) *The first thing the son received was a robe (v. 22):* This represents righteousness (Isaiah 61:10). The younger brother was being recognized as a son again. We must understand that in the father's eyes, the son was dead while he was alienated from him (v.24). When each of us was in the world doing our thing during our before-Christ days, we were ***"dead in trespasses and sins"*** (Ephesians 2:1 KJV). It was out of the Father's love and compassion (v. 22; John 3:16) that He showed us mercy and clothed us with righteousness. (There is just something about dads.)

6.) *The second thing the younger brother received was a ring (v. 22):* Rings are marks of honor (Genesis 41:42). When we receive the new nature and are born again and made righteous, God honors us. This, too, is not by works.

7.) *The third thing the younger brother received was a pair of sandals (v. 22):* Sandals are emblematic of one who has become a free man. It was customary for slaves to have their shoes taken away when they went into captivity. The moment we were adopted back into the family of God, we were set free from sin's captivity and became free to live as a son or daughter of God. More than that, we were set free from the Law.

8.) *The elder brother thought that he could win the father's favor through works (v. 25, 29):* It is easy to see the reunion of the prodigal son and his loving father as a happy ending, enough to make us rejoice and stop reading. Sometimes, people quit before they get to the end of the parable and forget about the elder son and his role in the profound truth of this story.

At first glance, the parable of the prodigal son seems a bit cutting. One might think that the elder brother had every right to be upset. Here he is, working long hours out in the fields, breaking his back and toiling hard, covered with sweat and straw, and the young screw-up gets all the reward? How can this be fair?

Unfortunately, the older brother had gone his whole life never understanding the heart his father had toward him as a son. He was too blinded by legalism and self-righteousness to experience the righteousness that the younger brother received, the righteousness that comes from Sonship.

Fellowship with God, according to Jesus, comes no other way except out of our new natures, a righteousness that was given to us because of Jesus Christ. As badly as the younger brother messed up, to his credit he quickly learned that wisdom is placing his dependence in fellowship with his father.

This is how it is with God, and what Paul is saying in Romans 8:8 (NKJV): ***"So then, those who are in the flesh cannot please God."*** The ones who were trying to please God through outward actions could not yet see that no amount of *action* could please God. They weren't yet His children through the second birth. The parallel between them and the elder son is that they needed to understand the heart their Father had toward them, and simply to *receive* that love.

The Father replied to the eldest brother's dismay by saying, ***"Son, thou art ever with me, and all that I have is thine"*** (v. 31). The Father was saying to the oldest brother, "Son, don't you know that you have always been my son? If at any point you had come out of the field and asked me for a robe, or a ring, or sandals, or a fattened calf, I would have freely given it to you."

Many people today are like the older brother, doing whatever they think is necessary to authenticate themselves before God. Some think that feeding the homeless gives them this validation. Others think it is ministry. And others think it is going to mass or saying Hail Mary's. The list of works goes on and on. The point is that *labor* does not earn us God's *favor*, nor does it advance us forward into fellowship with Him.

The Son of Man came to initiate a day where our relationship with God would be a delight. Jesus Christ is the eternal Sabbath (Matthew 12:1-8). It is in *His work* that we have eternal rest and an *enjoyable* relationship with our Father. We don't need to take vows or push ourselves to do things out of legalism. What we need is a revelation of Sonship. This is why Christ came, and it is the hour that we are in now. We must have the mentality of the younger brother, and get away from the self-righteousness of the older brother. As sons and daughters of God, we automatically please Him by simply being His children.

I recently watched a television show featuring a baby's birth. As soon as the newborn came out of its mother's womb, the father began smiling and couldn't contain his excitement. The show's commentator called him "a proud father."

I thought, *Gosh, a proud father? This child hasn't done a thing except be born.* That's all it took.

CHAPTER FOURTEEN

"Spirit" versus "spirit"

"By the time my playmates got to singing, the fire from the lighter was burning just as brilliantly on the numeric candle as was it on all the small candles that were resting half deep in icing. Not one flame had been diminished."

As much time as I spent reading Romans, the eighth chapter was a dreadful mystery to me. Only when the Spirit of God gave me a helpful key to understand it, did I begin to see what Paul was talking about. Romans 8 is the climax of Paul's argument in which he arrives at the true power of the Gospel: Sonship. It is central to the understanding of our relationship in Christ. The climactic point of Paul's legal explanation of righteousness comes in Romans 8. This could well be considered one of the greatest chapters in the entire Bible. If the Bible were a map of the world, Romans 8 would be like the San Andreas Fault. The activity in this chapter affects the way the whole Bible reads. I remember the way the Bible looked to me before I got a clue, and I know how the Bible looks to me after the Spirit of God showed me how to understand this chapter.

What unlocked this chapter to me was an understanding of the word "spirit." The original Greek has only one word, *pneuma*, which translates as "spirit". Context is the only way to understand whether it is the Holy Spirit or the reborn human spirit that is being discussed in the verses. In light of scriptures in John and the context of Paul's discourse in Romans, the majority of the time Paul refers to "spirit" in Romans 8, *he has in mind the human spirit that has been born of the second birth.*

The reason Paul so meticulously draws up the book of Romans, particularly this eighth chapter, is to help us understand that fellowship with God is done only out of the new man. Our walk with God now must be done *"after the spirit"* (Romans 8:4 KJV). The Holy Spirit has been given to assist us in this walk, as we will see, but it begins with the reborn life. This is what verse four is talking about.

I appreciate the translators' efforts. But as I went through Romans over and over and over again, I began to see that they may not have known what to do with many of the words "spirit," and capitalized *most* of them. This has shaded many of our understandings. In context with Romans, Galatians, and 1 Corinthians, this "Spirit" should be "spirit." Hence, I took the rightful liberty to remove the capital letters and make them lower case. Eyebrows rise whenever I mention this while teaching or preaching. Yet, I have studied the original Greek and can clearly show that the Greek word πνευμα (*pneuma*) is never capitalized once. If it were it would look like this in the Greek text "Πνευμα." Capital letters were rarely used in composing the Greek New Testament. Our insertion of them depends on context and still varies from translation to translation, an indication that it is something still open for an enthusiastic discussion.

Furthermore, it makes sense that Paul was discussing the new nature because that is where our walk with God proceeds from. Look what Paul shares concerning those who've been born of the second birth, *"But ye are not in the flesh, but in the spirit, if so be that the spirit of God dwell in you. Now if any man have not the spirit of Christ, he is none of his"* (Romans 8:9 KJV).

I will be completely honest. This verse used to confuse me (and I am a Bible College graduate and a preacher). I would think: "Ok, Chris. I am not in the flesh. Check. I am in the Spirit. Check. The Spirit of God dwells in me. Check. The Spirit of Christ dwells in me. Check. OK, now, what does all this mean? Am I a body? Do I have two spirits, plus my own spirit living in my body?" Then I'd shrug and close my Bible and think, "Well, one of these days I'll figure it out."

Sometimes we can fall prey to reading the words of the Bible, consenting to them because they are in the Bible, and never knowing what they mean or how they work in accordance with our lives. It wasn't until I understood John 5 (which was discussed in chapter 12) that this verse made sense. The "spirit" being talked about here is our reborn spirit, made up of the life of God. The Father gave this life to Jesus after Jesus's life had been quenched when He willfully took upon Himself our sin. In return, Jesus gave this life to us.

This life originated from the Father. Because the life of the Father is now inherent in us, we may say that the "spirit" of God dwells in us. Since this life had to flow through Jesus first so that it could get to us, we can say that we have the "spirit" of Christ. This being said, the "spirit" of God and the "spirit" of Christ are referring to exactly the same spirit. It refers to the light and life of the Godhead, which Adam lost when he sinned. Romans 8, then, is climactic because it *explains* the return of that life into mankind, affecting the way the whole Bible reads.

The way I can best illustrate this is to take you back to my childhood birthday parties. They were pretty much like else's birthday party, so I am sure that you'll be able to relate. When it came time to sing to me (my shining moment every year), my mother would bring out my traditional ice cream cake and slide it in front of me. There was the same number of candles on the cake as last year, plus one more to represent another year grown. Following the universal handbook of good mothering, my mom refused to let me light my candles. All parents think that fire and children make a bad combination.

For years, I was stuck watching my mom have all the fun lighting them. She had a procedure she always used. First, she would whip out the lighter. That lighter was the source of all the fire that in just a few seconds was going to visibly manifest itself all over my birthday cake. After lighting the big numeric candle in the middle of the cake that proclaimed how old I was turning, she would use that to light every other candle on my cake. By the time my playmates got to singing, the fire from the lighter was burning just as brilliantly on the numeric candle as it was on all the small candles that were resting half deep in icing. Not one flame had been diminished.

God, being the source of life, lit Jesus with life after He had paid the price of spiritual death and separation from His Father. The spirit of Jesus Christ was infused with the same life that was in His Father. When we came to believe on Jesus Christ, He rekindled within us a new nature with this exact life. The spirit that *God* has is made up of the same life that *Christ* has, which is made up of the same life that *I* have, which is made up of the same life *you* have, *if* you believe on Him. Though we are all separate

73

entities, it is still correct to say that, "I have the spirit of God." And it is just as correct to say, "I have the spirit of my elder Brother, Jesus Christ." This is how Christ can be *in* us. We share the same life together. He is my Brother and God is my Father. We are *His*. ***"And if any man <u>have not the spirit of Christ, he is none of His</u>"*** (Romans 8:9 KJV).

Look at what follows in Romans 8:10: ***"And if Christ be in you."*** *To explain, Christ is not literally in us as an entity inhabiting our body.* The Scripture tells us that Christ is now in heaven as our High Priest, ***"set on the right hand of the throne of the Majesty in the heavens"*** (Hebrews 8:1 KJV).

After His Resurrection Christ told us that He has a flesh and bone body, existing as our representative in the Godhead, the firstborn from the dead. ***"Behold my hands and my feet, that it is I myself: handle me, and see; for a spirit hath not flesh and bones, as ye see me have"*** (Luke 24:39 KJV). Because His glorified body is of flesh and bone, He can't be inside of us physically. He is at the right hand of God, literally in that body.

Rather, Christ is now in us by way of union. The union that we have with Christ is a family union, one that is made possible through our spiritual genetics. "Christ in me" means that we now have His genetic blueprint encoded within our spirit. This was made possible by *regeneration*, the restructuring of our genesis. What Paul was sharing in Romans 8 was a thesis on the composition of our spiritual DNA. This alteration in our spiritual stature makes us fit candidates to cooperate with the Holy Spirit, the only One that can lead this new man from glory to glory.

CHAPTER FIFTEEN

God Leads Us by the New Nature

**"A mature Christian is one who has mastered how to be led
by God and knows what His voice sounds like."**

God's Word is not a self-help book or *just* a manual that gives us principles for solving life's problems. *Instead, it is a playbook that goes into accurate detail, describing the redemption of mankind back to the original blueprint.* God gave us His word so that we may understand what we have become in Him, knowing that a full understanding of our identity would keep many of "life's problems" from entering our lives.

Every major, game-changing decision (and the smaller ones, too) that we make in life should have God's direction involved in it. When people foul up and make wrong decisions, usually affecting other people, it is safe to assume they missed God one way or another. God never leads astray, nor does He ever misdirect. It is my conviction that there is nothing more important and more crucial than to have a firm hold on: *1.) How to hear the voice of God,* and *2.) Understanding how He guides and directs.*

Without this knowledge, our insight concerning God will be dim, as will our perception of the events in life. Dim perception can hinder our walk with God in a way that can be extremely injurious. It is, after all, our perception of God's Word that enables us to follow after our righteous natures, stepping day by day into what He has made us. Again, what has He made us? And how does He lead us?

The very first foundational thing that must be understood before understanding anything else about God's leading is: God *rarely* speaks to our brains. Most of the time, we don't hear God at high volume through our ears. We hear God through the "still, small voice" inside of our spirit. This includes hearing His direction so that we can fulfill the assignment we have been given here on the earth. A *mature* Christian is one who has mastered how to be led by God and knows what His voice sounds like. *Maturity is the ability to discern the voice of God over the voices of ambition, self-gratification, and demonic deception.*

When we don't understand how God leads, we will end up like the person James describes: ***"For he who doubts is like a wave of the sea driven and tossed by the wind. For let not that man suppose that he will receive anything from the Lord; he is a double-minded man, unstable in all his ways"*** (James 1:6-8 NKJV).

Double-minded people say that God said one thing on Monday and another thing on Tuesday. In February, they said that God told them to stay single their whole lives. In April, God told them that the barista at the coffee shop is to be their spouse. In June, they are dating the youth pastor because God told them that the youth pastor is "the one." Six months later, they have discovered a new revelation concerning dating, and they are with an unbeliever. This is double-mindedness.

> *⁵For those who live according to the flesh set their minds on the things of the flesh, but those who live according to the Spirit, the things of the Spirit.*
> *⁶For to be carnally minded is death, but to be spiritually minded is life and peace.*
> *⁷Because the carnal mind is enmity against God; for it is not subject to the law of God, nor indeed can be.*
> (Romans 8:5-7 NKJV)

The mind is not our enemy. One of the greatest truths we can know about walking with God and fellowshipping with Him is that our minds play an important part in this. When positioned correctly, the mind becomes a tremendous asset to every believer. In the above verses, the believer who is walking in new life is contrasted with the Jew who refuses to come out from under the Law. ***"Those who live according to the flesh"*** are those Jews who are trying to please God out of their dead nature by keeping laws that can't transform them from the inside. In Romans 2:1, Paul puts them in the same class with those Gentiles who ***"hold the truth in unrighteousness"*** (Romans 1:18 KJV):

Therefore you are inexcusable, O man, whoever you are who judge, for in whatever you judge another you condemn yourself; for you who judge practice the same things. (Romans 2:1 NKJV)

Those who remain born of the first birth and refuse to go through the second birth possess a mind that can only pick up things from the dead, sinful nature. Often, I will hear someone say, "Can you believe that so-and-so did that?" If I know that they have never met Jesus, I will say, "Why, yes, in fact, I would expect that from them." Dogs bark, ducks quack, cows moo, and sinners sin. This is all that they can know because their mind is connected to the death that is dominating their flesh.

On the other hand, when one becomes a son of God through the second birth and is placed on the path that leads to everlasting life, the whole game changes. *He acquires the capacity to discern things from his reborn nature.* Learning things from our inner man is called spiritual mindedness. Being spiritually minded is one of the primary ways that we begin our fellowship with God. It starts when we begin picking up on the realities of our regeneration in Christ, truths that will go as far as illuminating us into our specific destinies as individuals. Though some people think that this is self-centeredness, Paul's whole revelation concerned, *"Christ in you [me], the hope of glory"* (Colossians 1:27 KJV).

When I have spoken these certainties to people or preached them in churches, they have been a tremendous blessing to many people. Yet, I have had others say: "Yeah, well, this is too deep. How does this help me? I am a mother and a housewife." Or, "I am a businessman. How do these apply to me?" Don't you see? It doesn't matter whether you are a housewife, or businessman, or truck driver, or president of the United States. What you *are* has nothing to do with your *job.*

"For as many as are led by the <u>spirit</u> of God, they are the sons of God" (Romans 8:14 KJV). Now that we have received the spirit of Sonship, it is out of this spirit that God is able to lead and guide us. The Spirit of God, here, refers to our new nature, not to the Holy Ghost. By no means am I suggesting that the Holy Ghost doesn't lead us. He does. Jesus said that the Holy Spirit, the third person of the Trinity, guides us into all truth (John 16:13). John tells us that the Holy Spirit teaches us

all things (1 John 2:27). Before Paul mentions the leadership of the Holy Spirit, however, he informs us that the Holy Spirit leads the new nature.

We don't have to go to the tabernacle and find a bunch of scrolls to help us get to God. Instead, God is able to speak to us as a father to a child, and to grow us up into all things. It is this new nature that is constantly in fellowship with God that gives us the direction we need to carry out the blueprint for our lives. Not only does our fellowship with God help us to hit the mark every time, it provides the direction that we need to walk down the road of righteousness until we receive the crown of righteousness and take up our glorified bodies as fully manifested and revealed sons and daughters of God. Romans 8:15 (KJV) joyfully reminds us, *"For ye have not received the spirit of bondage again to fear; but ye have received the* _spirit_ *of adoption, whereby we cry, Abba, Father."*

The work of Christ released us from the spirit of bondage to sin and fear, the barrier to being led by the new nature. The New Living Translation says, *"You have not received a spirit that makes you fearful slaves."*

Paul calls the old man "the spirit of bondage again to fear." The "old man" was a slave to sin, its master, and worked day by day for it, storing up in its account the wrath of God (Romans 2:5). The wrath account, getting bigger and bigger by the day, kept man distanced from God, fearful of Him, knowing that this wrath had to be satisfied. However, we now can *"have peace with God through our Lord Jesus Christ"* (Romans 5:1 KJV), no longer having to stay away from Him because of a fearful conscience. We can get right on the path of the just and let Him lead us all the way into Him because of regeneration and reconciliation.

By regeneration and reconciliation, God immediately adopted us into His family. This did not come through the unrighteous nature that was bound by the fear of wrath, but rather, through our born again nature that is made up of the life that is in Christ Jesus. Just as Jesus calls God Father (John 5:17) because of His nature, so, too, do we because we now have His life.

"This sounds great, but how can I be sure that I am reconciled to God and equipped with this life?"

When I was a young man in junior high, maybe about twelve or thirteen, I used to run up to the altar every time my youth pastor called for people to get saved. I must have gotten saved twenty-five times when I was in sixth grade. Every week I wanted to make sure that I was saved. As time went by, I learned more about salvation. One day, I just became confident that I was saved, and I haven't gone up for a call since. All of us need this assurance, to wipe out the fear. Where can we locate that assurance?

When you are adopted into the family of God, you will know because your inward man will begin to call God, "Father." This is our witness that testifies to us that we are born again and have begun our true fellowship with God. Once we enter into right standing, our heart thinks of God and we gleefully say: "Daddy!" He is my Father. My Father loves me.

> ***And because you are sons, God has sent forth the <u>spirit</u> of His Son into your hearts, crying out, "Abba, Father!"*** (Romans 8:15 KJV)

This reminds me of the look my one-year-old nephew, Michael James, gives my brother when he sees him. Twenty people may be walking around the room at the same time. As Michael James' eyes scan the room, once they lock onto his father, he grins with a smile that says, "Daddy!" He knows his father by instinct and won't hesitate to respond to his voice.

CHAPTER SIXTEEN

True Worship Unto God as a Son or Daughter

"Have you drunk this "water"? If the answer is yes, your spiritual genetics give you access into the Holy of Holies, where your Father now awaits."

A Samaritan woman is drawing water from a well. Jesus approaches, and tells her about water that will cause her never to thirst again. Jesus tells her, in fact, that this "water" is so amazing that it is a spring of everlasting life (John 4:14 KJV). Failing to understand, the woman naively asks Jesus for some of it so she'll never be thirsty again, and won't have to keep making long trips to the well carrying those heavy ewers. Jesus responds concerning her personal life. He accurately tells her, by a word of knowledge, that she has had five husbands and the man she is currently living with is not her husband. Whether she knew it or not, Jesus was getting to the root of her trouble, the old nature that drove her flesh.

> *21Jesus said to her, "Woman, believe Me, the hour is coming when you will neither on this mountain, nor in Jerusalem, worship the Father.*
> *22You worship what you do not know; we know what we worship, for salvation is of the Jews.*
> *23But the hour is coming, and now is, when the <u>true worshipers</u> will worship the Father in <u>spirit and truth</u>; for the Father is seeking such to worship Him.*
> *24God is Spirit, and those who worship Him must worship in spirit and in truth."* (John 4:21-24 NKJV)

This is another scripture that was puzzling for me. Looking back, I must have known that I didn't know exactly what it meant to worship God in spirit and in truth. I did know that I had to worship God from within. That was as close as I could get in understanding. Sometimes I would get emotional during a worship service or while I was worshipping God alone, and I would think, "This is it. I am worshipping God from within." I wasn't wrong. I was onto something. I just needed to take a few more steps into it.

The Message Bible states John 4:21-24 this way:

> *21-23 "Believe me, woman, the time is coming when you Samaritans will worship the Father neither here at this mountain nor there in Jerusalem. You worship guessing in the dark; we Jews worship in the clear light of day. God's way of salvation is made available through the Jews. But the time is coming—it has, in fact, come—when what you're called will not matter and where you go to worship will not matter.*
> *24 "It's who you are and the way you live that count before God. Your worship must engage your spirit in the pursuit of truth...God is sheer being itself—Spirit. Those who worship Him must do it out of their very being, their spirits, their true selves, in adoration."*

Here is what Jesus was saying to the Samaritan woman regarding the new nature:

1.) *The hour had arrived:* This was the fullness of time spoken of in Galatians 4:4-5 when Christ had come to redeem humanity from the sinful nature.
2.) *The way of salvation is made through the Jews:* This way of salvation was none other than the Messiah who stood directly in front of her. Jesus unequivocally told her, *"I am He"* (v. 26), and that through Him the *outer* worship of the Jews and Samaritans would end.
3.) *It is who you are that counts before God:* After Christ's death and resurrection, sacrifices no longer meant anything to God.

That which the sacrifices and tabernacle represented had already come: Christ. His work produced what sacrifices could not: everlasting life.

4.) *Those who worship Him must do it out of their new life:* After Christ, the source of worship is no longer an outward act. The spring of all worship is the new nature. In order to tap that spring so that it can shoot up like a geyser, revelation is required (Ephesians 1:17-18).

What Jesus was explaining to the woman at the well was revolutionary. When He introduced the woman to the "water" that gives everlasting life, He was not introducing her to another set of religious customs or practices. Jesus was introducing "water" that could regenerate her spirit and make her a daughter of the Almighty God (Titus 3:5). Of course, this is not literal H₂O, the essence of *physical* life. The "water" that Jesus was introducing was the essence of *spiritual* life, the life of God. This "water" would bring her out of the flesh (where she couldn't please God) and into everlasting spiritual life (where she could please God). Mankind's relationship to God was about to change *in Him* and *through Him*.

As we look at the Epistles in the New Testament, we will see statements such as "In Christ," "In Him," and "In Whom." I accepted these when I was a young man, but I felt that I was not fully grasping them the way I knew was possible. My own lack of revelation was keeping me away from obtaining them fully.

Then I grew into understanding the realities of the new life in Christ. It all began to occur to me (as I am praying that it is now occurring to you), that "*in*" is depictive of the new nature. To say "In Christ" means that I am now talking about the life that He received from the Father and gave to me. It implies sharing of the same genome or spiritual genetics. Here are some Scriptures that include "In Christ", "In Him," and "In Whom."

> ***In whom*** **we have redemption through His blood, the forgiveness of sins** (Colossians 1:14 NKJV).

> ***Through whom*** **also we have access by faith into this grace in which we stand** (Romans 5:2 NKJV).

__In Him__ also we have obtained an inheritance (Ephesians 1:11 NKJV).

Even when we were dead in trespasses, made us alive together __with Christ__ (Ephesians 2:5 NKJV).

And hath raised us up together, and made us sit together in heavenly places __in Christ__ Jesus (Ephesians 2:6 KJV).

I have been crucified with Christ; it is no longer I who live, but __Christ lives in me__; and the life which I now live in the flesh I live by faith in the Son of God, who loved me and gave Himself for me (Galatians 2:20 NKJV).

Look at Galatians 2:20. I remember coming across this verse when the Spirit of God opened it up for me. It completely changed the way I read Galatians and how I understood the New Testament. This verse illuminates how the ministry of sin is overturned by the ministry of righteousness.

1.) *"I am crucified with Christ"*: This "I" refers to the old man born of Adam under sin.
2.) *"Nevertheless I live"*: This "I" refers to the new man born of God as a son.
3.) *"Yet not I"*: This "I" refers back again to the old nature, born of Adam, that animated the flesh and drove it to do wrong.
4.) *"Christ lives in me"*: This refers back to the new man born of God as a son, the life of John 5:26.
5.) *"The life which I now live in the flesh"*: The flesh is now being animated by the genome that came from the original blueprint, the *Logos*. No longer is the flesh the seat where sin has its manifestation. Instead, the flesh has become the seat where the life of God has its manifestation.

Little did the Samaritan woman realize, the Prophet by the well was speaking of "water" that could change her genome and perfect her worship toward God. This would enable her to finally reach God with her inner man and cease from all attempts to reach Him with the outer man. Have you drunk this "water"? If the answer is yes, your spiritual genetics give you access into the Holy of Holies, where your Father now awaits.

CHAPTER SEVENTEEN

Our Down Payment

"The next time you wonder what is beyond the veil of death, just have a look inside."

I got my first good-paying job three months after I graduated college. I had never known what it was like to have money pile up in my bank account. I was accustomed to seeing sparse dollars in there. When my first paycheck came, I could have lived on it for a month. But, before I could spend a fourth of it, another paycheck came, followed by another, and then another.

By the time I had $7,000 sitting in my bank account, I decided to go get a nice set of wheels. I marched down to the Jeep dealership and sat in all of the newest Grand Cherokee editions. The salespeople looked at me funny. I was twenty-two, but looked probably nineteen. Doubtless they didn't believe I was serious about buying a brand new Jeep. After all, how much money could this young kid have?

When I decided I wanted the black one with the sunroof, they began drawing up the papers, still uncertain of how serious I was. Then, to their relief, I put $2,100 dollars on the table as a down payment. This money proved that there was more invested in this agreement than just talk. The money on the table was my earnest money. It was the cash down to prove that I had more where that came from.

Whether you like it or not, the old saying is true, "Money talks." The salesperson and her manager began to speak to me differently after that. They saw that I was completely, 100% sincere and genuine. The $2,100 plunked down in front of their eyes was proof that I planned to make the Jeep mine. I showed them the money.

Just as buying a vehicle is a process, God's redemptive plan is a process. It is not accomplished in one night. God's plan requires time to reach fulfillment. God spoke of this plan immediately after Adam sinned and, yes, it wasn't until 4,000 years later that the Redeemer came.

Likewise, salvation is just as much of a process. The moment we receive Jesus by faith, our new birth takes place, and redemption commences. We begin the journey down the path of the just, fellowshipping with our Father from our new nature, and the crown of righteousness awaits us at the end.

> *13 In whom ye also trusted, after that ye heard the word of truth, the gospel of your salvation: in whom also after that ye believed, ye were sealed with that <u>holy spirit</u> of promise,*
> *14 Which is the earnest of our inheritance until the redemption of the purchased possession, unto the praise of his glory.* (Ephesians 1:13-14 KJV)

In Ephesians, Paul talks about this *new nature*. The *new nature* came by hearing the Word of God (Romans 10:14-17), and trusting the word of truth, the gospel of our salvation (Ephesians 1:12-13). This *new nature* is *"the holy spirit of promise."* Just because the word "holy" proceeds the word "spirit" does not necessarily mean it is referring to the third person of the Godhead. Within Bible interpretation, *context* always determines meaning, not *isolated words*. In this *context*, "holy spirit" is not referring to the Holy Spirit, the third person of the Godhead. It is referring to our reborn spirit in Christ. In this case, "holy" is an adjective that denotes that the promised reborn spirit is sacred and set apart.

Ephesians 1:14 goes on to let us know that the new spirit that we have received is just a first payment, given by God to us, to prove to us that He has a plan in place that will eventually result in our full redemption and possession. The reborn life that we experience here on earth is just a taste of all that is to come. This first money down is proof of God's sincerity to redeem us from the death that is now at work in our flesh. As a result of receiving the new nature (or "that holy spirit of promise"), the believer is then qualified to experience the power of the world to come (Hebrews

6:5) through the complete union with the Holy Spirit (the Baptism in the Holy Spirit).

We are not at the finish line yet, for death is still at work inside of our bodies. Although I have met those who don't think so, I have yet to see the proof. Popes, bishops, pastors, evangelists, mighty apostles, valued prophets, and men and women who have had great revelation from Jesus Christ have all lain down in the grave. Despite all of the miraculous healings and creative miracles I have seen in my own life and ministry, the healing power of God cannot do away with mortality and death. Mortality has yet to be swallowed up in our physical nature. Just as Christ Jesus died physically, so will our bodies die.

Our new nature is God's down payment to us in this life, ensuring us that the adoption process will be made complete after physical death. This new nature, our born again spirit ("that holy spirit of promise" and "spirit of adoption") will be the life that comes to animate our brand-new spirit body that Christ first put on when He was raised from the dead.

> **But if the <u>spirit</u> of Him who raised Jesus from the dead dwells in you, He who raised Christ from the dead will also give life to your mortal bodies through His <u>spirit</u> who dwells in you.** (Romans 8:11 NKJV)

With this exhilarating statement, Paul's explanation of being a son and daughter of God through the second birth takes on a whole new dimension.

Paul was adamant that the process of physical death does not void our Sonship. Instead, it does the opposite; it accelerates it. Because of Christ, death has been reversed. Where death ought to have separated us eternally from God, now, ironically, through death, we are brought into the fullness of our inheritance as sons and daughters of God. This is part of the reason Paul said, **"For to me to live is Christ, and to die is gain"** (Philippians 1:21). For us to live as believers is to have the spirit of Christ living in us. For us to die as believers is to come one step closer to our full inheritance, our glorified bodies, promised to the adopted children of God.

Interestingly enough, Romans 8:23 says that we are "waiting for the adoption, the redemption of our *bodies*." It dawned on me one day when

I was explaining these verses to one of my friends over the phone. In fact, it hit me so hard I had to pause and very nearly put the phone down: the life that we received in our new nature is a sample of the life that we will one day receive in our glorified human bodies. Until that day, it is a living proof and witness that it is on the way.

Though our bodies are dying, a witness on the inside continually affirms that it will soon be changed. This is the earnest money of our inheritance, the holy spirit of promise. One day, when we get our full inheritance, the life that is in our spirit will be taken up by our glorified bodies, and our spirit and body will be forged together forever, never to be separated by death again. We will go throughout eternity with the life of God flowing through us continually. Should we ever doubt or become unsure of God's plan we can look to the down payment that God gave us: our new man. It serves as a persistent witness that death has been defeated. *The next time you wonder what is beyond the veil of death, just have a look inside.*

CHAPTER EIGHTEEN

What About Our Bodies?

"Let's be logical about one thing: Paul did not halt his systematic argument concerning the redemption of the human race to mention your arthritis."

"If you are bald headed when you sin, you will be bald headed when you get saved." This humorous statement from my spiritual father illuminates the truth that being reborn does not immediately affect our bodies. Unless some healing or creative miracle takes place at the moment of salvation, your body will look the same once you give your life to Jesus.

Paul understood that the Church at Rome was going to wonder, "Well, what about our bodies? What happened to it when the life of Christ came into me?" Now that the flesh had been animated by the life of God, and no longer by a sinful spirit, the question became, "What happens to my flesh? Are we going to suffer? Are we going to die? What is next?"

> *¹⁶The Spirit Himself bears witness with our spirit that we are children of God,*
> *¹⁷and if children, then heirs—heirs of God and joint heirs with Christ, if indeed we suffer with Him, that we may also be glorified together.* (Romans 8:16-17 NKJV)

"You see, Chris? The Bible says that we must suffer. I guess God gave me my arthritis to teach me a lesson, eh?"

Let's be logical about one thing: Paul did not halt his systematic argument concerning the redemption of the human race to mention your arthritis. No, the suffering he is referring to here is physical death.

Although we are heirs of God and joint-heirs with Jesus Christ, we still have an appointment with death: *"And as it is appointed for men to die once"* (Hebrews 9:27 NKJV).

Despite the new life that now is at work in us, death is still at work inside our flesh. This does not mean our bodies are sinful and evil, it just means that they are mortal, subject to death. The weaknesses that we deal with now are a result of our mortality. Some people insist: "Ah, yes. So that means we can expect suffering. We can expect sickness and disease." I am not sure why people want to think this way. No. Sickness and disease are the siblings of sin, and Christ defeated them on the cross, so they no longer have dominion over a child of God (Romans 6:14). *In light of the glorified bodies awaiting those who have become children of God, having to deal with this mortal body is considered suffering.*

Yet, that doesn't mean we have to suffer in pain. It means that the mortal body *pales* in comparison to what is soon and coming.

My good friend Sean got his license to drive before I did. As high school juniors, we were looking to expand our social lives beyond the lockers at school. The first car that his dad bought him was an old beater Buick. When Sean rolled that baby into the parking lot at school the first day, I didn't see an old, smelly pile of junk. I saw fun and freedom. We took that car everywhere, and by everywhere, I mean fishing every day. "The Fishing Mobile" was an amazing machine to us—*until* Sean's dad brought him a brand new GMC Envoy. I couldn't believe my eyes. This was the kind of car that a rich person would own. I didn't think 17-year-olds were even allowed to drive one.

Sean's dad didn't get rid of the old Buick right away. It sat on the driveway for weeks, sad because it had nobody to drive it. Sitting next to that Envoy, it looked dejected and miserable. One day we decided to climb into the Buick, for old time's sake. The stench! The stench that came out of that car when we opened the doors was absolutely stultifying. I said to Sean, "Can you believe we used to take this car fishing every day, and thought we were cool?" We just never knew what else we could have.

> *For I consider that the sufferings of this present time are not worthy to be compared with the glory which shall be revealed in us.* (Romans 8:18 NKJV)

Whether we want to believe it or not, the body that we look at in the mirror every day is an old beat up Buick. Each day that we take it out for a spin, we bring it closer and closer to the junkyard. The limitations and trouble that we face right now are largely because our bodies have yet to be redeemed.

> *¹For we know that if <u>our earthly house</u>, this tent, is destroyed, we have a building from God, a house not made with hands, <u>eternal</u> in the <u>heavens</u>.*
> *²<u>For in this we groan, earnestly desiring to be clothed with our habitation which is from heaven,</u>*
> *³if indeed, having been clothed, we shall not be found naked.*
> *⁴For <u>we who are in this tent groan</u>, being <u>burdened</u>, not because we want to be unclothed, but further clothed, that <u>mortality may be swallowed up by life.</u>*
> (2 Corinthians 5:1-4 NKJV)

In 2 Corinthians 5, Paul is comparing the present earthly body with the heavenly body that we are promised as children of God. One body has death working in it; the other has glory inhabiting it. Because death is now working in our present mortal bodies, there are some heavy-duty limitations imposed upon our flesh. Here is a small list of them:

1.) The possibility of getting sick (James 5:15)
2.) Susceptibility to temptation (James 1:13-16)
3.) Potential to deviate from the new nature by committing sin (1 John 2:1) When a *sinner* commits a sin, he or she is doing it *by* nature; it is bred out of his deadness of spirit. Because it is his or her nature, it goes on perpetually. Should a *believer* commit a sin, it is now *against* his or her nature. According to James, this is the flesh being tempted, drawn away, and enticed (James 3:14).
4.) Vulnerability to demon spirits (Ephesians 4:27; 6:12; 1 Peter 5:8-9)
5.) Vulnerability to false doctrine which can lead astray (1 John 2:26)

6.) Cares of this world (Mark 4:19)

7.) Deceitfulness of riches (Mark 4:19)

8.) Lusts of other things (Mark 4:19)

9.) The capacity to get into quarrels, unforgiveness, division, strife, and offense (Romans 16:17; 2 Timothy 2:23; Philippians 1:10; 1 Corinthians 1:10)

10.) The possibility of becoming a deserter to the faith, apostate, cast away from the family of God (2 Timothy 3:8; 1 Corinthians 9:27; Hebrews 3:6)

In understanding Sonship, Paul sought to explain just how far Sonship goes. Though our flesh will one day wear out, our right standing with God and our position as children of God do not end at physical death. By the time Paul wrote Romans, thousands of believers who had experienced the second birth had already died. The revelation that Paul received from Christ, however, accounted for Sonship in relation to the flesh and death.

> *But if the spirit of Him who raised Jesus from the dead dwell in you, He who raised Christ from the dead will also give life to your mortal bodies through His spirit who dwells in you.* (Romans 8:11 NKJV)

With this exhilarating statement, Paul's explanation of being a son and daughter of God through the second birth takes on a whole new dimension.

When I was twenty-two, I was a pastoral care minister. Day in and day out, I visited hospitals in and around the city of Detroit. I probably made around three hospital calls a day, five days a week, for two and a half years. I kept a record in my smart phone of every visit. At the end of my time with that church, I counted up my hospital appointments: over 1,600 visits.

The point is that I preached over 1,600 short sermons at the edge of a hospital bed. In order to make this feasible, I needed a stockpile of really good scriptures on healing. Romans 8:11 was one of my favorites. I would walk into that hospital with my dark hair all gelled up and say, "Sister so-

and-so, the same Holy Ghost that pulled up Jesus Christ out of that grave, that Holy Ghost is inside of you right now! And if you will believe it, then by golly, you will get off this bed!" I was a feisty, skinny little preacher at age twenty-two. (Now that I think of it, things probably haven't changed that much.)

I would walk out of the hospital room knowing that I really didn't have a grasp on the verse. Oh, don't get me wrong. I believed it to be true: I was walking in the light I had received about it. I just had an incomplete understanding. God wanted to open up the verse to me a little more.

One day, it hit me. The verse is not about our current mortal bodies being quickened by the Holy Spirit for a physical healing in this life. Instead, it is telling us that the life of Christ that is currently working in the new nature will eventually begin working in a body that is prepared for us on the other side of death. God delights in healing people for a variety of reasons, one of them being that healing is the evidence of a quickening power that exists. It is a taste of what is to come and gives evidence that there is more in store.

Notice:

1.) *The spirit of Him that raised Jesus from the dead*: In light of John 5:21, 26 (NKJV), I had this verse all wrong. The Holy Ghost didn't raise Jesus from the dead. The Father raised Jesus from the dead with His life:

> *²¹For as <u>the Father</u> raises the dead and gives life.*
> *²⁶For as <u>the Father</u> has life in Himself; so he has granted the Son to have life in Himself.*

2.) *Dwell in you:* Christ gave this life to us in the second birth. Through this life we have become just as much sons and daughters of God as Jesus has become. Jesus was the firstborn, and we all have taken a number right behind Him.

3.) *Shall also quicken your mortal bodies by His spirit that dwelleth in you:* Our bodies are currently mortal and, by definition, subject to death. The paradoxical element of death is that, through death, for those who believe, death is swallowed up by the life that exists on the other side. This new life working in our spirit is destined to get a hold of our fleshy material and work for us a new and eternal *body*, all according to God's redemptive plan.

So why can't we have our glorified bodies now instead of waiting around for all the vulnerabilities of the current body and the possibility of bad things? *That is because we have another, bigger, glorious responsibility to mankind.* The dispensation of grace that we are now living is a period that God allotted so that the world can be reconciled to Him. You may go to work every day as a truck driver, a nurse, clerk, businessman or businesswoman, but that is just your vocation. God has positioned you strategically within your vocation so that you may better handle your *real* assignment, the only thing that is keeping you here*: You are a minister of reconciliation.*

we are a minister

> [18]*Now all things are of God, who has reconciled us to Himself through Jesus Christ, and has given us the ministry of reconciliation,*
> [19]*that is, that God was in Christ reconciling the world to Himself, not imputing [charging] their trespasses to them, and has committed to us the word of reconciliation.* [20]*Now then, we are ambassadors for Christ, as though God were pleading through us: we implore you on Christ's behalf, be reconciled to God.*
> (2 Corinthians 5:18-20 NKJV)

As ambassadors of the Kingdom of God, we have been given the commission to endure the hardships of this unregenerate world as soldiers on foreign soil, to preach the word of faith (Matthew 28:18-20; Mark 16:15-18; 2 Timothy 2:3-4), and expand the Kingdom of God. Believers who are not consciously aware of this live their lives with only token purpose. *Those who place their earthly vocation above their heavenly assignment have reversed God's order, and have prioritized fleeting duty over eternal responsibility.* A greater revelation of eternal responsibility causes us to operate in it, all while nurturing our earthly vocation and temporary responsibilities. *The believer operating in the revelation of his high calling will be more joyful and less confused than the believer who sees only an earthly vocation as his purpose.*

Our Father has made us a promise called "salvation" and has given us proof of that promise: our new natures. At present, the completion of our salvation still remains a hopeful expectation. Though the work needful for salvation has been completed, we have yet to receive everything that has been provided through it. ***"Be sober, putting on the breastplate of faith and love; and for a helmet, the <u>hope of salvation</u>."*** (1 Thessalonians 5:8 KJV)

Eternal life is *now* our possession, but we have not yet received the completion of our inheritance: our glorified bodies. When our assignment is complete and this period of reconciliation is over, our corruptible bodies will put on incorruption, and our mortal flesh will put on immortality. This is known as *"the manifestation [revealing] of the sons of God."*

> ***For the earnest expectation of the creature waiteth for the manifestation of the sons of God.*** (Romans 8:19 KJV)

A revealed son or daughter of God has taken upon the likeness of Christ in nature, as well as the image of Christ in appearance. When Christ Jesus was raised from the dead, He came back with a glorified body. Not until we have these bodies, which are conformed to His present image, can we be considered a "manifested son of God." Though the life in us is exactly the same and our natures are no different than His, we—with all creation—still look forward to the day when the adoption process will be completed, and we take up glory in our bodies. Not only will we put on glory after this age, but also so will all creation. Notice:

> ***Because the creation itself also will be delivered from the bondage of corruption into the glorious <u>liberty</u> of the children of God.*** (Romans 8:21 NKJV)

This liberty is none other than freedom from death. There is another age coming, and we anticipate it with great expectation. Until then, let us keep our boots tied tight and endure the difficulties of being a good soldier. Perhaps the greatest way to do this, before we go any further with *our* journey, is to examine the life of one of God's best soldiers, the Apostle Paul.

Part II

Another Man's Journey

CHAPTER NINETEEN

Why Did God Choose Paul?

"Paul journeyed along a path of fellowship with God that did not end when his head hit the dusty floor of the Coliseum."

Buried within the Old Testament is a marvelous image of Jesus that could not come forth until the finished work of Christ was accomplished. Prophecies, especially in Isaiah, refer to the advent of the Messiah. With Jesus' life, crucifixion and resurrection, those prophecies were fulfilled.

Next, God needed to reveal the last aspect of the Gospel. It was no longer enough to hear about Christ's coming prophetically. It wasn't enough just to hear He had come in the flesh. Now, this was not *only* Jesus Christ; it was Jesus Christ *now in us, to us, and through us.* It was time for the next installation: who He now has become *in* us. The great Christian apologist C.S. Lewis wrote, "The Son of God became a man to enable man to become sons of God."

The Holy Spirit came onto the scene and began looking for a messenger He could show that image to, so that the messenger, in turn, could teach it to the Church and establish it as the foundation on which everything else could stand. God couldn't just pick Joe Anybody off the street for this task; Joe wouldn't have had the knowledge of the Law. God needed someone with a stellar knowledge of the Law so that He could get in there and, by the Holy Ghost, re-program His interpretation of that Law.

God selected Paul for this assignment. Paul's superior knowledge of Old Testament Law and the Prophets made him the perfect candidate. It is safe to believe that Paul had the Law memorized, as well as having a persuasive interpretation of it, so much so that it made him one of the leading Pharisees of his day. Paul had all the building blocks he needed to reveal Christ from the Old Testament, and how the Law now pertained to the new dispensation of grace.

> *15But when it pleased God, who separated me from my mother's womb and called me through His grace, 16to reveal His Son in me, that I might preach Him among the Gentiles.* (Galatians 1:15-16 NKJV)

When Paul was in his mother's womb, God marked him for the Gospel. The word *marked* is the Greek word, *aphorizo*, and means "to set off by boundary." Just as the end zone of a football field is ten yards, marked off by paint and orange posts, so, too, was Paul marked and set apart from the others who were born during his time. In explaining to the Churches of Galatia about his ministry, he says that he was "called." This is the Greek word, *kaleo*, and means, "to bid, name, call in a loud voice, invite, to give a name to." God marked him for a special encounter that occurred in Acts 9. This encounter turned Saul into Paul and changed the course of his life. It placed him along the path of transformation and literally made him into *another* man.

In appearing to Paul on the road to Damascus, Jesus appointed Paul to the special designation He had desired for him since the moment he was conceived. Yes, God intended for Paul to have this appointment. Through the divine hand of providence, Saul (Paul) unknowingly spent his whole life preparing for it. It was this preparation, combined with his conversion that made him the perfect candidate to champion the Gospel.

But what was it about Paul that made him shine above the rest? He gives his credentials and tells us:

> *4...If anyone else thinks he may have confidence in the flesh, I more so: 5circumcised the eighth day, of the stock of Israel, of the tribe of Benjamin, a Hebrew of the Hebrews; concerning the law, a Pharisee; 6concerning zeal, persecuting the church; concerning the righteousness which is in the law, blameless.* (Philippians 3:4-6 NKJV)

Other than Jesus Christ, no New Testament figure has had more impact on the proclamation and preservation of the Gospel than the Apostle Paul. If anyone ever took the journey of power and walked hand in hand with Jesus Christ, it was Paul. From his introduction in Acts 7 as Saul of Tarsus, to his last recorded words in Second Timothy 4, he is a prime example of one who steps onto the path of righteousness and walks it straight into eternity, leaving for us all the revelations he discovered during his journey.

It is commonly expected that once the call of God is fulfilled over one's life, he or she will get all kinds of honors, a library named after them, a wall full of plaques, and the respect of their spiritual sons and daughters, none of which are bad. As a matter of fact, I would love to have more plaques on my wall. Yet, I am simply setting a plumb line to put the understanding of our hearts into true alignment.

Look at snippets of what Paul said as his ministry was winding down:

> *⁶For I am already being poured out as a drink offering, and the time of my departure is at hand.*
> *⁷I have fought a good fight, I have finished my race, I have kept the faith.*
> *⁸Finally, there is laid up for me the crown of righteousness, which the Lord, the righteous Judge, shall give to me on that Day...*
>
> *¹⁰Demas has forsaken me, having loved this present world...*
>
> *¹³Bring the cloak that I left with Carpus at Troas, when you come—and the books, especially the parchments...*
> *¹⁴Alexander the coppersmith did me much harm. May the Lord repay him according to his works.*
>
> *¹⁶At my first defense, no one stood with me, but all forsook me...*
> *¹⁷But the Lord stood with me and strengthened me, so that the message might be preached fully through me,*

and that all the Gentiles might hear. (2 Timothy 4:6-8, 10, 13-14, 16-17 NKJV)

This in Second Timothy is the last we hear from Paul in the New Testament. The Great Apostle to the Gentiles finished his race as a prisoner in a murky, dank cell. Paul noted that even the believers he had poured Christ into didn't show up to defend him at trial, no doubt fearing they would get the same penalty as Paul's. If he had any retirement at all, it was listening to the henchman grind the ax as he awaited his beheading. He was ending his life without fanfare or kudos, in apparent disgrace.

What in the world could allow Paul to endure in such a state?

It was his walk with God, the same thing that got him going in the beginning. Out of that walk, the Jesus he witnessed in Acts 9:3-7 gave him the power to carry on until the end: No matter the calamity or humiliation, he said, *"The Lord stood with me, and strengthened me."*

Through divine revelation, Paul had seen a crown of righteousness in the hand of His Lord, named after the path of righteousness that he elected to take. Whatever the crown looked like, it was *not* given as a reward for his ministry. It was given to designate Paul throughout eternity as one of those who walked in Christ upon the earth. It earmarked him as part of the company of the redeemed, who, through great tribulation and trial, upheld his fellowship with God and, at last, received the end of his faith and the salvation of his soul (1 Peter 1:9).

Paul journeyed along a path of fellowship with God that did not end when his head hit the dusty floor of the Coliseum. Contrary to the mad thinking of Nero, which sought to terminate Paul's journey through death, the path of the righteous led straight out of Rome and directly into the high court of heaven.

The journey does not begin when one starts ministry or enters into Christian service.

The journey begins the moment an individual turns his or her life over to Jesus Christ by faith in His already accomplished work, and it ends in that one moment when the spirit stands completely undisguised before the One who gave him that new life, Jesus Christ.

Paul finished successfully and so can we. If we do what he did along the way, there won't be any doubt that we will end strong, just like Paul.

CHAPTER TWENTY

Paul Went Up by Revelation

"He comes on the scene with a new revelation that becomes the bedrock of Christianity, often referring to it as his gospel. Where did he get it if he had nobody there to teach him?"

After Paul encountered Jesus Christ on the Damascus road, his next meeting was receiving the Baptism in the Holy Spirit (which was, no doubt, accompanied by praying with other tongues, as in Acts 9:17). We are then given hints as to what Paul did shortly after his conversion and baptism experiences. The path that God placed Paul upon didn't lead him to go consult with the head honchos right away.

> *¹⁶I did not immediately confer with flesh and blood,*
> *¹⁷Nor did I go up to Jerusalem to those who were apostles before me; but I went to Arabia, and returned again to Damascus.*
> *¹⁸Then after three years I went up to Jerusalem to see Peter, and remained with him fifteen days.*
> *¹⁹But I saw none of the other apostles except James, the Lord's brother.* (Galatians 1:16-19 NKJV)

Paul has a radical encounter with Jesus Christ, is reborn in due season, and the Spirit of God leads him away from Jerusalem and into Arabia, particularly into Damascus (modern day Syria). Here, Paul spends three solid years.

Pride could have led him to go to Jerusalem immediately (where the Church leaders were), as a converted man, and show off his intellect and education. Paul knew more about the Law and the Prophets than all the other Apostles. He had gone to the best rabbinical schools, not to mention that he was smarter, with command of multiple languages and philosophy. But this would only have led to trouble, as it was neither intellect nor his current interpretation of the Law that God needed. (Nor did God need a clash between apostles.) God needed to reframe his interpretation of the Law, and for the first time, give someone a systematic and comprehensive spiritual understanding of it.

Look at what Paul said again: *"Nor did I go up to Jerusalem to those who were apostles before me"* (Galatians 1:17 NKJV). This is pretty strong language; Paul is implying that, by the time he was writing to the churches of Galatia, he was on the same level as the other Apostles. "They may have been apostles before I was, but I have finally caught up."

Then look at what Paul says about the Apostles just a few verses later:

> *But from those who seemed to be something—whatever they were, it makes no difference to me; God shows personal favoritism to no man—for those who seemed to be something added nothing to me.* (Galatians 2:6 NKJV)

Translate this into modern day speech. Paul was saying, "I finally met the head honchos after years of being away. We did what all preachers do when we get together. We had a conference. Although they were apostles before I was, they didn't add a drop to me at all." This indicates that Paul had found an accelerant that caused him to make up time and span the revelation gap that separated him and the Apostles.

So what was it that Paul had to accelerate his journey?

After spending three years in Arabia, Paul made an appearance in Jerusalem and stayed with Peter. From the account of Paul's travels, described in Galatians 1, the two apostolic giants had only fifteen days together. Peter, probably for the first time, conceded in 2 Peter 3:16 (NLT), *"Some of his comments are hard to understand."*

Paul was a thinker, and Peter was a fisherman. Except for their passion for Christ, it would have been an awkward stay. Needless to say, fifteen days was not enough time for Paul to glean all of the wisdom Peter had learned from walking with Jesus.

During those two brief weeks, Paul also met with James. James had been privileged to grow up in the same household as his elder half-brother, Jesus, but there is no way Paul could have learned all that James could have taught him. Two weeks and a day after he arrived in Jerusalem, Paul left, heading into the regions of Syria and Cilicia with what he had gained from his time with Peter and James. This wouldn't be enough, however, to build inside of Paul the revelation that God would use to save the Church from heresy. There had to be something else working.

Fourteen years after Paul visited Jerusalem, he went back. Only this time he went back an utterly different man. This was not the same guy who had stayed with Peter and conversed with James. Something had been installed into Paul's inner man that made him an authority in the Church, and God's man of the hour, even though he had never walked with Jesus the way the Apostles had.

And I went up by revelation. (Galatians 2:2 KJV)

What a difference in the way Paul compares how he visited Jerusalem. The first time, Paul said, *"I went up to Jerusalem."* The second time Paul said, *"I went up by revelation." The revelation of Christ now <u>in</u> the believer was what made all of the difference between his visits.* Unlike the first visit, Paul didn't go by himself and spend two weeks *learning* from Peter and James. He had experienced a serious growth spurt; he would now be the teacher.

Growth spurts make all the difference. I have a friend, whom I'll call Russell, who was such a dominant basketball player that I always thought he'd make the NBA. One day, I mentioned to him that I'd heard that another friend, Maurice, was on his team. Russell laughed, "Yeah, but he is a scrub. He's always riding the bench." I was surprised. I always thought Maurice's drive and determination would have gotten him farther.

A couple of years passed, and suddenly Maurice was in the newspaper repeatedly. As a high school junior, he led his team to the State Championship, and won. After his senior year, he received a scholarship to Michigan State University, played four years at Michigan State, and took his team to the Final Four during his senior year. Later, the Dallas Mavericks drafted him. I will never forget watching Maurice on television, remembering how Russell called him a scrub. (Russ did not make the NBA, by the way.) I finally asked Russ, "What happened to Maurice? You used to call him a scrub."

Russell said, "Chris, one summer he had a growth spurt, and he wasn't the same guy. Maurice came back to the team and became our best player." This growth spurt launched Maurice into success.

Paul, though not a basketball player, had a growth spurt of his own. As Maurice showed up on the court, a transformed ball player, Paul showed up in Jerusalem a transformed apostle. He even brought two of his understudies with him, a way of showing that he was already duplicating himself—the touchstone of a true apostle.

> **And communicated to them that gospel which I preach among the Gentiles, but privately to those who were of reputation, lest by any means I might run, or had run, in vain.** (Galatians 2:2 NKJV)

The man Saul would have wanted to rush right up to Jerusalem and tell the Apostles what they did *not* know about the Law and the Prophets. But the Spirit of God had grabbed him. This Paul was now humble. He laid out his whole doctrine for a thorough cross-examination of everything he had received as revelation. Paul was so certain of the path the Spirit of God was leading him on, that it made no difference if the greatest apostles alive examined it. It would hold to be exact and true.

Not only could *"those who seemed to be somewhat"* (Galatians 2:6 KJV) find no cracks in his foundation, they could add nothing to him. Paul had everything they had. All they did was urge Paul to remember the poor as he went to the Gentiles. No problem, he agreed, it was something *"I have always been eager to do"* (Galatians 2:10 KJV).

The story takes an interesting turn here. Later, while in Antioch, Paul got in Peter's face and corrected him on a matter of principle.

> *11Now when Peter had come to Antioch, I withstood him to his face, because he was to be blamed;*

12For before certain men came from James, he [Peter] would eat with the Gentiles; but when they came, he withdrew and separated himself, fearing those who were of the circumcision.

13And the rest of the Jews also played the hypocrite with him, so that even Barnabas was carried away with their hypocrisy.

14But when I saw that they were not straightforward about the truth of the gospel, I said to Peter before them all, "If you, being a Jew, live in the manner of Gentiles and not as the Jews, why do you compel Gentiles to live as Jews?" (Galatians 2:11-14 NKJV)

Peter had stopped eating the same foods that Gentiles ate and had begun eating only kosher food once again. He knew better. In Acts 10, Peter had already had a vision of an open heaven and a sheet that came down from it:

12In it were all kinds of four-footed animals of the earth, wild beasts, creeping things, and birds of the air.

13And a voice came to him, "Rise, Peter; kill and eat."

14But Peter said, "Not so, Lord! For I have never eaten anything common or unclean.

15And a voice spoke to him again the second time, "What God has cleansed you must not call common." (Acts 10:12-15 NKJV)

After a battle in his own mind, Peter had concluded, ***"God has shown me that I should not call any man common or unclean"*** (Acts 10:28 KJV). In other words, Peter started to see that anyone born of the new birth, Jew or Gentile, was now acceptable to God, having the life of Christ. Although Peter was obedient to God in Acts 10, he started to fall back from it. The issue was *not* what he was eating. The issue was that what he ate indicated what he *believed*. In Acts 10, God was trying to do much more than give Peter a menu. God was trying to deepen Peter's understanding of the new man in Christ Jesus. All through Scripture, Peter struggled with this revelation.

Therefore, it took Paul to declare, ***"There is neither Jew nor Greek, there is neither slave nor free, there is neither male nor female; for you are all one in Christ Jesus"*** (Galatians 3:28 NKJV). Peter still somewhat held onto the belief that it was his Jewish blood that gave him access to God. Unlike Peter, Paul came to understand that it was the new nature that gave mankind access to God. Therefore fellowship with God is not found in the keeping of Jewish customs. Despite the heritage of the outer man, anyone who places their faith in Christ receives this new life and is accepted by God.

Unholstering the revelation he gained in the seventeen years away from Jerusalem, Paul corrected Peter, Barnabas, and all other Jews who were caught up in this hypocrisy. Single-handedly, with the revelation he had gained, Paul saved the Apostles from drifting back into Judaism. Paul immediately laid it out in Galatians 2:15-6:15 (as well as in his other epistles), just after he tells how he corrected the pillars of the church.

When I saw this, I thought, *Ok. He didn't walk with Jesus. He was a Pharisee, and was like all the other politically religious Pharisees. He gets saved. He gets filled with the Holy Ghost. He comes on the scene with a new revelation that becomes the bedrock of Christianity, often referring to it as his gospel. Where did he get it if he had nobody there to teach him?*

CHAPTER TWENTY-ONE

Praying in Tongues Revealed the Old Testament to Paul

"All of Paul's considerable Old Testament knowledge began to get deciphered, as the Holy Ghost cracked for him that which had been locked up through the ages."

[10] Of this salvation the prophets have inquired and searched carefully, who prophesied of the grace that would come unto you,
[11] searching what, or what manner of time, the Spirit of Christ who was in them was indicating when He testified beforehand the sufferings of Christ and the glories that would follow. (1 Peter 1:10-11 NKJV)

Christ Jesus remained a mystery in the Old Testament. Although those writings painted a picture of the wonderful Messiah, those who prophesied and wrote about Him and those who were reading about Him could not see Him until the Holy Spirit came on the scene. Jesus had been adamant to the Disciples that they must not begin their ministry until the Holy Spirit arrived.

I thank my God, I speak with tongues more than ye all.
(1 Corinthians 14:18 KJV)

It was through praying in tongues, releasing forth the mind of Christ in a mystery, that the Spirit of God began to illuminate to Paul the revelation of God from the Old Testament. All of Paul's considerable Old Testament knowledge began to get deciphered, as the Holy Ghost cracked for him that which had been locked up through the ages.

Paul was God's super soldier from the day of his birth. At first, his zeal caused a great persecution against the Church. But, when Paul was finally chosen by God and baptized in the Holy Spirit, he found a new teacher in the Spirit of God. As the Holy Spirit sat as Paul's tutor, uncovering what the Law and the Prophets indicated about Christ, the mystery of Christ Jesus from the Old Testament went up in mystery form, and God sent it back in the form of revelation knowledge.

Before, no teacher had been able to do this. Paul said, ***"These things we also speak, not in words which man's wisdom teaches, but which the Holy Ghost teaches"*** (1 Corinthians 2:13 NKJV). The "things" that he speaks is the revelation of Jesus Christ that once remained a secret to the whole world. He acquired this from the Holy Spirit. Just as soon as Paul was baptized in the Holy Ghost and the Spirit of God began to assist him with his prayer language, the information began to flow.

"What information?" you ask. *It is the whole mind of Christ.* When the Spirit of God comes to teach you, He begins to fill you with the thoughts of God, including His plan of redemption in Christ.

> **For who hath known the mind of the Lord, that he may instruct him? but we have the mind of Christ.** (1 Corinthians 2:16 KJV)

Seventeen years of meditating the Law and the Prophets through praying in tongues became the accelerant that pushed Paul into revelation knowledge, making him the Great Apostle. This revelation steered Paul toward a true spiritual walk in God, leading the church away from carnal doctrines, meaningless traditions, and exclusive religion. It ignited a form of meditation that led him away from fleshly interpretations to preserve the Church that Jesus had built.

The journey accelerates and takes off when you grab your prayer language and begin praying in tongues. As Paul found, tongues is a door that opens up a whole new world of understanding, furnishing the components needed to make the journey. The revelation that it installs within your heart makes you effective in God's redemptive plan and a nuisance to hell. This, of course, cannot go unchecked by the Kingdom of Darkness.

CHAPTER TWENTY-TWO

Paul's Spiritual Struggle

"If God's people could get serious about their journey, counting it a joy to batten down the hatches when darkness arises, there would be a great breaking forth of light, a revival, in the land."

The more that you understand the mystery that surrounds Christ, don't think for one second that darkness will not notice. You are picking a fight. Many believers who come to understand this decide that a fight is not what they desire in this life. One person said fearfully: "I have a husband and a job. I just don't have any time to welcome Satan's attacks."

I understood her point. However, it goes back to our earthly responsibility that equips us to carry out our eternal purpose. If God's people could get serious about their journey, counting it a joy to batten down the hatches when darkness arises, there would be a great breaking forth of light, a revival, in the land. Currently, many Christians just want to marry, have babies, get a good job, attend church, tithe, and hear more about how to have a blessed life.

It is extremely unpopular to talk about Satan inside of most churches now. Trust me, I know. I once preached about this system of darkness in a church, and it turned out to be a train wreck. I could see the disgust in the people's faces as if they were thinking, "Who does this kid think he is, telling me that Satan targets people?" The enemy loves the fact that so many people have veered away from their journey.

Yet, God will always have a People. There will always be a sanctified few who, like bulldogs, remain resolute despite the pressure. Paul was one of these men. The degree he journeyed was the degree of opposition he faced from the enemy.

Romans 8 is a journey from start to finish. It begins with a new nature and goes right into deliverance from the Law, putting on the spiritual mind, taking up the Spirit of Christ, being led by the new nature through the witness of the Holy Ghost, the promise of our glorified bodies that awaits us at the end of our journey, the prayer language of the Spirit that catapults us in this life, and the promise of victory that we have through all the heavenly graces that have come from Jesus Christ.

Paul was the first man to understand the path of the just *to this degree.* Nobody had more revelation of God's mind than he. It was this revelation that he took on his four missionary journeys to pull the Church out of error and false doctrine, so that the Church could grow past infancy.

Satan wanted to crush the Church before it started changing culture and civilization. Yet this man, Paul, armed with his revelation, was one of the few reasons darkness could not succeed. Notice what Paul says regarding his experience:

> **[38]For I am persuaded, that neither death, nor life, nor angels, nor principalities, nor powers, nor things present, nor things to come,**
> **[39]Nor height, nor depth, nor any other creature, shall be able to separate us from the love of God, which is in Jesus Christ our Lord.** (Romans 8:38-39 KJV)

Paul was talking about things that he looked squarely in the face while on his journey, four of which included other creatures, angels, Powers, and Principalities. Let's not forget that the same guy who wrote Ephesians 6:12 also wrote Romans 8. The Apostle who revealed the dark caste system taught it wherever he went. It was part of his doctrine. Here Paul tells the church at Rome what he had met along the way:

1.) Other Creatures: The Greek word for "creature" is *ktisis* and means "any created thing." It is a vague word. I believe Paul was referring to Wicked Spirits, because they were an act of creation that is still vague to me, even after studying Athenagoras and other church fathers who sought to explain their existence. The chief studies on demons attest that they were created when fallen angels procreated with mortal women (Genesis 6) and produced the Nephilim, or giant races. These giants ruled the land, became gods among men, and eventually died, having no resurrection of their bodies (Isaiah 26:14). These giants, born of eternal beings, possessed spirits, however. With no body and no place to rest after they were separated from their physical existence, they still roam the earth today as Wicked Spirits, ruled by the Kingdom of Darkness. Paul, like other believers, encountered them first-hand.

2.) Angels: When Paul resisted those wicked little spirits, certain angels came and tried to shut down the light of the Gospel that was coming from his revelations. These angels, I am convinced, were Rulers of Darkness and messengers of wickedness that tried to block any invasion of light.

Paul ran into the Rulers of Darkness in Athens. In 2011, I visited the place where Paul delivered his Mars Hill sermon. It is a wide rock, red in color, overlooking the whole city of Athens. I thought, *if there ever was a place to preach and bring a city to her knees, this is it.* It would have been so for Paul, except the Ruler of Darkness neutralized him so, that after he got done preaching it says,

> **³²And when they heard of the resurrection of the dead, some mocked, while others said, "We will hear you again on this matter."**
> **³³So Paul departed from among them.**
> **³⁴However, some men joined him and believed, among them Dionysius the Areopagite, a woman named Damaris, and others with them."** (Acts 17:32-34 NKJV)

A Ruler of Darkness was not about to turn his jurisdiction over without a struggle. Just a few people, out of the countless citizens who inhabited Athens, were saved.

3.) Powers: Paul didn't quit. He kept going deeper into his calling as a sent one of Jesus Christ. When the discouragement he faced from Rulers of Darkness couldn't stop his ministry, Powers came along to belittle the power of God working in his life. Certainly, the enemy thought it sufficient to get into a power struggle with Paul. One of the many examples is found in Acts 16 in the city of Philippi. Having made the first convert on the continent of Europe, Paul and Silas awakened a power. No way would the enemy have it so. A spirit of divination met the two men of God, attempting to swallow them up.

Now it happened, as we went to prayer, that a certain slave girl possessed with a spirit of divination met us (Acts 16:16 NKJV).

The word *divination* is *python* in the Greek. In the Greek culture, the god Apollos killed a python that guarded the oracle of Delphi. Apollos became associated with a python and was recognized as the god of light, truth, and prophecy. The python spirit, then, was a spirit of light and fortune telling. It was a power that tried, like a serpent, to get in league with Paul and Silas and deceive them. Had it had been successful, the *pythonic spirit* would have elongated its jaw and swallowed them up. Trapped in the belly of the snake through deception, they would have been severed from their path, and would have been on the snake's path instead, resting in its stomach. Like Moses, Paul used his authority that he had received from God (2 Corinthians 12:12) and overcame this power.

4.) Principalities: Depending on the situation, Paul encountered Wicked Spirits, Rulers of Darkness, and Powers in and out of his ministry. It wasn't until the end of his life that a Principality finally stood up against him to shut him down. Paul had become so effective and had triumphed over everything darkness had thrown his way. In light of this, Paul wrote 2 Corinthians 11:23 concerning false apostles who boasted of themselves:

> *23Are they ministers of Christ—I speak as a fool—I am more: in labors more abundant, in stripes above measure, in prisons more frequently, in deaths often.*
> *24From the Jews five times I received forty stripes minus one.*
> *25Three times I was beaten with rods; once I was stoned; three times I was shipwrecked; a night and a day I have been in the deep;*
> *26in journeys often, in perils of waters, in perils of robbers, in perils of my own countrymen, in perils of the Gentiles, in perils in the city, in perils in the wilderness, in perils in the sea, in perils among false brethren;*
> *27in weariness and toil, in sleeplessness often, in hunger and thirst, in fastings often, in cold and nakedness-*

²⁸besides the other things, what comes upon me daily: my deep concern for all the churches.
²⁹Who is weak, and I am not weak? Who is made to stumble, and I do not burn with indignation?
³⁰If I must boast, I will boast in the things which concern my infirmity. (2 Corinthians 11:23-30 NKJV)

Many times it is never taken into consideration what was behind all of Paul's persecutions. A majority of them were the workings of the canopy of darkness trying to negate his apostolic efforts. This was his proof that he was a greater apostle than the false ones. In 2 Corinthians 11:12-15 Paul puts these false brethren in league with Satan, and contrasts himself, showing that the persecutions prove that he is working *against* Satan. To his credit, nothing listed in 2 Corinthians 11:25-28 (which coincides with Romans 8) could stop him. He had reached a place where nothing could take him off his path, so a Principality finally had to rise up and try to destroy him.

How do we know it was a Principality that finally got involved? A Principality is a spirit that guides governments and controls the highest earthly influences. When Paul first began teaching his revelation, his struggle came from common people and ordinary sects. Eventually, he landed in front of the world's greatest influences. When Paul gained access to them, the Principalities empowering them rose up to defend their subjects. This complicated Paul's journey. Toward the end of his ministry Paul was not upsetting just a few people here and there. He was making lots and lots of people angry. One example is found in Acts 23:12-13 (NKJV):

¹²And when it was day, some of the Jews banded together and bound themselves under an oath, saying that they would neither eat nor drink till they had <u>killed Paul</u>.
¹³Now there were <u>more than forty</u> who had formed this conspiracy.

Aided by his nephew, Paul escaped to Caesarea, guarded by two hundred soldiers, seventy cavalry and two hundred spearmen, all led by two centurions. It took 472 men to guard Paul from the crazy men who were bent on destroying him. This, no doubt, *was* a demonic plot.

Paul was then brought before Felix, the governor, where Ananias, the High Priest, via a professional orator named Tertullus, falsely accused him (Acts 24:1-5). Paul defended himself, and the trial was postponed for a few days (v. 10-23). Finally, Felix heard the Gospel from Paul's mouth and began to tremble. Unwilling, however, to accept the truth, he sent Paul away. From that point on, the only time Felix called for Paul was an attempt to lure him into bribery. Unable to escape the clutches of the government, Paul was imprisoned *for two years* until Festus succeeded Felix.

The Jews still intended to get their hands on Paul and kill him. The leading Jews met with Festus about Paul's future (Acts 25:1-4). Again, the Jews made false accusations they couldn't prove (v.7). Being a responsible governor, Festus gave Paul a chance to defend himself. Paul told the court that he was innocent, and he appealed to Caesar. After consulting with his advisors, Festus agreed.

Not knowing what kind of charge to make against Paul, Festus asked King Agrippa to hear Paul's case while he was in town. King Agrippa had Paul stand before him (Acts 26:1) and speak concerning the Jewish religion and Jesus Christ. Paul gave one of the most astounding sermons concerning the revelation of Jesus Christ. Astonishingly, King Agrippa said to him, ***"You almost persuade me to become a Christian"*** (Acts 26:28 NKJV). Having talked it over, although Festus thought Paul was crazy, based upon his defense of Jesus, they both admitted he was innocent and had done nothing to be consigned to death or chains.

Unfortunately for Paul, he had appealed to Caesar, and to Caesar he must go. Acts 27 tells of the unpleasant voyage to Rome, during which Paul suffered a shipwreck and nearly drowned before he washed up onto the island of Malta. The people of the island welcomed Paul, and built up a fire to warm his wet and icy bones. Because of the heat of the fire, a serpent crawled out from the wood and chomped onto Paul's hand, and just hung there, swinging back and forth. Paul merely brushed it off into the fire, while the people of Malta waited for him to swell up and die. Acts 28 tells of Paul's experience with the venomous snakebite that didn't kill him, much to the shock and amazement of the people of the island.

Finally, three months after the shipwreck, Paul was taken to Rome on a ship from Alexandria. While in Rome, Paul testified to the Jewish leaders about The Way, confirming that the Messiah had come and that Jesus was alive. Luke leaves us in Acts by telling us that Paul preached the Gospel in Rome for two years as he awaited his appointment with Caesar, the king of most of the world.

Paul *was not* a greater apostle than the false apostles because he had such trials and persecution. He *was* a greater apostle because he overcame this persecution caused by lower level spirits, until finally governmental spirits had to step in to try and shut him down. Even *they* could not prevail. What apostle of that day could boast of that kind of power and effectiveness?

CHAPTER TWENTY-THREE

Paul's Struggles Mirror Our Own

"It is common for readers to get carried away with this verse by overlooking the Apostle's reason for writing what he did: *an unveiling of Christ comes with a price.*"

¹It is doubtless not profitable for me to boast. I will come to <u>visions and revelations of the Lord</u>...

⁷And lest I should be exalted above measure by the abundance of the revelations, a thorn in the flesh was given to me, a <u>messenger of Satan to buffet me</u>, lest I be exalted above measure. (2 Corinthians 12:1, 7 NKJV)

Let me illustrate this further. <u>Who is powerful enough to enter the house of a strong man like Satan and plunder his goods? Only someone even stronger— someone who could tie him up and then plunder his house.</u> (Mark 3:27 NLT)

When I first started playing video games everything was eight-bit. For you gamers today who think that there were always open worlds, think again. Until technology improved drastically, gaming was confined to moving your character from left to right. You never were given the ability to move backward. Essentially, games were about progress. "How far have you gotten?" was the common thing to ask. Skill was determined by how many levels you overcame.

True to the cliché of early 1990's video games, levels were guarded by what my friends and I called "bosses." Oh, yes, you may have subdued the challenges that came along while you progressed through the level. But every kid holding those square controllers of a first edition Nintendo system knew that whatever great skill you demonstrated while blazing the journey through the level was soon forgotten as soon as the boss dropped from the sky, spitting snakes or throwing hammers at you to keep you from reaching the next level. Sometimes it would take hours, days, weeks, or in rare occasions, months to figure out how to beat these bosses. Having no internet back then, I'd have to consult my friends on the playground or beg my mom to buy me a $5.00 gaming magazine, hoping the answer was in there. Be as it may, video games successfully captured a great spiritual truth: a strongman (an enemy that uses its strength to hinder forward progress) guards every new level we desire to break into along our journey.

Paul Met the Strongman

2 Corinthians 12 is an interesting chapter, written by Paul, telling about his personal experiences in his journey down the path of righteousness. Needless to say, the Paul described here is not the same Paul who spent time at Peter's house learning about the mysterious Christ. With the ticking away of time, layers of mystery had been peeled back, unveiling to Paul the visage of the God-man.

Paul referred to what he had come to know about Christ by saying, ***"This boasting will do no good, but I must go on. I will reluctantly tell about visions and revelations from the Lord"*** (2 Corinthians 12:1 NLT). Some translations make us think that the Apostle Paul was saying, "I am determined to get more and more revelation from God," resulting in people confessing, "I will get revelation from God; I will get revelation from God." Such is not the case. The visions and revelations referred to here were the aspects of the mysterious Christ and the Gospel that Paul had already seen through the illumination of the Holy Ghost. They are the same visions and revelations that are available to us through the Holy Spirit.

The word *vision* in verse 1 is the Greek word *optasia*, meaning "to see and to bring into view." This is where we get our word "optometry," the study of the eyes. Having worn eyeglasses since I was six years old and contacts since I was thirteen, I understand optometry quite well. Over the years, optometrists, endeavoring to determine the strength of my vision, place a special machine over my eyes and cast different sized images on the wall with a projector. The machine is adjusted until it brings the images into view. With each click of the machine, the image gets clearer. When I can read the images perfectly, I have experienced *optasia*.

In Paul's case, after fixing his eyes on Christ in Acts 9, the Spirit of God was placed over the eyes of his heart, bringing the image of Christ clearer and clearer and clearer. This was the source of Paul's power and apostolic authority. He saw Jesus in a dimension of revelation that nobody during his day had experienced.

Paul speaks of this process of unveiling through *optasia* in Philippians 3:10 (KJV), **"*That <u>I may know Him</u>, and the power of his resurrection, and the fellowship of his sufferings, being made conformable unto his death.*"** The less a mystery Christ became to Paul, the more he came to know Him. This was made possible through a stronger vision of Christ.

Of all the glorious visions that Paul experienced, he highlights his firsthand experience of paradise where he was shown things beyond his mortal senses (2 Corinthians 12:2-4). It is common for readers to get carried away with Paul's mystical experience in 2 Corinthians 12 by overlooking the Apostle's reason for writing what he did: *an unveiling of Christ comes with a price.*

The enemy is not concerned about people who go to church. I once took this statement a little further while I was preaching, and said, "The enemy doesn't even mind it when you read your Bible and pray." The audience gasped. With that statement, I had them where I wanted them.

I went on to explain that going to church, praying, and reading the Bible can all become *religious activities* that are good for nothing. People who have a problem when I say that are those who have been taught that we need to be good Christians, achieved *only* through Bible reading, prayer, and going to church on Sunday (and Wednesday if we want extra points). Satan will never challenge a person who thinks that way. That is no threat to darkness. Religion never stopped the forces of sin.

"Well, how do I know if my praying, going to church, and reading the Word is religious or not?" Here is the litmus test: is it *optasia*? Is what you are doing causing you to encounter the living, walking, talking King of Kings and Lord of Lords? I don't mean facts or good thoughts about Jesus.

I mean a *true seeing* and *knowing* Who He is, where the mystery begins to be rubbed away.

There was a popular television game show I used to watch as a youngster called "Get The Picture." Kids were brought for each episode, divided into two teams of two, (Orange and Yellow), and given the chance to answer trivia questions. Across the stage stood a large screen, divided into sixteen smaller squares that corporately covered the image underneath it. When a team answered a question correctly, they chose a square, and part of the picture was uncovered. The more questions answered, the more squares were uncovered, until finally someone could guess the picture.

Our times of prayer, Bible reading, and going to church should have the same results as answering a question correctly on "Get The Picture." It should wear away part of the mystery that shrouds the Gospel plan and give us a further clue as to who Jesus Christ is and who He is in us. *This is what makes the enemy nervous, because the key to power and authority is in our revelation of Jesus.* As long as the enemy sees us busying ourselves with religion and tradition, having a do-gooder's mentality, he won't bother with us. As soon as we start uncovering the God-Man, the strongman is going to butt in, attempting to keep us from living at the level of revelation we received.

Paul's Thorn Was a Strongman

For whatever reason, Paul's thorn happens to be a subject of extreme interest. Every commentary I have ever read has its own explanation for what the thorn was. Poor eyesight and clubbed feet are just a couple of the suggestions I have come across since I began studying the Word. I am unable to understand why it is unclear to so many students of the Word when Paul plainly tells us what it is. Notice what Paul did *not* say: "And by reason of the exceeding greatness of the revelations, that I should not be exalted overmuch, there was given to me a thorn in the flesh, *clubbed feet*, that I might not be exalted overmuch." No, he was very precise, ***"And by reason of the exceeding greatness of the revelations, that I should not be exalted overmuch, there was given to me a thorn in the flesh, <u>a messenger of Satan to buffet me</u>, that I might not be exalted overmuch"*** (2 Corinthians 12:7 ASV).

Messenger is the Greek word *aggelos* and is translated "angel" all over the Bible. Angels are not some kind of nebulous thing; rather they assume the following characteristics:

1.) *They are personalities:* Angels are separate beings, one from another, each having their own identity, including name and responsibilities (Daniel 10)

2.) *They have passions:* Scripture notes that angels get angry (Revelation 12:12), lust (Jude 7), eat food (Psalms 78:25), or can be puffed up with pride (1 Timothy 3:6)

3.) *They possess spirit bodies:* These bodies have body parts just as our terrestrial bodies do. Based upon their description from Scripture, certain classes of angels resemble human beings (Genesis 18; Jud. 13:6)

4.) *They are influences:* To be influential requires intelligence, wisdom, knowledge, and the ability to communicate, all of which angels are seen in Scripture to possess (Ephesians 3:10; 1 Peter 1:12; 1 Corinthians 13:1; 2 Samuel 14:20)

Paul was dealing with a spiritual entity that had come with a definite reason and a precise purpose. Based upon how the Apostle Paul wrote about his experience, we know that he understood this because he says that the messenger of Satan "was given" to him and that Paul wanted it to "depart." The being came from somewhere and someone, and could leave and go back to where it came from, or go to another assignment.

The words, "there was given," is a term that means "to give someone what is due; to pay wages." Paul received his revelations from the Lord, then he was paid a visit by this angelic being. This is a great insight as to how the Kingdom of Darkness works.

Satan is referred to as a snake from the very first time that he is mentioned in Scripture (Genesis 3:1). The law of first mentions is a very important aspect of Bible study. This rule basically states that in order to grasp the fundamental meaning of a doctrine or concept from Scripture, the student must discover where it is first mentioned, and study it from that point, to lay a general foundation whereby all other concepts concerning the same doctrine or concept will rest. Before Satan is referred to as "Satan," "devil," "accuser," or even "Lucifer," he is referred to in the Hebrew as *nachash*, or *serpent* in English. Classic theology implies that there was an actual snake that roamed the garden and spoke to Adam and Eve. Scholars offer further proof that the serpent was literal because God cursed the serpent after the fall.

I am not suggesting that such isn't the case. However, it would still make sense to me, almost more sense, that the word *nachash* was *just a description of how Lucifer functioned.* For Moses to call Lucifer *nachash* would be a statement to let the readers know that, although the being that appeared to them was full of wisdom and light, it was a serpent seeking to deceive. Because God cursed the literal serpent, humanity could look at the way a serpent behaves and know that Satan behaves the same way. This could be the reason enmity exists between human and snake, because a snake is a continual reminder of how the enemy of humanity lives and behaves.

Notice that John calls Satan ***"that old serpent, called the Devil, and Satan"*** (Revelation 12:9 KJV). Ask yourself why John chose to declare the devil as a serpent, even before devil and Satan. I believe it is because the Scripture describes him as a serpent first, and John is adhering to the importance of the law of first mentions.

"Well, then, what was in the Garden of Eden?" you may ask. I believe Adam and Eve saw a being of great beauty and light (2 Corinthians 11:14), whose rotten core was full of illusion and deceit. In interpreting the story, Moses said that under all of his beauty he was serpent-like. God cursed the serpent to serve as our example in understanding the Kingdom of Darkness, and Satan, the highest *Principality* (the indoctrinating influence that governs the masses).

While walking down the path that leads to life, Paul encountered a snake—a boss if you will—that craved to make it difficult for him to walk any further into the light of the glorious Gospel of Christ (Proverbs 4:18; 2 Corinthians 4:4). When bosses arrive on the scene, a decision awaits: Do we stop and call it quits? Or do we push and keep going?

Having discovered a greater Help, Paul kept on going. And so should we.

CHAPTER TWENTY-FOUR

Paul's Reliance Upon the Spirit

"His walk with God became leaner, as the carnal fat of his flesh and its passions were purged and trimmed off by the Holy Ghost."

> *⁷And lest I should be exalted above measure through the abundance of the revelations, there was given to me a thorn in the flesh, the messenger of Satan to buffet me, lest I should be exalted above measure.*
> *⁸For this thing I besought the Lord thrice, that it might depart from me.*
> *⁹And he said unto me, My grace is sufficient for thee: for my strength is made perfect in weakness. Most gladly therefore will I rather glory in my infirmities, that the power of Christ may rest upon me.*
> *¹⁰Therefore I take pleasure in infirmities, in reproaches, in necessities, in persecutions, in distresses for Christ's sake: for when I am weak, then I am strong.* (2 Corinthians 12:7-10 KJV)

As we said before, Paul's thorn was a demon spirit that stirred up persecutions, lack, want, hunger, conflict from other believers, problems in his churches, and a barrage of other things that yanked the handles of his flesh and attempted to pull him around and around, opposing his call and violating his progress in God. Some got the idea that Paul was some kind of masochist and enjoyed these pleasures. Some today even pray for a thorn in the flesh. (A bad idea, seeing that Satan will accommodate your willingness.)

Rather, Paul was saying that he gloried in his infirmities because it was in these very infirmities when he noticed that the power of Christ came to rest all the more upon him. *The reason that Paul became strong in his infirmities is because he tightened up his reliance upon the Spirit of God.* His walk with God became leaner, as the carnal fat of his flesh and its passions were purged and trimmed off by the Holy Ghost.

The moment those difficulties challenged Paul, he immediately turned himself over to the Holy Ghost and allowed the Spirit of God to locate any handle in his life that could allow the attack to be effective. If there were any, the Holy Ghost purged it. This worked more glory in Paul's life and brought him out on the other side even stronger.

As we continue to increase in revelation knowledge, our forward motion in God begins to grow exponentially. It is this kind of exponential growth that brings us into a walk of power that becomes threatening to hell. People who only go to church or who are only having a Bible study in a coffee shop do not threaten Satan.

No, Satan gets threatened when people begin to grow in revelation knowledge and, as a result, become dependent upon the operation of the Spirit. Using this dependency in prayer and intercession, the people of God begin to drive back demonic powers that are still illegally at work in their area. When this happens and the Kingdom of God starts to grow, the eyes of people's hearts are opened, *"Through mighty signs and wonders, by the power of the Spirit of God"* (Romans 15:19). Demonstrations of power, followed by the preaching of the Word of Truth, serve as witness that the Christ has *"spoiled principalities and powers...made a shew of them openly, triumphing over them in it"* (Colossians 2:15 KJV). Satan cannot tolerate this happening in his kingdom, so he launches a counterstrike.

God's Word provides us the exact pattern for how the process goes, and delivers us the solution:

1.) A child of God, through revelation knowledge about Christ in him, begins to advance in authority and begins to launch out in power (2 Corinthians 12:1-6).
2.) The Kingdom of Darkness, always monitoring this kind of thing, takes notice. A counterstrike is launched to stop the child of God from advancing.

3.) When the strike comes, the child of God turns himself over to the Spirit of God, forcing reliance upon the Spirit, and the Spirit of God fortifies him against it (2 Corinthians 12:7-10).

4.) The child of God overcomes the scheme of Satan and comes out on the other side triumphantly, with more peace and contentment than he had before (2 Corinthians 12:9-10; Philippians 4:12-13).

Paul was our forerunner. More than apostle, theologian, philosopher, or whatever else Church history can consider him, he blazed the path of transformation and left us an example of what to expect as we run *our* race. His revelations and writings are the map that he left behind to help us reach the same place when it is all said and done.

Now, back to *our* journey!

Part III

How To Walk Out
Your Journey

CHAPTER TWENTY-FIVE

Introducing the Holy Ghost

(Limitless Teacher, Convicting Agent, Fortifier, Protector)

"But to ensure that you overcome the limitations of the flesh, fulfill your high call, and finish the course of righteousness, inheriting everything that I have said that can be yours, I will send heaven down to you."

In light of all the weaknesses and susceptibilities our body now has during this age of reconciliation, Paul answers some very important questions: "What did God do to help us in this weakness? How are we supposed to deal with the limitations imposed by our flesh?" Surely, God didn't just leave us here with a hunk of flesh to contend with, having no help from Him to deal with it. After all, we are busy with our ministry of reconciling the world unto God. We wouldn't be able to do that very successfully if we didn't have help to deal with our own limits.

> *22For we know that the whole creation groans and labors with birth pangs together until now.*
> *23Not only that, but we also who have the first fruits of the Spirit, even we ourselves groan within ourselves, eagerly <u>waiting</u> for the adoption, <u>the redemption of our body.</u>*
> *24For we were saved in this hope, but hope that is seen is not hope; for why does one still hope for what he sees?*
> *25But if we hope for what we do not see, then we eagerly wait for it with perseverance.* (Romans 8:22-25 NKJV)

After we were born again, we were placed on a road of Sonship that would take us right into everything that we lost in the first birth and into those things we have been called to inherit in the second birth. What God could not do was take us to heaven right away because He needs us as His ministers to reconcile lost mankind to Himself. But in His master plan He did something astounding. He said, "Child, I cannot take you to heaven right now to be with Me. But to ensure that you overcome the limitations of the flesh, fulfill your high call, and finish the course of righteousness, inheriting everything that I have said that can be yours, I will send heaven down to you."

This came in the person of the Holy Spirit, also called the Holy Ghost. He comes to fortify and purge us of any weakness and to build up our most holy faith so that we can tear up hell so bad, it won't know what hit it. Jesus sent us Heaven's very best. *It is up to us to learn how to use Him.*

Imagine the faces of the twelve when Jesus said some of the things that He said. I can picture Judas nodding his head, pretending to understand. I can see young John and his innocent face indicating he is a bit lost. Thomas is contemplative, weighing Christ's words in the balance. Then there is old Peter, speaking before his brain can process what was actually said.

For three solid years Jesus spent every day with His twelve disciples, teaching them things concerning the Kingdom of God. Three years, although it can go by pretty quickly, is a significant amount of time. I am sure Jesus repeated Himself on many occasions, and the disciples must have heard Christ's teachings over and over again as He spoke to crowds in different cities and regions.

Even after He taught them long hours, the disciples still had to pull Jesus aside, as Luke 8:9 (KJV) records: ***"What might this parable be?"*** They just couldn't get it; it was so new and unlike anything anyone ever heard before. Jesus constantly scolded His disciples for their slowness of heart, ***"and upbraided them with their unbelief and hardness of heart, because they believed not"*** (Mark 16:14 KJV). How many times was He going to have to tell them?

The problem the disciples had (and the rest of the world) was not external; it was internal. They did not have a nature that could fully understand God. Although the New Testament begins in Matthew 1:1, the actual New Testament didn't take effect until Matthew 28:1, when Jesus rose from the dead. The disciples were unable to take up the new nature until regeneration became available through the Blood of Christ. Until this regeneration occurred, man was not completely reconciled to God, and the Old Covenant was still intact. Jesus walked with the disciples while in this state. It is no wonder they did not get it—their nature was still separated from God and unable to understand spiritual things.

Then, Jesus said something astounding in John 16:7 (NLT) that once I wished He had not said. ***"But in fact, it is best for you that I go away."*** How could that be? Can you imagine what the disciples thought when He said this? If they couldn't understand while He was with them, how in the world were they to move on into the Kingdom of Heaven without Him there to guide, and explain, and expand?

This was one of those verses I did *not* highlight. It didn't make any sense to me. Didn't Jesus know who He was? He cast out devils with His word, the blind saw when they left His presence, paralysis was weak near Him, and even death couldn't even tell this Man no. But, after raising Lazarus from the dead, Jesus drops the bomb on His disciples. "It is best for you that I go away."

Had I been at the Passover feast that night with the disciples, I probably would have been the one to blurt out: "But, Jesus! How can you say that? You are the Messiah. It doesn't get any better than You!" Jesus might have looked at me with His eyes, living pools of love, patient with me despite having interrupted Him, and gone on with His sentence, *"because if I don't [go away], the Advocate won't come. If I do go away, then I will send Him to you."*

An Advocate? A Helper? What did He mean? Did He mean it just for the disciples, or was it for all of us, for the whole world, for all time? What would He look like? Would He look like another human? And how were we to utilize this Helper?

In Greek, this is called the *Paraclete*, and it means, literally, Comforter, Counselor, Helper, Empowerer, Advocate. He is the Holy Spirit, the Holy Ghost. After we are born of God, the Holy Ghost comes in. The Holy Ghost is a person, though He is unseen. *And beyond that, the Holy Spirit is a master teacher for all those who are in Christ. What makes this so exciting is that the Holy Ghost is introduced as One who literally comes alongside us and teams up with us.* Right as we come from the womb of the second birth, we are given a personal Mentor and a Teacher (John 14:17-18). His only interest is to get you into His classroom and begin teaching you all about your elder Brother, Jesus Christ, your new nature, and your new inheritance as an adopted child of God. Skilled with the ability to ensure success, this Tutor has no other purpose besides that of causing us to overcome.

The Helper is to ensure that we inherit every Heavenly thing that is rightfully ours, despite any obstacle that may attempt to hamper our success. This Helper's duty is to take us by the hand, to mentor and teach us, and to help us to cross the finish line victoriously (2 Timothy 4:7-8).

Limitless Teacher

When I was twenty-six, I began preaching on the Holy Ghost everywhere I went: East Coast, West Coast, Europe, Caribbean, you name it. Someone finally asked me (in a religious tone), "Why do you always preach on the Holy Ghost? Aren't you supposed to be preaching on Jesus?"

I shocked the person with my answer: "Immaturity in the Body of Christ is a result of people who do not know the role and function of the Holy Ghost and how to use Him. My job is to turn people over to the Holy Ghost, so that the Holy Ghost can turn people over to Jesus."

"Why is that important?" they might ask. "Don't we have preachers to teach us? Aren't *you* supposed to teach us?"

Here is my greatest limitation as a preacher: I cannot change your heart. I can stand before congregations and tell them how wonderful Jesus Christ is. Opening the Bible, I can share revelation from the Word that I have accumulated over the years. I can jump on chairs, holler and scream; I can even swing from the fan, do a somersault, and land in the aisle. But what I cannot do is to open up your heart and pour in the revelation knowledge that is going to completely change the way you live. Only the Spirit of God can do this.

When we are first born again, it is only to be expected that we will cling to our spiritual parents and mentors. It is like any infant who is developing and needs help. But, the more a person grows in wisdom and revelation, the more he or she should begin to depend less and less on human leadership, and more and more on the Holy Ghost. We turn to the Holy Spirit in prayer, and ask for help and guidance, and it is given. Not as the world gives, mind you, but as God gives.

Did you know that every apostle, prophet, evangelist, pastor, and teacher in the Body of Christ has limitations? *A great blunder is when congregants walk vicariously with God through their pastor, apostle, or favorite preacher of God.* Although we should honor them and follow their leadership, we are to have *our own* walk with God that is not limited by any one person. The moment we begin to walk with God through another person, we take upon ourselves that person's limitations.

No matter where I go or how far away one place is from the next, it is rare to find people who understand that the Kingdom of God is larger than one particular church or denomination. When people believe that God is moving *only* through their ministry or circle, they become unbalanced in their perspective. "You wouldn't believe what God is doing in this church! Our man of God is so anointed! We just stand amazed at all that He does!" There is nothing wrong with saying these things, *if* they are being said with the understanding that there are, in fact, others just as anointed and just as amazing.

Should one of these "amazing" and "super anointed" leaders fall, what happens to your walk with God? Major leaders have fallen, and their churches have come right down with them. All of us have seen this happen more than once. Those who have looked only to the leadership of a human, neglecting the Holy Spirit's ministry as the Great Teacher, will be devastated and disappointed, sometimes beyond recovery.

If there is anything that is true in life, it is this: the only one who will not let you down or disappoint you is God. The ascending Christ gave us "Ministry Gifts," found in Ephesians 4:11, not so that ministers could take people into everything that God said they could inherit. *No, these Gifts were given to help each and every member of the Body of Christ turn himself and herself over to the Holy Ghost, so that the Holy Ghost could teach them out of their new natures, and that they would, in turn, begin to look more and more like Jesus.*

Convicting Agent

The Holy Spirit has yet another job, infinite in its importance, given to those who have yet to accept the second birth:

> *⁸And when He has come, He will <u>convict</u> the world of*
> *sin, and of righteousness, and of judgment:*
> *⁹of sin, because they do not believe in Me;*
> *¹⁰of righteousness, because I go to My Father and you*
> *see Me no more;*
> *¹¹of judgment, because the ruler of this world is judged.*
> (John 16:8-11 NKJV)

To convict means to prove. When something is proven, it becomes settled. Jesus was clear that the job of the Holy Ghost was to do the convicting, the proving. When the Holy Spirit is doing His job, the following takes place:

1.) *The Holy Spirit proves to an individual he is a sinner and needs to accept Jesus:* When a human attempts to do the job of the Holy Ghost, an altar call becomes composed of people who want to "give Jesus a try." Life may need a touch-up, so they try "the whole Jesus thing." I know from experience that these individuals will eventually pick up something else when "the whole Jesus thing" doesn't work out. Because there was no conviction, there can be no inward transformation, since it has not become settled in that person's heart that they need Jesus Christ.

Conversely, when the Holy Ghost convicts a person's heart, He opens it up and convinces that person that he or she is a sinner. In 1 Corinthians 12:7 (NKJV) it says, ***"The manifestation of the Spirit is given to each one for the profit of all."*** This word *manifestation* is the Greek word *phanerosis*, meaning, "making visible" or "a flash of light." This is one way the Spirit of God operates in conviction. He flashes to a sinner's heart what they really are. They get a revelation of sin and its grossness. When this happens, the person will never want to pick it up again, because they have seen sin the way God sees sin. Instead of becoming just a religious convert and a nominal believer, this person becomes sold out for Jesus.

In my ministry I have seen many people instantly changed, beginning with this moment of conviction that is initiated by the Spirit of God. Conviction is the spark plug that produces the energy for one to get off the path of destruction and make the first move down the path that leads to life.

Tom, a good friend of mine since high school, had this flash of experience. I met Tom in the 8th grade in youth group. Funny, smart, and cool to be around, Tom still did not look like a very happy kid. His family life wasn't the greatest, and he had grown up around a lot of religion. Tom made it clear to us that he wasn't interested in God.

During the autumn of sophomore year, the youth group was having a youth retreat and Tom decided to go. (We later found out there was a girl at the retreat that he was interested in.) Maybe just to appease our begging, Tom answered the altar call the last night. He came up to receive Jesus into his heart. *Wow!* we all thought. *Would you look at that? We did it! We got Tom saved. If he can get saved, who can't we get saved?*

It was just a few weeks later that Tom completely dismissed the fall retreat and was the same old Tom.

Then something happened that completely changed the course of Tom's life. Another fall retreat came along. We had abandoned all our hopes of "getting Tom saved," and had decided just to leave him alone. One afternoon while we were fishing, our friend Adam said to him, "So, Tom, why are you running from God?"

My jaw just about unhinged when I saw what came next. Tom paused from reeling in his line. It was literally like something seized him. He couldn't find words intelligent or witty enough for the moment. It was like an unseen force had halted him; his whole being was captured. His mien looked as though he had seen a flash of something that would not leave him untouched.

Adam began to preach to him the "word of truth" (Ephesians 1:13). In about twenty-five minutes, tears began to roll down Tom's face as he got on his knees and surrendered his life to Jesus Christ. Finally, as time grew late, we began to walk back to camp. Suddenly, Tom stopped. He came up to me, put a marijuana pipe in my hand and said, "Take this from me. I don't need it anymore." Since Adam had a longer throw than I did, I handed it to him. Adam sent that pipe flying into the abyss of Spring Lake, where it remains today.

When we got back to camp, I can't think of one person who didn't say, "Tom! What happened to you? Your face looks so different!" I can tell you exactly what happened to Tom. Tom got convicted by the Holy Ghost. The Holy Ghost turned him over to Jesus, and Jesus set him free.

2.) *The Holy Ghost will begin to convict people in righteousness:* To do righteousness means to live the right way, out of your reborn human spirit. Notice that it is the Spirit of God's job to convince people to walk down the supernatural path of righteousness, not a human's job. (It certainly had not been up to us boys to convict Tom to be saved, regardless of what we thought at the time.) Conviction produces initiative. Initiative from the Holy Ghost is one of the most powerful forces that can be received. Ask yourself these questions.

a.) How much initiative do I have to step into everything Jesus said I could have in the second birth?

b.) Where did my initiative come from? Did it come from my pastor? Did it come from my ambitions? Did it come from my own desires to conquest and conquer? Did it come from the Holy Ghost?

c.) To what extent will my current initiative carry me?

When you operate from initiative that comes from any other source other than from the Holy Spirit, you run the risk of being stopped in your tracks by any unforeseen obstacle that may block your way. Divine initiative does not come from the motivation to impress your pastor. It does not come from the intent to build a work for God. Divine initiative does not even come from the determination to do ministry. Thousands of years of church history have proven that religious leaders cannot beat initiative into people so that they serve God. This only buries people neck deep in religion and people pleasing.

Paul is the greatest example of one who operated in divine initiative. The Holy Spirit took hold of his heart and flashed the revelation of what he could receive and accomplish as a child of God. God's revelation injected Paul with so much divine initiative that nothing could stop his forward progress down the supernatural path of the new birth. Believe me, he had a lot of logjams that might have stopped him cold. But, through all these terrors, Paul was faithful because he had the initiative from the Holy Spirit.

3.) *The Holy Spirit warns of the judgment to come:* Without a fair warning of judgment, people might actually be able to accuse God of being unfair. The Holy Spirit, at some point in a person's life, will bring before them an internal awareness of a coming judgment. Ministers cannot do this themselves. This is why standing on a street corner and yelling, "Repent! The end is near" rarely works—this act doesn't usually get into the heart. The Holy Spirit looks at this and says, "I have already tried to tell them that." It is the Spirit of God's desire for His people to hear Him on how to take further what He has already warned sinners about. This may include an act of love, a word of knowledge, a word of wisdom, healing, or anything else to validate the witness of that judgment and provide a way of escape. Therefore, warning of judgment is a spiritual operation, not a fleshly operation—it is a task for the Spirit of God.

Fortifier and Protector

You remember why you were given the Holy Ghost, right? Jesus sent Him to come along side you, as He did Paul, and help you with anything hell could possibly throw your way. Isn't it exciting to know that God has so fully planned for your success as a child of God that He sent heaven to you in the person of the Holy Ghost? The third person of the Trinity is now teamed up with your new nature to fortify you against the weaknesses of the mind and of the body. If that weren't enough, He has become our first line of protection, defending us from false doctrines and demon spirits who desire to lead us astray.

Being in the church world my whole life, I have seen just about everything in the book, including hucksters and clowns who sneak their way into the pulpits and sheer the wool off the sheep. I remember one in particular who created quite a stir, boasting of outrageous miracles and extravagant encounters. He mesmerized his followers. Finally, I met an "ex-follower" in the airport. I felt badly for this guy. He was drained, confused, and still unable to make sense of the whole thing. The preacher still had his heart but common sense made him break away. He told me of all the money he gave this preacher, the time he spent with him, and how, in the end, the preacher bullied him around and treated him poorly. The bottom line was that, through it all, there had been no real change produced in this follower.

Don't think for an instant that the Holy Spirit had not tried to tip this man off. I am sure He did. Somewhere, there was a disconnect and a failure to listen. The Spirit of God knows the hearts and motives of every teacher. When He directs someone to a particular ministry, He does so knowing what that ministry will add to advance them along in their journey. If the ministry is harmful, the Holy Spirit will never lead someone to it.

The Apostle Paul encountered his share of hucksters and clowns in his day. As a matter of fact, his greatest challenge was protecting the churches he set up from them. Often in his letters he would validate himself and discredit them. In 2 Corinthians 11, Paul does just that by saying,

> *21-23 Since you admire the egomaniacs of the pulpit so much (remember, this is your old friend, the fool, talking), let me try my hand at it. Do they brag of being Hebrews, Israelites, the pure race of Abraham? I'm their match. Are they servants of Christ? I can go them one better.* (2 Corinthians 11:21-23 MSG)

After this, he lists that horrendous litany of persecution he had undergone (v. 24-28).

The proof that the Holy Spirit was Paul's source was not discovered in his achievements. It was found amidst his troubles. The fact that he had overcome so many times proved that he was cooperating with a Greater Power. Paul was saying, "Do you want to know what comprises an *authentic believer*? It isn't a fancy sermon. It isn't loud prayers. It isn't the activities of religion. It isn't even success in ministry or miracles. It is a strength that goes beyond the obstacles that have set themselves against my forward advancement as a child of God."

The only way that this divine strength can come is when the Holy Ghost captures a person and fortifies their new nature. If we learn right from the start to depend on the Spirit of God, fortification will begin immediately and supply us with the strength that we would otherwise hope to get from false teachers. When we are fortified from the inside out, we cannot be led astray by ill-intentioned teachers who make outrageous claims to hold feeble hearts in captivity. The Spirit of God will drive in us enough strength to overcome anything that comes our way, be it shipwreck, persecution, dangers, and yes, the enticing words of slick speakers.

When we fully yield to the mighty Holy Ghost, depending wholly on Him, nothing can stunt our growth in God. Among His myriad of functions, He promises to teach us, convict us, fortify us, and protect us—if we will just allow Him. *Gladly for us, Paul taught us how we can turn ourselves over to Him.*

Let me introduce you to praying in the Holy Ghost.

CHAPTER TWENTY-SIX

Tongues 101:
Praying in the Holy Ghost

"I had been changed by it in a powerful and significant way. No lecture I ever heard against tongues could take that away from me."

"So," people ask me, "you are a tongue-talker, are you?"

"I am," I reply.

"What are you saying when you do that?"

"I don't know. It is unintelligible speech in my ears."

"I see," the questioners typically mutter with an exasperated sigh. Yet, the same people will also ask me why I frequently glow. They desire to know what causes the light to spark behind my eyes.

"Very simple," I say. "It is the revelation of Jesus that has come through this unintelligible prayer language that God has given me." And they sigh again.

Praying in Tongues (also called Praying in the Holy Ghost or Praying in the Spirit) has been a subject of controversy for many believers, even mature ones. In Bible school, it was embedded within our sixteen fundamental truths that had to be upheld to receive licensing and ordination from the University.

Down the interstate, however, another denominational university was teaching that speaking in tongues passed away with the Apostles. Some even went to extremes in saying that it was of the Devil. This made Bible College a place where discourse never ran dry. Oh, the hours I spent defending my theological stronghold from foreign doctrines, as though I were a medieval knight fighting off hoards of dragons.

Once, a new, sharp, well-spoken professor began to take praying in tongues to task in our *own* university. I was infuriated. However, I respected him enough to hold back assaulting him with questions during class. Instead, I led a small revolt in the corner of the library where we studied at night. I was like a buzzing honeybee, teaching the essence of tongues without being critical of the professor's knowledge and expertise (which were far greater than my little Bible College mind). Despite my inadequacies in theological training, one thing gave me the strength to stand against the heavy-duty reasoning against tongues: I had been changed by it in a powerful and significant way. It was the source of revelation I was receiving from the Word of God. *No lecture I ever heard against tongues could take that away from me.*

In my four years in Bible College, I had become known as the guy who really knew the Word of God. Chats with frustrated students often ironed out their confusion. I wasn't the valedictorian or the salutatorian, but I bore a solid understanding of God's Word. It wasn't brilliant speaking, nor was it profound discourse. Rather, it was revelation spoken with authority, *of which I attribute to the regular time I gave toward praying in tongues.*

There are schools of thinking that believe tongues fell away with the Apostles. In other words, when the last Apostle died, the gifts of the Spirit (including tongues) passed away with him. However, more than the eleven disciples (twelve, including Matthias) received tongues. One hundred twenty people received it on the day of Pentecost in Jerusalem; a group of men received it in Caesarea; twelve received it in Ephesus. There is no way of telling how many others received it all over the known world during that time. Considering the ratio of how many times tongues is mentioned in the relatively small book of Acts, we can safely project it was breaking out everywhere. If records were not kept of all of Jesus' miracles and supernatural happenings (John 21:25), they were certainly not kept of all of the disciples', either.

Acts deals mainly with the ministry of Peter and Paul in relation to the establishment of the Church. It is not an exhaustive archive of miraculous experiences, although it includes those that are necessary to show the founding of the Church. For one to suggest that tongues died off with the Apostles is to make a tremendous presumption that is not supported anywhere in history, scripture, and definitely not in experience.

In my own travels all over the US and the world, I meet Pentecostals who are, themselves, speaking in tongues and reporting to me how people in their country are getting this experience. Surely, all these people aren't self-deluded.

So, after long years of hearing about this experience and waiting to receive the gift themselves, one hundred twenty faithful believers, including Mary, the mother of Jesus, and the eleven disciples, received the Baptism of the Holy Spirit, and began to speak in tongues.

> *¹And when the day of Pentecost was fully come, they were all with one accord in one place.*
> *²And suddenly there came a sound from heaven as of a rushing mighty wind, and it filled all the house where they were sitting.*
> *³And there appeared unto them cloven tongues like as of fire, and it sat upon each of them.*
> *⁴And they were all filled with the Holy Ghost, and began to speak with other tongues, as the Spirit gave them utterance.* (Acts 2:1-4 KJV)

As we said, they were filled with the Holy Ghost <u>*and*</u> began to speak with other tongues. The Greek word *and* is the word *kai* and can mean "even, also, or too". In other words, two separate yet seamlessly integrated experiences were occurring here. A Baptism of Power joined together with new tongues. In the other instances where this Baptism is received, tongues is right there accompanying it.

> *⁴⁴While Peter yet spake these words, the Holy Ghost fell on all them which heard the word.*
> *⁴⁵And they of the circumcision which believed were astonished, as many as came with Peter, <u>because that on the Gentiles also was poured out the gift of the Holy Ghost.</u>*
> *⁴⁶<u>For they heard them speak with tongues, and magnify God.</u>* (Acts 10:44-46 KJV)

How did Peter and the Jewish believers know that the non-Jews (Cornelius and his kinsmen and near friends) had received the Baptism in the Spirit? "For they heard them speak with tongues." Tongues were outward evidence (a tangible and immediate manifestation) that proved this Baptism had been received.

It happens again in Scripture. In this instance it is in a different city other than Caesarea (Ephesus), Paul is the minister instead of Peter, and it happens to a completely different group of people who, more than likely, never met Cornelius and his Gentile kinsmen and near friends (disciples of Apollos). Yet the experience is exactly the same.

> *⁴Then said Paul, John verily baptized with the baptism of repentance, saying unto the people, that they should believe on him which should come after him, that is, on Christ Jesus.*
> *⁵When they heard this, they were baptized in the name of the Lord Jesus.*
> *⁶And when Paul had laid his hands upon them, the Holy Ghost came on them; <u>and they spake with tongues, and prophesied.</u>*
> *⁷And all the men were about twelve.* (Acts 19:4-7 KJV)

In this case, prophecy (inspired speech in an understandable language) was integrated with this Baptism. It is very possible that this prophecy included the interpretation of these tongues, considering that tongues plus interpretation equates to prophesy, according to 1 Corinthians 14:5.

Be that as it may, it is vital to understand that when the Spirit of God comes upon us with force, it opens us up to experience whatever spiritual gifting the Holy Ghost deems appropriate at that moment. Gifts of healing, discerning of spirits, miracles, special faith, word of wisdom, and all the others may, in fact, happen right at the moment of being baptized in the Spirit. Then again, they may not. What is important to realize is that whatever experience transpires during this Baptism, tongues will always be included. Tongues is infallible proof that the Baptism of the Spirit has been received.

Baptism In the Spirit is Distinct From Tongues

Jesus told His disciples that this marvel would occur as soon as His earthly ministry had ended. In light of this, He gave strict orders for them not to begin their commission until they had received the fullness of His Spirit.

> *And, behold, I send the promise of my Father upon you: but tarry ye in the city of Jerusalem, until ye be endued with power from on high.* (Luke 24:49 KJV)

John the Baptizer, as the Greek text calls him (Mark 1:4), referred to this experience as a Baptism. The word "baptize" means, "To plunge, immerse, dip fully into." The meaning later evolved into a ceremonial rite and ritualistic observance. Technically, you "baptize" your body in water every time you jump off a diving board into a pool. Obviously, this is not the water baptism from Scripture.

Interestingly, in Scripture there are multiple kinds of Baptisms. Five to be exact: Baptism in water (Matthew 3), Baptism in suffering (Luke 12:50), Baptism in the cloud and sea (1 Corinthians 10:2), Baptism into Christ (Romans 6:3-7), and finally, the Baptism in the Holy Ghost, as foretold by John the Baptist in Matthew 3:11 (KJV):

> *I indeed baptize you with water unto repentance, but he that cometh after me is mightier than I, whose shoes I am not worthy to bear: <u>he shall baptize you with the Holy Ghost, and with fire.</u>*

Around three years after John spoke of this Baptism, Jesus declared it and told His disciples what to expect upon receiving it. Then, He ascended into heaven:

> *But ye shall receive power, after that the Holy Ghost is come upon you: and ye shall be witnesses unto me both in Jerusalem, and in all Judea, and in Samaria, and unto the uttermost part of the earth.* (Acts 1:8 KJV)

Mistakenly, it is frequently thought that the Baptism of the Holy Ghost means *only* receiving the ability to speak in tongues. Although tongues *always* accompany Baptism in the Spirit, it is more than just that. *Baptism in the Spirit is the clothing of power upon the believer for outward Christian service.* The Greek word for *power* in the verse above is *dunamis.* It means, "might, deed, power, wonder, miracle, capability." Our English word "dynamite" is derived from this exceptional Greek word. When does this power come upon us? Luke says, ***"After the Holy Ghost is come upon you."*** The word *come* is the Greek word *eperchomai* and means "to move upon, arrive, or to come against someone with force." *Upon* is the Greek word *epi* and is used to answer the question "where." The answer is *us.*

Therefore, from this we can reason that *dynamite miraculous capability comes upon us after the Holy Ghost moves upon, arrives, and meets us with force.* Just as most dynamite is intended for the purposes of demolition, this dynamite power from the Spirit of God is used to destroy the strongholds of Satan and demolish the fortresses of thinking he has erected in the minds of those who are lost (2 Corinthians 10:4-5).

Like a backpack for a hiker, the Baptism in the Spirit with tongues is a major part of the believer's equipment while on the journey. Do you have your backpack on?

CHAPTER TWENTY-SEVEN

Tongues 201: How Do I Get It?

**"It does demonstrate one great truth: To get the Baptism
of the Spirit off the chalkboard and into our lives,
we must hunger and thirst."**

Once I was preaching on the Island of St. Thomas for two weeks back in August 2010. One muggy evening as I sat surfing the web in the villa's lounge, my good friend Arthur called. As soon as I answered there was an immediate presence that overtook me. I could tell it had already been upon Arthur before he phoned me. As many times as I had told him about the Baptism of the Spirit and tongues, he had just listened intellectually and considered it. Nothing really ever dropped into his heart, until now. "Chris, I want it. I know I need it," Arthur groaned. How interesting this was. Arthur grew up in a denomination and family that forbade tongues. Something had grabbed hold of his spirit that was deeper than the teaching he had heard for over two decades. A hunger brewed in him that was now spilling into his emotions and into his will.

I walked back to my room as I listened to his plea. I said, "Arthur, after receiving Jesus there is one major qualification for this."

"What is it? Tell me. Please."

"Jesus said, 'If any man thirst, let him come unto me, and drink. He that believeth on me, as the scripture hath said, out of his belly shall flow rivers of living water.' Arthur, Jesus looks at our hearts and examines our desires. He right now knows how your whole being wants to go deeper." By this time, I could hear Arthur crying.

Suddenly, with a gentle force I said, "Arthur, speak." And as fast as I could finish saying those words, his mouth broke open into heavenly ecstasy. The words flowed exactly as how Arthur's Savior said they would, "as rivers of living water."

The next evening he called to say he had continued to pray in tongues for an hour and a half after we hung up. And while working all that day, he prayed in whispered tongues while he operated his press at the tool and die company.

Arthur never gave up his prayer language and discovered that it was an avenue that led him into the fullness of God's plan for his life. Less than two years later he found Paige, the love of his life and another Spirit-filled believer. Interestingly enough, although they did not know each other at the time, Paige had been learning and practicing the same things as Arthur. But through this supernatural prayer language, God was setting them up for a life of power, together. Today, they attribute much of this success to their good friend, Mr. Praying In Tongues.

Laying On of Hands To Receive

Arthur's experience is custom fit for him and is not a template for everyone. He received it over the phone, he and I being separated by over 2,000 miles. Yet, there are other ways it can be obtained. According to the Word of God, laying on of hands was—and is—a common way that the Baptism of the Holy Ghost was ministered.

> *[14] Now when the apostles which were at Jerusalem heard that Samaria had received the word of God, they sent unto them Peter and John:*
> *[15] Who, when they were come down, prayed for them, that they might receive the Holy Ghost:*
> *[16] (For as yet he was fallen upon none of them: only they were baptized in the name of the Lord Jesus.)*
> *[17] Then laid they their hands on them, and they received the Holy Ghost.*
> *[18] And when Simon saw that through laying on of the apostles' hands the Holy Ghost was given, he offered them money,*

> [19] *Saying, Give me also this power, <u>that whomsoever I lay hands, he may receive the Holy Ghost</u>.* (Acts 8:14-19 KJV)

The same thing is noted in Acts 19:6:

> *And <u>when Paul had laid his hands upon them, the Holy Ghost came on them; and they spake with tongues, and prophesied</u>.* (Acts 19:6 KJV)

I attended a powerful prayer meeting in the summer of 2010 where believers had gathered to pray for a woman in her late twenties who was battling cancer. I was the only minister present and unofficially led the majority of the assembly. As we were finishing the service, the young lady sat in a chair in the middle of the room and we all laid hands on her. I happened to be behind most of the people and placed my hand on the shoulders of the gentleman in front of me.

When we finished, a woman asked if I would mind praying with her husband to receive the Baptism in the Holy Ghost, something he had been longing to experience for some time. To my surprise it happened to be the gentleman whose shoulders I had placed my hands on.

"Honey, I got it!" he said.

"What are you talking about?" his wife asked.

"When Chris placed his hand on my shoulder I immediately started speaking in tongues!" It was amusing but, nonetheless, a splendid testimony of God's power.

It appears that God uses the hands of His people as a point of contact to transmit the power of God to those who are looking for it. Simon recognized this immediately and asked the disciples how he could get in on it, going so far as to offer them money. He saw the money he would put up front as a small investment, thinking he would get it all back by charging people to receive this power. To his chagrin, he learned that the power of God is not a commodity that can be purchased. Rather, it is a free gift that is available to those who thirst for it. Laying on of hands is one of the ways it can come.

Believing God To Receive

Though God uses the hands of His servants, this is not always the case. I personally have led people into receiving this power without ever laying hands on them. Once, I told a friend of mine that if she believed God, she could get the Baptism of the Holy Ghost by the time we got off of I-696 and onto I-275 (a span of around twelve miles). She looked at me as though I was being blasphemous.

I said, "God wants you to have it now. What are you waiting for?" She must have roused because she began to ask the Lord for it. Sure enough, she began speaking in tongues by the time we had reached I-275. When she got home she was giggling and told her mother. Before the night was over, her mother too, had received it. Neither of these two women had anyone lay hands on them. This is also Scriptural. Notice two incidents in Acts where believers were Baptized in the Spirit, never having a minister, mentor, or guide to lay hands on them.

> *¹And when the day of Pentecost was fully come, they were all with one accord in one place.*
> *²And suddenly there came a sound from heaven as of a rushing mighty wind, and it filled all the house where they were sitting.*
> *³And there appeared unto them cloven tongues like as of fire, and it sat upon each of them.*
> *⁴And they were all filled with the Holy Ghost, and began to speak with other tongues, as the Spirit gave them utterance.* (Acts 2:1-4 KJV)

> *⁴⁴While Peter yet spake these words, the Holy Ghost fell on all them which heard the word.*
> *⁴⁵And they of the circumcision which believed were astonished, as many as came with Peter, because that on the Gentiles also was poured out the gift of the Holy Ghost.* (Acts 10:44-45 KJV)

Whether the Baptism of the Spirit is ministered using the laying on of hands or without the laying on of hands, what God is looking for is the ardent desire to go deeper into the things of Him. It does demonstrate one great truth: *to get the Baptism of the Spirit off the chalkboard and into our lives, we must hunger and thirst.* There are two types of hunger that will lead us into it.

1.) *A hunger for the Baptism in the Spirit*: Jesus told His disciples *exactly* what to expect and seek after (Luke 24:49; Acts 1:8). Their time of seeking in the upper room in Acts 2 was for this experience. In our lives, once we believe Jesus' promise and go seeking for it, we can be sure that He will give it to us. Jesus said:

> *⁷Ask, and it shall be given you; seek, and ye shall find; knock, and it shall be opened unto you:*
> *⁸For every one that asketh receiveth; and he that seeketh findeth; and to him that knocketh it shall be opened.* (Matthew 7:7-8 KJV)

2.) *A hunger for Jesus:* There have been a great many occasions where people just simply know they need Jesus and give their lives to Him without even knowing about tongues. Right then and there, they get filled with the Holy Ghost and speak in tongues. Afterward, someone has to explain to them what happened. It is important to remember that God knows our heart even when we don't.

Someone might object, "Hey, God gave them something they may not have wanted." Not so. If their heart had not wanted it, they would not have been given it. God sent it because *He* knew what they wanted even if *they* didn't, yet. Paul tells Timothy, *"If we believe not, yet he abideth faithful: he cannot deny himself"* (2 Timothy 2:13 KJV). *Our heavenly Father is so faithful that He delivers what our heart is reaching for, even when we are not sure of what that is.*

One woman who had heard me preach on tongues approached me after service. Oh, how she wanted to enter in, but timidity prevented her. "I am scared I will get a devil." I can certainly understand that concern.

When I was fifteen I was ignorant of my authority and position in Christ, and was always afraid of demons.

We do not have to be concerned about getting a devil when asking for the Holy Spirit. The airtight seal of fellowship we have with our Father cannot be broken by a scheming, sinister entity. I said, "Sister, there is no need to worry about this. You are in a fellowship with your heavenly Father. No devil on earth can get in between your asking and receiving of Him." Then I reminded her of the words of Jesus:

> *[11]If a son shall ask bread of any of you that is a father, will he give him a stone? or if he ask a fish, will he for a fish give him a serpent?*
> *[12]Or if he shall ask an egg, will he offer him a scorpion?*
> *[13]If ye then, being evil, know how to give good gifts unto your children: how much more shall your heavenly Father give the Holy Spirit to them that ask him?* (Luke 11:11-13 KJV)

What determines our receiving is the state of our hearts. Even when our minds get jumbled up or fearful, if there is something in our heart, however small, that God can work with, the Holy Spirit will use that tiny willingness to bring us to the place we need to be to receive. When He begins to work on our heart in this sort of way, what builds in our heart will override what is in our head and replace it, erasing all the wrong teaching that has confused us over the years.

The Mechanics of Man's Makeup

After believers receive tongues (or even before, if they are searching,) they occasionally question what I like to think of as "the linguistic process of tongues." By this, they want to know how tongues work, mechanically. Though it is not a requirement, it can indeed be explained. Just as it was not required for us to know that the earth revolves around the sun, curious minds took to finding out how. We can do the same with our prayer

Greek
Sophia
wisdom

language. The chief question is, "How do I know it is not my mind telling me what to say?"

Believers truly wonder how the mind relates to all of this, seeing that 1 Corinthians 14:14 (KJV) says, *"For if I pray in an unknown tongue, my spirit prayeth, but my understanding is unfruitful."* This Scripture leaves people scratching their heads. Another blanket statement, "Well, we must take it by faith," has been thrown over this to smother the fires of curiosity. Of course, it is not vital to our salvation to figure this one out, but wouldn't it be nice to know? It is possible. To do so, we have to grasp an understanding of humankind's makeup.

In 1 Thessalonians 5:23, we are given the three main parts that make up each individual as a whole: spirit, soul, and body. The spirit is your eternal man, your immortal self, the part of you that communes with God. Your soul is your mind, your will, and your emotions, and is housed within your body. And finally, your body is your "earth suit," the exterior human that enables you to interact within this physical dimension. As distinct as they are from one another, they are seamlessly welded together and operate as one collective unit. This is what makes you, you.

Wrong teaching suggests that they can operate apart from each other. When Paul said, *"my spirit prayeth, but my understanding is unfruitful,"* he was *not* saying that his mind has no part in this. Rather, he was saying that his mind couldn't understand the language that was being spoken from his mouth. However, the mind is still involved in the process. In Ephesians 1:17-18 (KJV) there is a circuit that explains how this process mechanically works:

> *That the God of our Lord Jesus Christ, the Father of Glory, may give unto you the <u>spirit of wisdom and revelation</u> in the knowledge of him: The eyes of your understanding being enlightened; that ye may know what is the hope of his calling, and what the riches of the glory of his inheritance in the saints.*

There are a couple of things to notice. First, it speaks of "the spirit of wisdom and revelation." Wisdom is the Greek word *sophia* and it means "broad intelligence." This would be the Holy Spirit. The Holy Spirit

152

cooperates with man by sharing His broad and limitless understanding. This includes the hearts of people (discernment), future happenings, past happenings, and other things we could never know without His help.

Revelation is the Greek word *apokalypsis* and literally means to "make naked." It gives the impression of undressing something. In English it would be to *reveal*. The undressing part comes into play when we consider that all through the ages Christ, the God-Man, was a mystery (Colossians 1:26). Even among His own people, the Jewish nation of Israel, the religious leaders could not see that He was the Messiah because He was clothed with mystery. Because they rejected Him, the Holy Spirit was grieved and did not assist them in uncovering His identity (Mark 3:22-29). However, the same Holy Spirit stands by saints and will personally reveal as much of Jesus to them as desired. This is His ministry (John 14:26; John 16:13). Though He shows us many things out of that broad wisdom, His primary revelations to us are "in the knowledge of Him" (Ephesians 1:17), the great truths and aspects of Jesus Christ, and who we are now in Him.

"But how?" you ask. Verse 18 is the answer. Notice that it says, ***"The eyes of your understanding being enlightened."*** The Greek word for "eyes" is *ophthalmos*. It is not a mere reference to the physical eye, but is a reference to much more. The best translation for it would be, "seeing with spiritual understanding." The Greek word for *understanding* is the word *dianoia*. Although this refers to the intellectual faculty of man, it refers to a specific region of it: the *imagination*. Clement of Alexandria uses the word *dianoia* as a reference to such. And last, the word *enlightened* is the Greek word *photizo* and means, "to shed light." The root word of *photizo* is the Greek word, *phos*, which simply means "light." Couple *phos* with the Greek word for write, *graphe*, and you have the English derivative *photograph*, an image written with light.

When we back up and take a look at what is literally being said here we gain a powerful insight of how the Spirit of God operates with our spirit and mind: "The Spirit of broad understanding and intelligence, who undresses the mystery of Christ for us, does so in the form of spiritual understanding. This spiritual understanding occurs when He moves upon our spirit. Once our spirit gains the insight, it sends that insight up to our minds, particularly the imagination, and floods it with images of light."

This is why it is not uncommon for people who pray in the Holy Ghost to have imaginations (ideas and inspiration) pop into their minds. The Holy Ghost drops it into their spirit, and their spirit sends it up to the mind. If their mind is renewed, it has no problem receiving what the spirit sent up. Revelation and guidance can then be clearly understood, and walked in, in daily life. If the mind were not engaged, we would be unable to walk in what God has shown our spirit. The mind is needed if we are going to understand the language of the Spirit as He moves upon our own spirit. This transfer from our spirit to our mind happens in a fraction of a second and is almost unnoticed.

Once, I was visiting a mentally ill person in a psychiatric hospital. During the visit I was watching a young man across the room, and I sensed a tremendous burden for him. As I continued my stay, the burden grew larger and larger. It was as though a call to action was being summoned in my inward man. I do know the Spirit of God had gotten a hold of my spirit.

As soon as I walked out of the hospital, imaginations of how to help the mentally ill community exploded in my mind. I instantly knew exactly what to do. I could tell it wasn't an imagination conjured up by myself because of the effect it produced in me: faith, thankfulness, excitement for the Kingdom, and a love for God that caused me to immediately enter into worship just as soon as I got in my car. I would never have made the connection unless my spirit was able to push what it had received from the Holy Ghost through to my mind.

The Science of Tongues

This being the case, consider the prayer language itself. It is no different. The Spirit of God gives the words to your spirit. Your own spirit takes those words and sends them to your mind, and your mind gives the order to your mouth to speak them out. Because the words passed through your mind and imagination, another part of your brain also gets in on the action. This would be our memory. If you are quiet enough to hear yourself think, you can hear the tongues in your brain that you have previously spoken forth. God designed it to be this way because He wants you to pray in the Holy Ghost at all times (Ephesians 6:18). We should not make the faulty assumption that just because tongues are now a part of our mind it is no longer sacred. The fact that God made this prayer language to be absorbed by the brain makes it all the more divine.

The ultimate chapter on Praying in Tongues is found in 1 Corinthians 14. No other place in the Bible deals as directly with it as this passage. Paul writes:

> *For he who speaks in a [unknown] tongue does not speak to men but to God, for no one understands him; however, in the spirit he speaks mysteries.* (1 Corinthians 14:2 NKJV)

In the original Greek manuscript, the word *unknown* is not found. This has been a point of argument for literal textual critics. Yet, translators added that word because the Greek word for "tongue" is *glossa,* meaning "foreign, unintelligible, mysterious utterances." Some also say it means "celestial and mysterious utterances." It describes speech that happens during spiritual elation. This goes hand-in-hand with 1 Corinthians 13:1 (KJV), *"Though I speak with the tongues of men and angels."*

Isaiah, the eagle-eyed prophet, spoke of this prayer language when he prophesied in Isaiah 28:11-12 (KJV):

> *For with stammering lips and <u>another tongue will he speak</u> to this people. To whom he said, <u>This is the rest wherewith ye may cause the weary to rest; and this is the refreshing;</u> yet they would not hear.*

Thousands of years later when Jesus walked the earth, He declared this linguistic phenomenon while commissioning His Apostles:

> *[15]And he said unto them, Go ye into all the world, and preach the gospel to every creature.*
> *[16]He that believeth and is baptized shall be saved; but he that believeth not shall be damned.*

> *[17] And these signs shall follow them that believe; In my name shall they cast out devils; <u>they shall speak with new tongues;</u>*
> *[18] They shall take up serpents; and if they drink any deadly thing, it shall not hurt them; they shall lay hands on the sick, and they shall recover.* (Mark 16:15-18 KJV)

Again, the Greek word used in this passage of Mark above is the word *glossa*. Though the word *glossa* can refer to the tongue as an organ, when coupled with the word "new" it takes on deeper meaning. "New" is the Greek word *kainos*. It carries the meaning of something that is new, strange, or unknown. Even more, it brings along the idea of news: "What is the latest news? What has happened that I haven't heard?"

New tongues refers to strange speech that has yet to be seen, known, heard or witnessed by humankind. This is most certainly the speech identified by Isaiah, guaranteed to bring *rest* and *refreshing* to the people of God. Being so, speaking in tongues is not a concept that was intended to fill hours of classroom discussion or to coat the pages of endless theological works. Instead, it is an experience that God's people are to encounter, whether our logic can clearly frame it or not.

The fact is that our minds are so far behind spiritual experiences that we may never, in this lifetime, build up enough brainpower to clearly understand them. However, as long as these experiences are Scriptural and doctrinally sound, we can enter into them without fear. All we must do is yield.

CHAPTER TWENTY-EIGHT

Yielding to the Problem Solver

"The reality, however, is this: a person's prayer is usually not the answer to a difficult problem. The answer to the problem is a relationship with the Holy Ghost."

> *26Likewise the Spirit also helps in our weaknesses. For we do not know what we should pray for as we ought, but the Spirit himself makes intercession for us with groanings which cannot be uttered.*
> *27Now He who searches the hearts knows what the mind of the Spirit is, because He makes intercession for the saints according to the will of God.* (Romans 8:26-27 NKJV)

One thing I kept in mind while I was studying theology in Bible school, and still keep in mind when I am out ministering, is this: Life is real. Real people have real problems, and oft times, cannot find real solutions. If we take a quick account of our lives, we will recognize limitations: limitations on our thinking, limitations upon our understanding, limitations upon our bodies, in our wills, emotions, desires. God knows this. He realizes our finiteness as human beings. With all that limitation, we certainly do need a Helper.

One of the greatest needs today is for believers to begin to yield to the Holy Ghost. Paul understood this. These two short verses, Romans 8:26-27, are the starting point for discovering how we can *consciously* and willingly begin to turn ourselves over to the Holy Ghost for help, comfort, and guidance in every situation.

In the family of God, each believer is 100% unique. Every problem, circumstance, and situation is different from the next person's.

"Yeah, but Brother Palmer, what if two people are dealing with the same thing?"

People might appear to have the same problem on the surface, but if you talk to them, you will usually find that they are dealing with the problem for different reasons or for a different root cause. All of the variables that trigger people to do what they are doing are never the same. In fact, even if you *seem* to be having a problem that you've had before, the situation and your current understanding will make it different, and thus the answer should be different. The human answer and the Holy Spirit's answer frequently prove to be diametrically opposed. *Generic answers to people's problems will only get us so far.* Even if generic answers help, one day a tidal wave of problems will come along and be so devastating that no static set of instructions could possibly apply.

My friend, Katharine, knows this to the core of her being. When faced with a decision, she will say, "I'll turn it over to the Holy Spirit." She understands that even what appear to be small decisions may, indeed, have long-reaching ramifications for her life, and for others. Once, while visiting friends in Colorado, she had responded to a problem in her usual manner: "I'll turn it over to the Holy Spirit."

Finally, her attorney friend asked, "Don't you ever try to do anything for yourself?"

"Gee, I try not to," she answered, pleased. She thought he was commending her, and it didn't occur to her until much later that he thought she should do everything for herself until there were no other answers. "Why would I want to do that?" she says. "Why not turn it over to the Holy Spirit first? Then we don't have to struggle to figure it out with our mortal mind. Plus, the Holy Spirit's answer means it is perfect for all concerned." Perhaps her friend did not understand that once the problem had been turned over to Holy Spirit, she would do what she was led to do. She would not simply sit on her hands.

She understands that, indeed, the Holy Spirit is there as our Counselor, and Advocate, and Guide. The Holy Spirit was given to us to help us know what to do. Even when there isn't time to pray about a situation, she will think, "I give this to the Holy Spirit," knowing that the Holy Ghost doesn't require human time. Holy Spirit requires only a little willingness. And, after that, even if the decision may appear to be odd or fractious, she has learned that in the long run, it has proven to be correct.

A Living Problem Solver

The Spirit of God is not a dead letter, but a living entity. When we entered the family of God, God didn't give us a list of one, two, and three answers for every problem. Instead, He gave us the divine source of wisdom in the person of the Holy Ghost. A dead set of rules cannot take into account those things that are ruining your life, and calculate a new solution for you. But the Holy Ghost can. Though Paul did outline some house rules and give tangible instructions in some of his other letters, he taught that the most important thing for each individual believer was to develop a close union with the Holy Ghost.

Jesus taught this to His disciples:

> *¹⁶And I will pray the Father, and He will give you another Helper, that He may abide with you forever—*
> *¹⁷the Spirit of truth, whom the world cannot receive, because it neither sees Him nor knows Him; but you know Him, for He dwells with you and will be in you.*
> (John 14:16-17 NKJV)

"Dwells with you" and "will be in you" are terms that denote not just any relationship, but a very close relationship. Hearing these words should have branded the brain of every disciple. Jesus was telling them that the key to their success in Him was to get acquainted with the Comforter, the Advocate, the One who was being sent by Him to come alongside and be their help. Jesus Christ's church was founded with the help of this Helper, and God intends that this same Helper carry on the mission of the Church. Success in the Kingdom of God and in our personal walk with God as Father is largely dependent on what we do with the Holy Ghost that was given to us.

Get To Know the Problem Solver

"Likewise the Spirit also helpeth our infirmities" (Romans 8:26 KJV). Another correct way of saying this, based on what Jesus taught about the Holy Ghost, would be, *"Likewise the Helper also helps in our weaknesses"* (NKJV).

When Jesus called the Holy Ghost the Helper, He obviously knew that we were going to need lots of support on the earth after He went away. There are few days when I don't say, "Oh, Holy Spirit, I need your help." Am I the only one? Have you had a moment this month, this week, today, or in this last half hour where you said, "God, help me!"

Being a minister, people ask me for prayer all the time. It isn't unusual for me to preach and minister for two hours, praying for the sick, casting out devils, and doing whatever else is necessary, and then minister to a line of people who are requesting prayer. It is my joy to do so. People are in need, and my heart is full of compassion for them (Matthew 9:36).

However, I do notice that some people don't come back just one, two, or three times for prayer. No, they come back week in and week out, with the same problem. I have even met people years later, and they tell me that they are dealing with the same issue, and request the same prayer.

I have a practical mind. I don't throw logic to the wind because I am now spiritual. It would be safe to assume that if the problem that is being prayed for now is not working, and hasn't worked for years, then it may not be the answer to the difficulty.

"Chris, how dare you suggest that prayer may not work?" I dare suggest it because it isn't working. Sometimes we get into a frame of mind and think, "If I just say enough prayers," or, "If I have the right person pray the right thing over me, things will be okay." If things don't improve, these will be the same people who visit every conference, every ministry, and every church looking for that one special prayer.

The reality, however, is this: A person's prayer is usually not the answer to a difficult problem. *The answer to the problem is a relationship with the Holy Ghost.*

My mom had a close friend whose life was in disarray for many different reasons. Her husband was rebellious toward God, and was a poor provider for the home. Her kids were not turning out the way she wanted, and it always seemed as though there was another ugly thing popping up its head. Because her husband would rather hunt and fish instead of providing for his family, my mom's friend worked long hours. The family was barely getting by.

I have compassion for people like this. *However, compassion is about accuracy and efficiency.* When Jesus had compassion on people, He didn't go over and put his arm around them and say, "There, there now. Isn't that devil just a meanie? It's all right. Things are going to be okay."

No, Jesus got right to the solution. Ever since I have known my mother's friend, she has had these problems, but she would never lift a finger to go to church to hear the Word of God. Anytime she wanted to reach out to God, she would ask my mom, "Could you just please have Christopher pray for me?"

Finally, one day I told my mom: "Mom, tell her I am not praying for her, because prayer is not the solution to the problem. Tell her that if she is serious about God, come to my ministry meeting this month, and we will lay hands on her and minister to her." I wanted to see if she was serious about getting a touch from God.

When that service came along, I spotted her in the back of the room as I was preaching. She had finally come. I knew she was going to get a touch from God. She was an asthmatic, and when I called for those who had sickness, she responded, and I prayed for her. To this day, she has not needed an inhaler.

However, just because she got healed of asthma, her problems at home did not dissolve into thin air. A few months went by, and it was more of the same. "Chris," my mom would say, "my friend is asking you to pray for..."

I cut my mom off and said, "Let me guess: her husband, kids, and finances. Mom, I want you to tell your friend this. Currently, her prayer life is not up to par even to begin to change her circumstances. As a matter of fact, her biggest problem is the person she looks at every day in the mirror: herself. Please firmly tell her that her answer is not your prayers, or mine. Her answer is a relationship with the Helper that Jesus gave her, the Holy Ghost." When we get to know the Problem Solver, every answer to every question becomes available to us. He is at our disposal anytime we need Him. If you will take time to yield and let Him work with you, then you will find that your "problems" have met their match.

CHAPTER TWENTY-NINE

Filthiness of Flesh and Spirit

"The year 2009 became the year that God killed Minister Palmer."

Before I became a full time evangelist, I spent two and a half years being the young, single, hot shot minister at the largest church in the state of Michigan. In my world and in my bubble, I was the cat's pajamas. I walked the halls of my church confidently, as people went out of their way to say: "Good morning, Minister Palmer. Great sermon yesterday! Well, hello there, Minister Palmer, did you get a haircut? I like it. Hey, Minister Palmer, can you tell me what your favorite book is? You have such a fire about you! I want the kind of relationship you have with God!" It didn't stop in the hallways. After church on Sundays and Wednesdays, congregants would come up, seeking prayer and momentary counsel.

During my tenure, the United States, and particularly Michigan, was facing one of the greatest financial crises it had ever seen. Often times, a struggling husband and father would come up and say: "Minister Palmer, I have given to God 20% of my finances. I confess the Word every day, and I am out there looking for a job constantly, but nothing seems to be working. What should I do?"

I hate to admit this, but the genuine compassion that I had for these folks was mingled with a sense of enjoyment that came with being what, I thought, a source of answers and solutions to people's most difficult problems. "Brother, all you need to do is have faith! Believe! Rejoice that it is all done. You know that the Scripture tells us that God supplies our every need. Why can't you accept that and just trust Him?" I clearly remember a few times walking out of the church feeling like a soldier who had just given his all for God's people. I would think: "People just don't get it. I guess this is why God called me into ministry. I am so full of wisdom.

Yet, look at how humble I am. I could be a business man or a lawyer, but I have chosen ministry." With those thoughts I would start my car and drive home from church, clearly a superstar in my own mind.

Something changed in 2009. My church was sending me out into the evangelistic field as a full time evangelist. No longer would I be solving people's problems at the church. No longer would I work in a pastoral care position. I didn't know much about starting a ministry or running an evangelistic operation, but hey, I was Minister Palmer. I'd make it happen. I was so full of ambition. I was so full of dreams.

As the date of my departure drew closer I noticed that there was just one problem. Not only did I have nowhere to preach, I was taken off salary at my church. That wonderful slip of paper that appeared on my desk every other Friday wasn't going to be magically showing up anymore.

On December 31, 2008, I walked out of my church for the last time as "Minister Palmer." The jig was up. No more answering people's questions, no more compliments in the hallway, no more paycheck on my desk, no more limelight to stand in. A feeling hit me right in my gut, releasing this paralyzing thought, *What am I going to do?* I knew one thing was for sure: I was about to find out what I was made of.

The year 2009 became the year that God killed Minister Palmer.

As the evangelist with no place to preach, I discovered I had an awful lot of time on my hands. As days turned into weeks, and weeks turned into months, as winter turned into spring and as spring turned into summer, I discovered that I was not the spiritual superstar and faith giant that I thought I was. Not having compliments to keep me moving forward, I began to sink lower and lower into a depression. The first things I experienced when I opened my eyes in the morning would be the last things I wrestled before falling asleep: the torments, fears, doubts, uncertainties, intense discouragement, and an oncoming sense of hopelessness. I spent seven months racking my brain, and found not one answer. Having nowhere to preach and making no money were now the least of my troubles. I became overwhelmed with things within myself that I never knew existed: bitterness, fear, torment, unbelief, care, and discouragement.

Even when I was given a rare opportunity to preach, I'd sometimes cry afterwards, because I could see that there was no power in my preaching. It was all empty words of doctrine and things I had heard other preachers say. For months and months all of these things churned inside of me like a cyclone. I knew if I could just pinpoint the problem, I could find an answer. I thought it was all because I had no money and no place to preach.

Little did I understand that having no money and no place to preach weren't the issues. They were being used to bring out the *vanity* and *pride* that existed in me while I was "Superhero Palmer" at my church. The false identity I had built on my title and position at the church would be of no avail. The false sense of security that came with being paid every week did not give me the faith I needed to help me win this battle. I felt like a helpless man, in the middle of the ocean being tossed in every direction, having no idea which way to swim. I did not know what to do.

There was no doubt that I was born again. I had come through the new birth when I was about twelve years old. I was a Holy Ghost-filled preacher of God's Word. So where were these attacks coming from? How long had they been dormant? How did they arrive into my life?

Once, I was sharing my story, and someone suggested that it was all assaults from Satan and demons. Now, I believe in demonic attacks, but this was not a demonic attack. I have had my share of attacks from the devil, and this wasn't one of them. Instead, I was beginning to notice all the parts of my life that needed to be purged.

> *Therefore, having these promises, beloved, let us cleanse [purge] ourselves from all filthiness of the flesh and spirit, perfecting holiness in the fear of God.* (2 Corinthians 7:1 NKJV)

Notice that Paul is writing to the "beloved." The beloved were his brothers and sisters in Corinth who had come through the new birth. Despite having become sons and daughters of God, according to Paul, it is needful for us to *"cleanse [purge] ourselves from all filthiness of flesh and spirit, perfecting holiness in the fear of God."* Filthiness of flesh and filthiness of spirit are barriers and obstacles to our flesh and spirit. When we yield to them, most of the time unknowingly, they stop our forward progress in God and block us from going any further down the path that shines more and more unto the perfect day.

Filthiness of Flesh

Filthiness of flesh is a term that is used to describe those things that come along to slow down your development in God, appealing strictly to your weak flesh. These are low-level temptations that derive from the appetites of the mortality still at work inside of the body. Naturally, they appeal to the carnal man and his self-gratification. Many times when a believer is being tempted by filthiness of flesh it is not coming from a demon source. ***"But every man is tempted, when he is drawn away of his own lust, and enticed"*** (James 1:14).

When an individual gives in to the filthiness that appeals to their flesh, it indicates that this area has not yielded to the "joint help" that Jesus came along and sent us for our building up and edification. If experiencing the new birth had done away with all of the weaknesses that remain in our bodies, then it would not have been necessary for God to send us a Comforter, Helper, and Advocate, whose sole purpose is to locate the thing that is causing our weakness and blow it out of the water.

There are areas that please the flesh and ease it from any tension that it may be under. They all bring temporary enjoyment and are limited to destroying the individual involved. Here are some contemporary examples of filthiness of flesh that are common today:

1.) *Lust:* pornography, promiscuity, sexual fantasies
2.) *Substance addictions and dependencies:* smoking, alcoholism, nicotine, narcotics, and any other substance that is depended upon regularly
3.) *Eating disorders:* gluttony, bulimia, anorexia
4.) *Pride:* haughtiness, arrogance, exaggerated sense of self-importance
5.) *Greed:* consumed with accumulating money, too much priority placed upon increasing wealth, an unhealthy and competitive drive to be rich
6.) *Narcissism:* an unhealthy obsession with self.
7.) *Filthy talking*

There is, however, another tier involved in the filthiness of flesh. These more directly involve the soul (the mind, will, and emotions). Whereas the ones above primarily destroy just the one person involved, the items below are more severe, because they destroy others as well.

1.) *Anger*: bitterness, resentment, and hatred toward those who have offended you
2.) *Unforgiveness*: the inability to release someone from the offense that they committed toward you
3.) *Gossip*: non-edifying language used to destroy and assassinate the character of a particular individual
4.) *Lying*
5.) *Jealousy*: obsessing over what another person has; not wanting someone to have something because you don't have it

Filthiness of flesh has a definite process to it that is very destructive. It is used as a weapon against your flesh, to assault you and destroy you. The most difficult thing about filthiness of flesh is that, because it appeals to self-gratification, most of the time it is something enjoyable. Often times, a child of God never advances into more of what Jesus said they could be, because they get caught up in this vortex of self-indulgence.

Here is how filthiness of flesh begins to delay a believer's progress.

1.) *Neglecting to cooperate with the Holy Ghost:* Not praying in the Spirit, or meditating the Word, or worshipping God regularly. Done regularly, these produce revelation knowledge. Revelation knowledge produces spiritual motion in our lives that causes us to go forward into our inheritance as children of God. When we do not have a constant flow of revealed knowledge at work in our lives, we stop identifying with our new natures and what God's Word has said about us. If revelation stops pouring in, the things which entice the flesh become alluring, and it will not be long until they draw us away from walking in our authority as sons and daughters of the Most High.
2.) *Lust is conceived*: When a child of God gives in to those things that have enticed his flesh, he goes against his new nature. This is "missing the mark," the mark that is the holiness of God. As long as we walk according to our new nature (Galatians 5:16), we

will never give in to the weaknesses imposed upon us by the lusts that target our bodies. By neglecting to look into God's Word to remind ourselves of who we are (James 1:25), lust is given an opportunity to hatch sin. When sin is born, it slows down the believer and begins to hurt his or her confidence before God.

3.) *The conscience begins to condemn:* The conscience is the inner voice of our spirit. In Romans 9:1 (KJV), Paul mentions the conscience: ***"I say the truth in Christ, I lie not, my conscience also bearing me witness in the Holy Ghost."*** The conscience is not the Holy Ghost; notice that it is something that Paul already possessed. The purpose of our conscience is to give us direction out of our new man. When we are born again, our new man has a voice. Anytime we start to do something that conflicts with that our reborn nature, the new man will say, "Hey, I wouldn't do that if I were you."

Some usually ask, "What is the difference between the voice of the conscience and the voice of the Holy Ghost?" The voice of conscience is the voice of *our* spirit; the voice of the Holy Ghost is the voice of *God*. After our spirit hears the voice of God, it bears witness to the rest of our being through this voice of conscience. Just like our outer man, our inner man has a memory. On many occasions, our spiritual memory recollects what it has heard from the voice of the Lord and communicates this to our outer man through this voice of conscience. Therefore it isn't *always* God speaking to you. It could be your inner man who is remembering what it has received over time from the Spirit of God. Be it the voice of conscience or the voice of the Lord, they are both sources that can be absolutely trusted.

Who is the conscience talking to? It is talking to the part of us that is weak: the flesh. The conscience has the approval of the Holy Ghost. When the inner man begins to speak to us regarding something, remember once again, it has received instruction and guidance from the Holy Ghost. Have you ever noticed that the voice of your conscience is so convicting and confident? It has every right to be; it has heard from the Holy Ghost, and not a scintilla of doubt remains.

Nonetheless, it is possible to ignore this voice. After you ignore it, the same voice that said, "Don't do that. It isn't good for you," will turn around and tell you, "See! You shouldn't have done that. Now look what has happened." This is different from the condemnation that comes from the devil. This is the witness and voice of the inner man that realizes that the flesh has gone against the new nature.

4.) *Confidence before God weakens:*

> ²¹*Beloved, if our heart [conscience] does not condemn us, we have confidence toward God.*
> ²²*And whatever we ask we receive from Him, because we keep His commandments and do those things that are pleasing in His sight.* (1 John 3:21-22 NKJV)

Asking and receiving is a normal thing that happens between a father and a son. We have every right to approach God and ask Him for something without ever having to feel that we are asking too much. This comes from being in right standing with Him. Though our position in righteousness came from the work of Jesus Christ, our execution of what we have become is based largely on how confident we are in that.

I have an older brother who, when we were kids, always found new ways to get into mischief. I was the goody-two-shoes, and my brother was the one who usually got the spanking. Once, my brother was swinging a bat around outside and accidentally bashed out the taillight of my dad's car. I saw it all go down and started laughing because I knew how much trouble he would be in. Not being a tattletale, though, I waited for Mikey to go and tell our dad what he had done. Instead, Mike stuck it out, hoping that our dad wouldn't notice.

For weeks, I watched how my brother was acting around my dad. Something was eating away at him. Feeling guilty, he couldn't look our dad in the eye. When our dad found out, he forgave my brother, and didn't treat him any differently than he treated me. My brother's position as a son didn't change, neither did my dad's graciousness toward him. What had changed was my brother's confidence.

The devil wants to see us fall into filthiness of flesh because he knows it will destroy our confidence to go before God, having missed the mark of holiness. Because of yielding to filthiness of flesh, believers today can't confidently pray for the sick, cast out devils, or walk anywhere near the authority that God fully intends for them to walk in. The Holy Ghost has been given to help them to fortify themselves against the weaknesses of their flesh and secure their confidence, but they refuse to use Him.

5.) *The conscience becomes seared:* Every time the conscience is ignored, sin begins to close up the voice of the conscience more and more. Paul tells Timothy that people would turn away from the faith (become redirected from going forward down the path of righteousness) because of **"having their conscience seared with a hot iron"** (1 Timothy 4:2 KJV).

Cauterization involves heating a knife and placing it upon an open wound or blister to close it up. When people get caught up in the process of filthiness of flesh, it becomes easier and easier to sin, because the voice of the conscience becomes duller and duller, as it is extinguished time and time again. A cauterized conscience is the reason why people begin walking further and further out of their salvation, while the grace and power of God empowers us to walk further and further into it.

6.) *The desire to get out of filthiness of flesh disappears:* As long as the Holy Ghost, through our conscience, is still bearing witness with us concerning the filthiness of the flesh, there will be the initiative to desire to be free from them. What causes a person to respond to an altar call, seeking deliverance? What causes someone caught up in the snares of lusts to start praying in the Holy Ghost again? When people fall into the slime pits of temptation, there has to be a force that drives them to put their hand on the first rock and begin the climb out. This force is initiative, and this initiative comes from the voice of the inner man, who is cooperating with the Holy Ghost.

Sadly, there are some people who have reached a place where they no longer desire to be delivered. This occurs when all initiative is quenched by the heaviness of sin. When this occurs, it leads to an even greater grief: filthiness of spirit, caused by doctrine that has been skewed and contaminated.

Filthiness of Spirit

Now the Spirit expressly says that in latter times some will depart from the faith, giving heed to deceiving spirits and doctrines of demons. (1 Timothy 4:1 NKJV)

³For the time will come when they will <u>not endure sound doctrine</u>, but according to their own desires, because they have itching ears, they will heap up for themselves teachers;
⁴and <u>they will turn their ears away from the truth, and be turned aside to fables</u>. (2 Timothy 4:3-4 NKJV)

Doctrine is not a man-made idea, nor is it a boring set of teachings that should put us to sleep while we are in Sunday school. Doctrine is the established, divine truth concerning God's plan for man. Placed next to each other, divine truths provide the blueprint for any child of God to be *"complete, thoroughly equipped for every good work"* (2 Timothy 3:17 NKJV).

When doctrine is in pure form it can provide reproof, correction, and instruction for every child of God who is walking further and further down the road of righteousness. Because doctrine is divine and supernatural, it contains the unique ability to penetrate our hearts. God chose the simple act of preaching as a way of inseminating mankind's heart with His divine doctrine. It is this doctrine that purifies the spirit and plays a major part in the new birth.

But Paul tells us that the same thing that led us onto this road is exactly what can lead us off this road. When doctrine becomes contaminated and harmful it becomes filthiness of spirit. Filthiness of spirit is the corruption of our spiritual minds through false doctrines. Filthiness of spirit is more serious than filthiness of flesh because it does more than just stop one's progress in God: *it reverses it.* Filthiness of spirit slips into men's hearts three ways:

1.) False teachers influenced by the spirit of antichrist (1 John 2:18-19)
2.) False angels of light (2 Corinthians 11:14)
3.) Lasciviousness (Jude 4)

Lasciviousness is the consistent involvement in filthiness of flesh, far beyond just a slip-up or two. This occurs when one shuts down the voice of conscience and starts living in sin, no longer thinking twice about not participating. More than the actions themselves, the greatest danger of lasciviousness is that those involved with it begin to turn, twist, and alter the pure forms of doctrines that were delivered to us by God, which is the start of filthiness of spirit.

> *For there are certain men crept in unawares, who were before of old ordained to this condemnation, ungodly men, turning the grace of our God into lasciviousness, and denying the only Lord God, and our Lord Jesus Christ.* (Jude 4 KJV)

When a doctrine begins to lead one further and further out of salvation and deeper and deeper into pleasure and sin, filthiness of spirit is at work. Of all the many deceptions that filthiness of spirit has produced, Jude gives the most pointed example: *"Turning the grace of God into lasciviousness"* (Jude 4). (In other words, using grace as a license to sin.)

The grace of God is empowering us to go further and further into our new nature, refusing temptation and lusts along the way. When we begin to head in the opposite direction, mistakenly calling it grace, we are being deceived by a false doctrine. John encountered people who had gotten into filthiness of spirit, turning the grace of God into lasciviousness, to justify their participation in the filthiness of flesh.

> *⁶If we <u>say</u> that we have fellowship with Him, and <u>walk</u> in darkness, we lie, and do not practice the truth.*
> *⁷But if we <u>walk</u> in the light as He is in the light, <u>we have fellowship</u> one with another, and the <u>blood of Jesus Christ His Son cleanses us from all sin</u>.*

> **⁸*If we say that we have no sin, we deceive ourselves,
> and the truth is not in us.
> ⁹If we confess our sins, He is faithful and just to forgive
> us our sins and to cleanse us from all unrighteousness.***
> (1 John 1:6-9 NKJV)

This verse is the focus of confusion for many. People have said to me: "Uh, so, do we say we have sin, or don't we say we have sin? Which is it?"

I have learned enough by now to realize that if a verse is confusing, one of the reasons might be because there are two different parties being represented in the dialogue. It was common for New Testament writers to go back and forth in their writings, representing two different kinds of people. The two people represented here are:

1.) Those who *say* they walk in the light, but walk in darkness
2.) Those who really *do* walk in the light as He is in the light

Again, the Light is the life that Jesus received from the Father and passed to us in the new birth (John 5:26). Our fellowship with God is based upon whether or not we live out of the new nature, putting the mortality in our bodies under subjugation. The first man is the lascivious one. He claims that he has fellowship with God but he is walking in darkness. When we read this, we sometimes take for granted that the lascivious man knows that he is wrong. This is not the case. Through filthiness of spirit that came from lascivious living, the first man legitimately thinks that he is walking with God while he is actually in sin.

Filthiness of spirit is powering this belief. In some form or another, his doctrine has bent grace to allow for sin under the guise, "The Blood of His Son Jesus Christ cleanses us from all sin so I am free to do what I please now."

John comes in and says: "No, no, no! The Blood is only effective when grace has not been skewed. Grace is not a license to sin. Grace empowers us to walk out of our reborn spirit, free from the dominion and power of sin (Galatians 5:16). If you are using grace promiscuously, it isn't grace." If the lascivious man says that he is not in sin because of grace, he deceives himself, and the truth is not in him (1 John 1:8). Another way of saying that the truth is not in him is to say that his doctrine has been tampered with, and is now faulty.

Finally, John provides a solution out of this filthiness of spirit (1 John 1:9). The person involved in it has to call his sin, sin. The only way that God can pull that person out of lasciviousness would be if he gave God the faith to do so. This would require him to have a revelation that his doctrine has been polluted by filthiness of spirit, after which he turns back to the pure form of doctrine that was delivered to the saints by the Holy Ghost (Jude 3). This will throw the man out of reverse and launch him back down the road of righteousness where he can again begin to inherit those things that rightfully belong to the children of God.

Doctrine is just that important. A good doctrine saves a man, and a bad doctrine damns him. Islam, Buddhism, Hinduism, etc. are all false doctrines that have come into the world through a spirit of deception. These doctrines get so lodged into a person's spirit that they become strongholds, never allowing the person to receive Jesus Christ and go through the new birth (2 Corinthians 10:4-5).

When Paul said that he was the chief of sinners, he was referring to the time *before* he had met Christ (1 Timothy 1:15-16). Paul wasn't the chief sinner because he killed Christians and sent them to heaven. Paul was the chief sinner because he was the chief propagator of a dead religion that had people reject Christ, sending them to hell. His whole life, before he met Christ, was devoted to tangling up the world in religious strongholds that would make it harder and harder for people to receive Jesus and come out of the new birth as sons of God. When Paul met the Holy Ghost, the Holy Ghost immediately drove Paul right out of this filthiness of spirit and purged out of him everything that played a part in getting him there in the first place. God's intent in doing this was for a lifetime of ministry. I may not have preached much in 2009, but God did something far deeper. God was exposing the areas of my life that needed to be eliminated so that I wouldn't fall into those things that could reverse me from my journey.

Are you frustrated with where God has you today? Don't be. Unknown to you, the Spirit of God may be undoing some of your greatest issues.

CHAPTER THIRTY

Joint Help to Combat Satan's Subtle Schemes

"The great problem was the shallow relationship I had with the Holy Ghost that wouldn't harness enough power to my emotions to brace me up against something like this."

Back in the year that God killed Minister Palmer, there were zones in my walk that had not been fortified due to my negligence and busyness. Ploys of darkness began to grind on me to such a degree that the torment, disquiet, and anxiety almost shut my ministry down before it began. Jesus spoke of other barricades that come to neutralize our forward progress in God. It was these subtle wiles of Satan (1 Corinthians 2:11) that pressured me when I first entered into full time evangelistic ministry.

Satan is a military genius. He has been studying humankind for over 6,000 years, knowing that with every generation there will come a new group of people who have not yet gained any experience in spiritual matters. It stands to reason that if he has had great success in past ages neutralizing believers with his tactics, then he sees no point to switching methods. It is up to us, then, to be aware of his schemes and learn how to combat them.

Just as filthiness of flesh and filthiness of spirit work on the mortality that preys upon the part of us that is unredeemed (our flesh), so, too, do these subtle wiles. The schemes of Satan listed below are sent to do the same thing: neutralize your walk with God and barricade your progress down the road of righteousness. Having the same purpose, their source is a bit different, however. Filthiness of flesh and spirit come generally as a result of a body that has not yet put on glory, many times, without any help of the Kingdom of Darkness. Though devils, demons, and false angels of light perpetuate many false doctrines, this usually comes only after lasciviousness is conceived within the mind of the believer.

The schemes of Satan, however, are strictly employed from an *outside source*, the Kingdom of Darkness, and come to put so much pressure on a believer that he or she is rendered ineffective as a child of God. The plots of Satan have done more to prevent believers from developing in their potential than any other thing.

The word devil in the Greek is *diabalos*. This literally means, "penetrator." Some think that "the devil" is the enemy's name. However, it is simply a term that describes what he does. A cook cooks, a mechanic tunes up machinery, a pilot flies planes, and a devil penetrates. Satan's greatest asset is that he is not in a hurry with us. His warfare tactic is to add pressure, increment by increment, until he has split us in half.

When I was in the sixth grade, I had to get a massive amount of construction done on my teeth. This smile of mine didn't come cheaply. Braces, headgear, spacers, rubber bands, retainer; you name it and I had it on my face. Included in my orthodontic arsenal was what is called a "palatal expander."

A "palatal expander" is a fancy term for a large piece of steel, hung in the roof of the mouth, which slowly, with maximum pain, puts a gap in your teeth. It wasn't so bad when they first put it in. They sent my mom home with a little key and told her to turn the notch on the expander once a week. At first, I didn't notice much of a change. Then, all of a sudden, things got merciless. The worst part of my week was when my mom came looking for me with that dreaded key. Oh, the pain was excruciating. Then one day, I noticed something in the mirror. I had a huge gap in my teeth. Although it seemed to have appeared overnight, it hadn't. The steady, constant pressure onto the roof of my mouth widened my gum-line and split my teeth in half. My sixth grade dating life was ruined.

Similarly, Satan will use day-by-day pressure through his wiles to begin to split us in two. God's Word says, ***"Your adversary the devil walks about like a roaring lion, seeking whom he may devour"*** (1 Peter 5:8 NKJV). Peter is telling us how the penetrator works, like a hungry lion roaring because it is looking for prey. We have all seen African safaris on television where the Australian narrator explains how the male lion targets a herd of zebra. A hundred times out of a hundred, the lion finds and isolates the weakest one. Once he gets it positioned, the lion pounces, and he and his lion friends feast on the poor, weak victim.

The Holy Ghost did not inspire Peter to write this verse to scare us. We are told how the penetrator operates so that we can:

1.) See that the devil targets weakness
2.) Become motivated to fortify ourselves against those weaknesses

The Five Handles

[14] The sower soweth the word.
[15] And these are they by the way side, where the word is sown; but when they have heard, Satan cometh immediately, and taketh away the word that was sown in their hearts.
[16] And these are they likewise which are sown on stony ground; who, when they have heard the word, immediately receive it with gladness;
[17] And have no root in themselves, and so endure but for a time: afterward, when affliction or persecution ariseth for the word's sake, immediately they are offended.
[18] And these are they which are sown among thorns; such as hear the word,
[19] And the cares of this world, and the deceitfulness of riches, and the lusts of other things entering in, choke the word, and it becometh unfruitful.
[20] And these are they which are sown on good ground; such as hear the word, and receive it, and bring forth fruit, some thirtyfold, some sixty, and some an hundred. (Mark 4:14-20 KJV)

The Word that is being sown into the hearts of men is the Word of truth (Ephesians 1:13), the Word of faith (Romans 10:8), and the doctrine that inseminated our hearts and sent us through the new birth onto the road of righteousness (1 Peter 1:23). Our progress down the new birth is a major threat to the kingdom of hell because the more revelation that we receive concerning our Sonship, the more authority we will begin to harness to push back darkness.

As I mentioned before, revelation knowledge of the truth is spiritual motion that sends us forward with authority. If we continue to progress as students of the Holy Ghost, it won't be long until we enter so much revelation concerning who Jesus is and what we have been made in Him that we will begin to lift people out of wheelchairs, see the blind and the lame made whole, and reap all sorts of other proofs that the Kingdom of God has arrived.

Satan is seeking to kill that Word that brings revelation and draws out the authority that has been bestowed upon us as children of God. He knows that if he can deactivate its place in your life, he can neutralize your forward progress. Operating like a roaring lion, he begins to isolate your weakness and examine your life for handles.

"Handles" are those unchecked areas of our lives that we have neglected to give to the Holy Ghost for His leadership and guidance. As soon as Satan finds a handle in your life, he isolates it and yanks, deploying one of his schemes. If it is to any degree effective, it will set you back and negate you from walking the life that Christ said that we could have. In teaching on the Kingdom of God and how it operates, Jesus didn't waste any time getting to these. They are:

1.) *Affliction: Burdens, tribulations, and trials that weigh you down and slow your progress.* Afflictions can be expected the minute you decide to lock in and go forward in God. Have you ever seen someone who gets a little revelation that is enough to launch them into a serious pursuit of going deeper? What I know by now is that I better begin to pray for those individuals because a cloud of affliction is on its way and will hang over the believer as long as it can. These afflictions are the first order that Satan uses to weaken the believer. Although they come in many forms, they often go unnoticed as having a spiritual source.

When revelation knowledge begins to spurt forth with greater force in my life, unleashing more authority in me, I become vigilant (1 Peter 5:8). Others may say, "God is taking me deeper! Yippy!" It won't be long until a cloud of affliction comes along to rain on their parade. *As much as the blessings are supposed to follow the believer, they are limited to the believer's submission to the Holy Ghost.* Afflictions don't steal our inheritance or eat our blessings that are rightfully ours in Christ. They have no authority to touch the things given to us by Jesus Christ.

Instead, they come to us and pull on any weakness that we might have exposed, chaining our hands from receiving the blessings. They can come especially when we are fatigued or pressed for time. We just have to remember *who* we are as quickly as possible, and tune in to Holy Spirit's comfort.

Once, I was returning from Europe after preaching for three weeks in Bulgaria, Greece, and Turkey. I was electric from the meetings, and couldn't wait to tell my family about the miracles I had seen. Because of flight delays and airline difficulties, I had to drive eleven hours from New Jersey to Detroit, all night, after already going through eighteen hours of travel. The next day I had to be in Texas to preach, so I could not wait for another flight home. This might have been the worst travel experience of my life, but as I neared the home stretch it all eased. All I could think about was my warm bed.

Suddenly, I noticed a flashing red and blue light in my rear view mirror. I was being pulled over by a state trooper. I thought, *This officer will see how tired I am and let me off easy.* Au contraire. The cop wrote me a $140 ticket and sent me on my way. My fatigue gave way to creeping rage. "How could this happen? I just got home from preaching. I am God's soldier! I deserve better than to get a $140 ticket!" It took only a few minutes for the Holy Ghost to remind me that afflictions come for the Word's sake.

2.) *Persecution: A relentless pursuit that engages you.* This pursuit begins when you start to receive revelation knowledge from God's Word and enter through the door of authority and power. Though it can take the form of demonic harassment, by and large, it comes *from others.*

"You mean to tell me, Chris, that when I start going forward into what Jesus said that I can be that I am going to have something pursuing me?" Yes. I am not telling you this to make you fearful. I am merely forewarning you; soon we'll be talking about how to work within Holy Spirit to bring you peace and overcoming and to drive you further into the Kingdom of God.

Did you know that there are countless believers worldwide who would prefer not to get into an authentic relationship with God because they *know* it will change them, and their families will begin to notice? "Well, Brother Palmer. You know I can't be that radical about God. It will create friction in my family." Friction is not what they are concerned about. *They are concerned about the persecution that is going to come with the decision to leave the old life behind and shine on unto glory.*

Anyone can handle a little friction in the family. If you look at your cousin wrong, you may get a little friction. Some people enjoy friction. God forbid that the family begins to ostracize you because now you have become "better than the rest of us." If the family wants to do things that you no longer want to do because you are going in the opposite direction, they will look at you like you just landed from the planet Zoron. Of course, this is because they saw you a few years ago, not only doing the things they are still doing, but instigating people to join in.

The persecution that comes from family members is one of the toughest forms of persecution around. Husbands have neutralized wives. Wives have neutralized husbands. Parents have neutralized young folks. And extended families have neutralized cousins.

"Ever since you found Jesus, Thanksgivings just haven't been the same." Or, "Oh, so you don't drink anymore? So *I* am going to hell?" Or even, "Why do you have to leave our church? We have so many friends here. You have become a radical."

Persecution overcomes the believer and halts him or her from stepping into what God desires. And God forbid you should go into the ministry. That will take the persecution to a more difficult level. Step out of line for just one moment, and they will make sure that you are well aware that you are a minister. Though it is easy to make light of, this is a very real persecution that has handicapped the walk of countless believers.

If family persecution weren't enough, we now have a society that has become hostile toward Christians. *Christians have become a speed bump in the social agendas of the world.* Many times when Christians advocate or tolerate liberal agendas, they say that they are trying to "understand" the world. "Well, you know, Chris, I was once in the world and I couldn't stand how Christians forced their beliefs down my throat."

What they are really saying, whether they know it or not, is that they are attempting to alleviate some of the persecution that would come from being a "close-minded Christian," as we are "slanderously reported" (Romans 3:8). There is a difference between offensively forcing our beliefs upon society, and defensively standing for our beliefs that shape and mold future generations. If believers dismiss the obligation to stand for Christian values, they are trying to appease the persecutors.

Some people relegate persecution to being killed by a group of rogues in a far off country for preaching the Gospel. Though that ultimate form of persecution is more prevalent than we think, family persecution and social persecution cannot be underrated. They will pursue and neutralize a believer at the drop of a hat if he or she is not fortified against it. Persecution in any form is a relentless attack designed by the enemy to stop the revelation of what we are now in Him, stripping us of our authority and hampering God's plan for our lives.

3.) *Cares of this world: Pressures from an outside source that lay hold of your emotions.* There are few things that move a person swifter than emotions. No outside force does a better job of laying hold on our emotions than do the cares of this world. As with persecutions and afflictions, *the cares of this world are a form of pressure from the outside*, looking to diminish your faith to nil. This ploy of Satan is masterful at applying pressure to our *emotions* in order to abort the progress that we have made in God. Our emotions are a part of our *soul*, the faculty that holds our mind, will, and emotions. Even after coming through the New Birth and receiving the life of Christ, our soul has to be constantly attended to in order to keep it in line with the authority that we have rightfully received in Christ. Our emotions should be yielded continually to the Holy Ghost so that He can send them into the right direction, taking you with them. Turn the cares of the world over to the Holy Spirit, and trust Him.

Most of the people that I counseled concerning their finances were being dragged around by the cares of this world. Just the look on their faces, and sometimes even the sweat on their forehead, was enough for me to see that worry and concern had set into them because of care. No longer was their focus on going further into God and taking another step down the road of righteousness, but instead, it had become the never-ending chore of trying to "fix" the care.

Indeed, many people's relationship with God has become based on His meeting their needs and quenching their overwhelming cares. Conferences and seminars that are *cares-oriented* frequently attract more people than conferences that teach *how to know God deeper and more authentically.* Care has consumed people's lives so voraciously that there is a constant need for people to hear: "It is going to be alright." "God is going to turn it around!" "God will make sure the devil pays you back!"

All this is true, but unless the believer understands how to eradicate the care and unhitch emotions from the torment caused by the cares of this world, he or she will become dependent on the temporary soothing of a preacher's voice. It is possible to get to a place of peace in God where care has no way of engaging you, even if the whole earth is removed and the mountains be carried into the midst of the sea (Psalms 46:1-2 NKJV).

As God began to teach me by His Holy Spirit, I learned that much of the torment and paralyzing fear I experienced when I first started my ministry was the *cares of this world.* Looking back, it wasn't that I did not have money coming in, nor was it that I had no places to preach. The extreme emotionalism this produced wasn't even my worst problem. *The great problem was the shallow relationship I had with the Holy Ghost that wouldn't harness enough power to my emotions to brace me up against something like this.* Having become so comfortable making a nice salary as a staff minister at my church, I had neglected to develop the kind of relationship with the Spirit of God that would act as a resisting force should I ever face a financial barrier.

"What about the new nature? Where is the new nature when you are going through all of this?" The new nature was buried under layers and layers of emotions being ruled by cares. The only answer to reeling in my emotions so that my new nature could begin to dominate them would be if I had help. I needed a Helper and a Comforter, one who could show me how to get back on track.

For the first two years of ministry, seeing the bills on my desk was one of the most discouraging things I have ever experienced in my life. Here I was, a full time evangelist, but I had no place to preach. I had to find something to occupy my time. Daily checking my post office box gave me the sense that I was working. It provided me with an ounce of hope that someone had finally seen the greatness on my life and sent me the million-dollar check that I was convinced I was due. That check never came. As a matter of fact, back then, the only check was from one of my four partners who was sending $5.00 a month. I never knew if I should be happy or cry when I got that check.

Once, while I was showering, the Lord said, "What would you do with a check for $1,000,000 if it came, son?" I thought about it and said, quite naturally, "Well, I'd slice the first, oh, maybe $60,000, right off and use it to pay my salary for a year."

The Lord interrupted. "Yes," He said, "you would first ease the care in your life so you could go on thinking that you are a big faith giant."

Of course, God wanted me to prosper. I got by that year. But if God had laid on me a million dollar check it would have destroyed me. My foundation would still have had a crack in it, the crack that was caused by being dependent on a salary, and not on God. God was slowly purging this dross from my life. Like a thoroughbred horse, God was championing me to run my race, free from the susceptibility to be overwhelmed by care. It wasn't long before God showed me how to put the Comforter into use to build up my most holy faith.

4.) *Deceitfulness of riches:* When persecutions, afflictions, and the cares of this world begin to apply pressure from the outside, the individual under attack immediately begins to *look for a way out.* The next two handles, deceitfulness of riches and lusts of other things, *are a bit different.* These are not coming from an outside source, but instead, they are coming from the mortality that is still working inside the range of our flesh. When deceitfulness of riches and the lusts of other things arise, the individual *looks for a way in, and resists a way out.*

Once, early one morning, I was praying to the Lord. I was dedicating myself to Him, telling Him: "Lord, I am your willing servant. I am a bondservant and have given my life to You. If You take me to Korea, I will go. If You take me to the remotest part of the world, I will follow. This life is not my own. If I should have everything stripped away from me, here I am."

In usual custom, the Great Master stopped my babbling. "What if I put a million dollars into your hands? Will you still serve Me?"

I was lying on the floor by my nightstand with a wool blanket over me. I popped my head up and thought, *Huh?* It seemed there was a switch of roles here. Last time, I wanted the million dollars, and God wasn't going to give it to me. This time, I was refusing the million dollars, and God was threatening me with it. What was this about?

Examining it, I began to notice that the cares of this world and the deceitfulness of riches would produce the same kind of filthiness in me, although they are polar opposites. The cares of this world are the anxiety and torment that come from *not having.* The deceitfulness of riches is the pride and madness that comes from *having* or *coveting to have.*

Often times, the cares of this world come first and keep people under submission so long that they never have the opportunity to dream the possibilities of having abundance. Not until the Holy Ghost comes into the mess and begins to aid you, do you begin to see the tremendous potential and authority that you have as a child of God, to prosper and to grow financially.

When this happens, the Holy Ghost has to get on the other side and say: "Okay now. Through My ability, I have protected you against the anguish that comes from *not* having. Now, I have to start the *real* operation on you. I must begin to protect you against the subtle pride that comes from *having.*" And He promptly goes to work on your susceptibility to deceitfulness of riches.

Many forms of religion have noticed the ugliness of the deceitfulness of riches. They have tried to deal with this by beating into themselves a synthetic desire not to want anything. The most extreme version of this is the vow of poverty that goes to the gross extreme of self-mutilation. Similar doctrines say, "God wants us poor," or "Jesus was poor, and so should we be."

Little do these people realize, they have noticed ugliness inside of them that would be set afire if God put a little bit of money into their hands. Jesus was very clear that money was never the problem, but rather, mammon (the spirit that drives people to live for money) was (Matthew 6:24). In harmony with Jesus' teaching on mammon, Paul says, ***"For the <u>love</u> of money is the root of all evil: which while some coveted after, they have erred from the faith, and pierced themselves through with many sorrows"*** (1 Timothy 6:10 KJV).

Often people mangle this verse, "Well, I don't know, Chris, about that prosperity stuff. Money is the root of all evil." Wrong. The **love** of money, which is mammon, is the root of all evil. Behind mammon is a *spirit or demon* that Jesus warned people about. It comes along, using the deceitfulness of riches, and begins to tempt people away from the Kingdom of God, drawing upon their lusts and playing upon their pride. "I am rich, I must be a good man." Nonsense.

Notice the effects of mammon: ***"Some <u>coveted</u> after, they have <u>erred</u> from the faith, and <u>pierced themselves</u> through with <u>many sorrows</u>"*** (1 Timothy 6:10b KJV). Paul was referring to a select group of believers who had not yielded to the Holy Spirit's operation in their life as the Joint Helper and Comforter. When mammon came along, it roped these people in through the deceitfulness of riches and carried them off of the trail of righteousness.

People who deny themselves money and stand for poverty are not dealing with the root of the problem: themselves. Not wanting to covet, they try to get as far away from money as they possibly can, not realizing that as far away from money as they might be, they are as close to the problem as ever. They are still susceptible to the deceitfulness of riches. God doesn't honor a man who has religion and false humility that stays away from money. They are never any better because of it.

God honors a man who has yielded his life to the Holy Spirit's joint help to such a degree that his mortality and carnal appetites have been purged, and so that mammon and the deceitfulness of riches could never cause him to err, even if a million dollars were placed in his hand. God could give him massive amounts of money, and pride would be nowhere to be found because the Holy Ghost dealt with it, up front. These are the kinds of people God is looking for to give Kingdom money to and to finance the Gospel.

> *5.) Lusts of other things:* A companion to the deceitfulness of riches, the "lusts of other things" is an overwhelming desire to do things that have nothing to do with the call of God on our lives. This is a susceptibility that is born from lack and/or abundance.

I went to a Bible university for four years where I earned my degree. In this time, I met so many students who were giving their lives to ministry and, even if they weren't planning on being in *full-time* ministry, they were going to serve the Kingdom in their vocation. Because of social media, I can keep up with many of these classmates. What I have noticed is that most of them (70% at least) are not doing what they originally set out to do for God. What happened? Working through lack and/or abundance, the lusts of other things drew their hearts away.

"Well, Chris, how does it do that?" I thought you would never ask.

The lusts of other things can work only when we have *not* entered into a state of true contentment that comes from the Holy Spirit's joint help at work in us. Having been under the gun because of pressure and selfish-ambition when I first entered into evangelistic ministry, I was the world's least contented person. Pressure is employed by the cares of this world, and selfish-ambition is employed by the deceitfulness of riches. With these two knuckleheads chasing each other inside of me, I was secretly looking for a way out or up. Oh, sure, I was going to stay in ministry, but these things had cunningly become a part of me, and I had not even noticed.

I remember the days when pressure forced its way in over selfish-ambition and was steering me. On these particular days, no matter where I went, I was envious of the people who had 9 a.m. to 5 p.m. jobs, believe it or not. I would walk into my bank and think, "Now look at this. This is what I should have done. I should have gotten a job in the private sector. I could come into work at 9 a.m. every day, make a consistent paycheck, come home and make dinner, watch my television show, and do it all over the next day. Then, on weekends, I could go to football games and hang out with my friends." Pressure was looking to find security. I didn't even know I had that problem; I had not allowed the Holy Ghost to reveal it to me in His joint help.

Then, of course, there were days when selfish-ambition was subdued, and pressure steered me. During the days when pressure controlled me, I felt a sense of *low self-esteem*. Conversely, selfish-ambition days were marked by *false confidence*. On one particular day, I heard that there was a financial seminar going on in town. I didn't have anything better to do, so I went. The seminar itself was free, but I managed to get some of their material. I thought, *Hmm, who is to say that I can't be a world evangelist and be a real estate mogul at the same time?* If I were turning over properties at the drop of a hat and making millions, I wouldn't need support. I'd be self-supported and self-made. Then I could show the younger guys how to do it. Self-ambition was looking to find accomplishment. That went on until I turned myself over to the Holy Ghost. Thankfully, I didn't lose too much time or money.

The Force of Contentment

The joint help of the Holy Ghost is the only way to recognize and overcome the schemes and tactics of Satan. When the Spirit of God gets control, He will build in us one of the greatest spiritual forces that exists today: *contentment*. This force makes us invulnerable to hell. Once it is built within us, Satan's schemes are rendered ineffective and they cannot stop our forward progress as children of God.

> *[11]Not that I speak in respect of want: for I have learned, in whatsoever state I am, therewith <u>to be content</u>.*
> *[12]I know both how to be abased, and I know how to abound: everywhere and in all things I am instructed both to be full and to be hungry, both to abound and to suffer need.*
> *[13]I can do all things through Christ who strengtheneth me.* (Philippians 4:11-13 KJV)

Philippians 4:13 is one of the most widely used verses today, seen on everything from refrigerator magnets to bumper stickers to picture frames. *In understanding the completeness of Paul's thinking by reading the context, the power to do all things was being harnessed through the force of contentment.* When the Spirit of God installed contentment into him, it charged him with ability to overcome and to do anything, no matter what state that he found himself in.

Paul was saying: "After becoming a child of God I have yielded myself over to the joint help of the Holy Ghost. This has brought me into a state of being called contentment. Now, the pressure of care cannot overcome me. Furthermore, if I abound I am not anymore enflamed by pride and greed, because I have been purged from the deceitfulness of riches and the lusts of other things. I have been rendered invulnerable, and there is nothing that hell can throw at me that can get me to stop my progress in God. I am fulfilling my call, and the devil can take everything from me or load my hands with riches, and it is not going to stop me. I can do all things without being stopped because I am now living out of my new nature, seeing that the Holy Ghost has delivered me into contentment." Isn't this glorious?

CHAPTER THIRTY-ONE

A Dense and Heavy Peace

"'Ah, wonderful. They are ready for another dimension of life and power.' Then He takes the hedge trimmer and starts chopping away dying and diseased limbs."

I remember hearing preachers say: "We must abide in Christ! We need to abide in Him and let His Word abide in us!" After working up a sweat they would sit down and never tell me how. What is the use if I have the initiative to do it but have no instruction to apply it to my life? Being the Great Teacher, Christ didn't leave us without instruction on this matter. He was very clear as to how we can lend ourselves to be purged and to walk in greater dimensions of the new nature.

Jesus, knowing that He was implementing the new nature, still made a point to tell His disciples that if they weren't constantly undergoing *pruning*, the mortality in their flesh would restrict them from living out of their new position in Christ. This would render them carnal, not spiritual. Jesus' greatest aspiration for His disciples was to see them produce fruit, even after He went away.

> *¹I am the true vine, and My Father is the vinedresser.*
> *²Every branch in Me that does not bear fruit He takes away; and every branch that bears fruit He prunes, that it may bear more fruit.*
> *³You are already clean because of the word which I have spoken to you.*
> *⁴Abide in Me, and I in you. As the branch cannot bear fruit of itself, unless it abides in the vine, neither can you, unless you abide in Me.*

> *⁵"I am the vine, you are the branches. He who abides in Me, and I in him, bears much fruit; for without Me you can do nothing.* (John 15:1-5 NKJV)

Even with a new nature and the promise of redemption awaiting them, Jesus informed the disciples that the only way they would constantly produce fruit in their lives was if they remained in Him. Abiding in Him means to live out of the new nature, the life that He lights us with in the second birth.

So often there are believers who don't produce any fruit in their lives. If you get them to be honest with themselves, they will admit that their life isn't much different from the life they lived while they were in the world, except for the fact that they are going to heaven. What a shame it is to live this way, when the Lord has given us everything that we need to be victorious and walk in the glorious new life that He dealt us in redemption. Likening Himself to the vine and us to branches, Jesus said the greatest thing that will keep His life flowing into our lives is constant purging.

1.) *The Father is the Husbandman:* When the Father sees a branch that is producing fruit out of its new nature, He comes along with the pruning shears and purges more and more layers of the mortal flesh. In our pea-brained thinking, many times we believe that if we produce fruit God will leave us alone, or if anything, pat us on the back. Instead, He will say, "Ah, wonderful. They are ready for another dimension of life and power." Then He takes the hedge trimmer and starts chopping away dying and diseased limbs.

2.) *The Father sent us the Comforter and Helper to <u>execute</u> the purging process:*

> *But the Helper, the Holy Spirit, whom the Father will send in My name, He will teach you all things, and bring to your remembrance all things that I said to you.* (John 14:26 NKJV)

The purging that we receive from God is directly connected to the joint help of the Holy Spirit. When Jesus told His disciples in the next verse

(John 14:27 NKJV), *"**Peace** I leave with you, My **peace** I give to you; not as the world gives do I give to you. Let not your heart be troubled, neither let it be afraid,"* He was introducing the disciples to the *result* of the purging process.

Think about the difficulties that Jesus encountered in His life, yet He stayed anchored in that peace. In just three years of ministry, Jesus was tempted multiple times by the devil himself, threatened with death, taken to the top of a hill to be thrown off, was almost stoned, walked in dark and dangerous places, almost had His boat sunk by a sudden violent storm—all on top of being betrayed and having to drink from the cup of His Father, which was His passion. Yet, Jesus walked so close to the joint help of the Holy Ghost that there was never one handle of weakness that Satan could find on Him. Look at what Jesus said concerning the success of His life and ministry, *"For the ruler of this world is coming, and he has nothing in Me"* (John 14:30 NKJV).

In all of this Jesus wasn't moved one time. *The Holy Ghost had helped Jesus to live as a human to such a degree that Jesus proved the efficacy of the Holy Ghost's ministry.* The Holy Ghost's end is to lead us unto the full and perfect attributes of God: pure and untainted peace, joy, love, and faith. As long as there is any dross in the measure of those virtues that we are currently walking in, the Spirit of God still has work to do.

Jesus, after displaying the peace of God to His disciples for over three years, turned to them and said, "Now, this peace can be yours." This must have been an incredible statement. Can you imagine what the disciples must have thought?

If they were anything like normal human beings, Peter was thinking, *Uh, yea, well, I don't know about Thomas over there. He is kind of a doubter. Not really sure he could ever walk in that kind of peace with all the doubting he does.*

Andrew must have thought, *Eh, I don't know about John. He is kind of young and inexperienced. Once he grows up a little more, experience will have its way with him.*

James may have thought, *You have got to be kidding. Peter? Having peace? The guy can't even get along with himself.*

No matter who was doing the thinking, it made no difference. Jesus was well aware of what was in their hearts. However, He was quite confident of the surety of the Spirit of God's ministry. The Holy Spirit was now going to assist in the ultimate conflict between the Kingdom of Darkness and humanity: the cross. No matter where the disciples were in their own development, the Father was getting ready to release to them this awesome Helper.

After Pentecost, this Helper would immediately start working with the disciples' born-again nature, purging them from any handle of unbelief, fear, torment, care, greed, lust, or whatever else may place a limitation on their walk with God. The more they allowed the Spirit of God to purge them, the more they would begin to see the purifying of the peace, joy, and other virtues of God that they had working in them. This purification process would bring them closer and closer toward the glory that they would one day completely inherit in their glorified bodies. In the meantime, it would deliver them into more and more unshakeable peace. And so it is with us.

The Peace of God

Peace is a word that is always taken for granted due to its commonality in our language. The kind of peace that Jesus is talking about, however, is a supernatural peace that cannot come from the natural realm. Paul came to know this peace and described it in Philippians 4:7 (KJV), saying, ***"And the peace of God, which passeth understanding, shall keep your hearts and minds through Christ."***

This is not peace *with* God, but rather it is a peace that makes up a part of God's glory. God didn't obtain this peace from anywhere; it exists because it is a part of who He is. This kind of peace is so dense and heavy, it cannot be moved by the pressures of care and anxiety.

In attempting to describe this peace to the Church at Ephesus, Paul likened it to the sandals that Roman soldiers wore in battle (Ephesians 6:15). Designed as all-terrain footwear, the sandals had traction that kept soldiers' feet in place as they were fighting. Peace, like a Roman soldier's sandal, is the force that will keep us from being moved when we are engaged with our adversary. It is such a strong and powerful force that, if implemented correctly, will provide the sustenance and endurance that we need to outlast any amount of difficulty that we may encounter.

The schemes of Satan cannot overtake a person who is overcome with this peace because, in that peace, the believer sees things the way God sees them. This peace outweighs the limitations of the flesh by anchoring our emotions and keeping them from being carried away from the torment, anxiety, and the other emotions that Satan's scheme produce. It was this force of peace that James refers to as "patience."

> *²My brethren, count it all joy when you fall into various trials* [any one of Satan's schemes],
> *³knowing that the testing of your faith produces patience.*
> *⁴But let patience have its perfect work, that you may be perfect and complete, lacking nothing.* (James 1:2-4 NKJV)

The peace of God is referred to as patience because it is describing what that peace does when it clashes with one of Satan's schemes. The moment a child of God is attacked, peace kicks in and drives its stakes down. Despite the length or intensity of the storm, the emotions are not going anywhere, because the constitution of the anchor is greater than the force of the storm.

Once I was up north fishing in Michigan when we had to bring our boat in because the waters were beginning to get rough. My friend quickly tied the boat to the dock, and we took cover inside. As the storm rolled in we began to see the boat being tossed all around by the waves. It was comical to see how such a little rope could keep that boat in place despite such a grand storm. I thought, *Hmm. This boat is not going anywhere anytime soon.*

When God sent us the joint help of the Holy Ghost, it immediately became His job to do whatever is necessary to anchor that kind of peace in our lives. Once that peace becomes a part of us it will not move, and as a result, neither will we. I am sure if that boat could talk it would say, "Yea, these storms happen all the time. I never worry, though. I am always anchored right." If you belong to the Holy Ghost, He will always use peace to anchor you, so that you can remain in Christ through every storm. The next time the wind begins to rip and the waves begin to beat, take a lesson from the boat and rely on your anchor.

CHAPTER THIRTY-TWO

One Peculiar Night, Two Peculiar Experiences

**"I had layers and layers of flesh restricting
the life of God from flowing brightly out of my lamp."**

*²⁶Likewise the Spirit also helps in our weaknesses. For
we do not know what we should pray for as we ought,
but the Spirit Himself makes intercession for us with
groanings which cannot be uttered.*
*²⁷Now He who searches the hearts knows what the
mind of the Spirit is, because He makes intercession
for the saints according to the will of God.* (Romans
8:26-27 NKJV)

It is one thing to know *about* the Holy Ghost. It is a completely different
thing to have an ongoing walk *with* the Holy Ghost. As I teach and preach
around the country and in different parts of the world, I have found that
Christians primarily fall into one of three categories when it comes to the
Holy Ghost:

1.) They *don't* understand the Holy Ghost and have *no* walk with
Him
2.) They *do* understand the Holy Ghost but still have *no* walk with
Him
3.) They *do* understand the Holy Ghost and they *do* have a walk with
Him

Looking back on my tenure at the church, I had a walk with the Spirit, but it was not where it is today. This is evidenced by the fruit and by the triumph that I have seen and am continuing to see on a regular basis. You can literally get to a place of walking with the Holy Ghost where you wholeheartedly *know* that He is much larger than anything that may come your way. This is a result of seeing Him, time and time again, do whatever is necessary in you to cause you to overcome.

Most of the time overcoming has more to do with you than it does with your circumstance. When a basketball team is constantly defeated by a rival, they don't sit around hoping that their opponent gets worse next year. Instead, they begin to work on themselves. They hit the gym harder, take more shots at practice, watch more films, and stay longer hours on the court. They realize that if something inside of them changes, they will have the potential to defeat their rival next year.

As a child of God, there lies a tremendous potential in you, and He has given you the Spirit of God to extract that potential and use it to secure your victory. "Yes, I know this, Chris. But *how*?"

Ah, yes, the great question now becomes *how*. We have seen *how* God redeemed us and made us His children. We have seen *how* we go through the second birth. We have even seen *how* we have been made righteous. We have seen *how* to overcome filthiness of flesh and spirit. We have seen *how* to combat the schemes of Satan. But, *how* can we cooperate with the Holy Ghost and allow Him to help us? It is not enough to know that He is a Help. *We need to know how we can help Him to help us.* This will turn us into believers who don't just talk about the Holy Ghost, but rather, those who have a true ongoing relationship *with* the Holy Ghost.

When you have an ongoing relationship with the Holy Ghost, you become a self-sustaining source of energy and power. You don't go to church to "refuel." Baby Christians need to "refuel" at church. *When mature Christians come to church, they add their own fuel to the communal supply, because mature Christians are constantly refueling during their private times with God.* Congregations that are into taking will drain their pastor and leave him or her exhausted. Congregations whose members have their own walk with the Spirit of God charge up their pastors and breathe fresh life into their churches.

A Peculiar Experience

I wasn't long in the evangelistic field before God sent me a mentor to help while I was feeling alone and helpless. This mentor somehow understood where I was, and empathized. I wasn't a bad person. It wasn't that I was in any kind of sin. *I just didn't know that I didn't know.* I had layers and layers of flesh restricting the life of God from flowing brightly out of my lamp. I jokingly say now that I was like a dingy lantern. The dirt and dust that was caked on my outer shell dulled the light that was trying to shine outwards.

So, my new mentor arrived on the scene. "Chris, you have nowhere to go on Saturday nights? You aren't preaching anywhere on Sunday mornings? Why don't you come and join me at my church for prayer on Saturday night at 9 p.m.?"

I thought, *Hmm. That's awfully late to start praying.* I asked, "How long do you intend to go?"

"Until 6 a.m.," he said, nonchalantly.

"Huh? That is eight hours." I said to myself. "Uh, ok. That's cool, that's cool. I'll come, I guess." I still remember driving over to the church that night thinking, "God, what in the world did I do by saying yes to being an evangelist? I was once in front of a massive congregation, praying awesome prayers, getting cheers and applause. Now, I am going to a dusty church to pray all night. In the dark. And I'm not even getting paid."

I didn't lie to myself, and I'm not going to lie to you. I was very angry at God. Here there were guys like myself, my age, with a schedule so full of preaching engagements that they were turning things down. And me? Well, I was in a church praying alone, and nobody wanted to hear me preach badly enough to buy me a plane ticket and let me come. When I faced these facts, I just got angrier.

When I arrived at the church I saw that it was going to be just the pastor and me. "Pray in tongues the whole night and don't stop," he said. I had done a lot of praying in tongues in my day and thought, *Well, this shouldn't be hard. I am an expert at praying in tongues.* Eight hours, however, was a bit of a challenge. I had only done it once, and that had been a while back. Well, it was time to add another long session of prayer to my spiritual resume, so I was happy to begin. The night went by steadily and nothing happened. I drove home in the morning, thinking, "I wonder how many other preachers prayed this long last night? I'm the one who should be preaching, God. Not them."

A few days later the phone rang. It was my pastor friend. I thought he might want to tell me he noticed it was incredibly easy for me to pray eight hours in the Holy Ghost and was calling to compliment me. "Hey pastor, how are you?"

"I'm good, Chris. Hey, are you preaching anywhere on Sunday?" I hated when people asked about my schedule back then. My identity was in my schedule and, ultimately, so was my security and self-esteem. "Uh, well, you know, no."

"How about coming by Saturday night and joining me again in prayer." Hesitantly, I agreed. And so, another Saturday night went by and I prayed for eight hours in the Holy Ghost. After that, I dropped into a routine of praying at pastor's church on Saturday nights. Despite everything, I had some kind of witness in me that kept saying, "This is what you need to be doing right now."

Pastor would often take a break from praying and disappear into his office to go over his sermon notes for the next morning. This usually left me pacing back and forth in the sanctuary alone. It was on an August night after a few weeks of constant praying in the Holy Ghost that I noticed something peculiar. Different from the previous times of prayer, I felt a very large heaviness resting in my stomach area. As time went on, it got stronger and stronger.

Prior to this, every time I had an experience with God it produced feelings that left me in tears or overwhelming joy. This feeling was different. Heaviness like this, I would normally think, would be demonic. However, there was no inner witness inside telling me that it was from the devil. Actually, I had a witness telling me to continue praying. Soon, that heaviness rose all the way from my stomach and into my chest. By the time it reached my neck, I noticed that the heaviness exploded out of me in the form of bitter tears and loud moans, forcing me to my knees in an almost fetal position.

I may have lost control of my body, but my mind was still intact. While sobbing and moaning, I thought, *Is this some kind of emotional thing I have worked up? Maybe the pressure has finally gotten to me. Maybe I am having a breakdown.* My mind paused from thinking and, in a flash, checked what was going on and gathered the data from my spirit. "No, this is not an emotional breakdown," said my brain. "Something is going on right now inside of you and I don't have the answer. Just let the process run its course."

While it did, I turned to reasoning to make sense of it. "Well, obviously this isn't you. Why would you want to cry and put yourself into this position? You can't gain any attention this way. Nobody is around. And, even if there were people around, why would you want attention like this? You look dumb." For over thirty minutes I was in this state, unable to figure out what was going on.

Toward the end of this experience, I noticed something that helped me make sense of what was happening. My spirit began to flash up images of a particular family member, whom I'll call Todd. When I came in the door to the church to pray, I had a serious bitterness toward him. This wasn't the animosity that is created from an average spat or small offense. This was one of those roots of rancor that takes years to get into your heart and is constantly watered over time by annoyance. This root of bitterness was responsible for creating emotions of disgust, anger, and resentment. These emotions were the reason why for several years I had been treating Todd terribly.

As soon as Todd's face flashed before me, the groanings intensified so severely that the tears stopped flowing. I don't know why. Perhaps my body was saying, "Ok, we can't do both now. If you want to groan this loud, we have to stop making tears." It was a terrible feeling. It was torment. I didn't want to endure. I didn't think I could stand it for one more second. Just at this point, it came to its climax and left. The moment it left, the tears started up again.

And there I was. As weak as a mother who had just given birth, I was lying helpless in a pool of my own salty tears. While tasting my tears, my spirit started flashing Todd's face before me again. This time I couldn't find the bitterness. Anger, resentment, and disgust were gone. And suddenly, I realized the tears were coming from a new source. Where the tears began from hatred, these new tears were flowing from a source of intense love. It was as if the pause between tears was someone shutting down the conduit of bitterness and had turned on the pipeline of love.

When everything calmed down, I stopped praying for a moment. I needed a minute to gather myself. When I came to, I thought about Todd again. *Oh, my,* I thought. *If it weren't so late I would leave this church and go find him, just to hug him.* All I could think about was seeing Todd the next day and showing him love. I started praying again. This time, it was as though I ran with hind's feet. As I prayed, I began to feel that I was taking control of my life. Literally, it felt like I had grabbed hold. Needless to say, I had quite the night. That Sunday I saw Todd and hugged him as I had not hugged him in a very long while. I was so happy to see him. To this day, that love is still being constantly renewed and generated out of my heart.

Another Peculiar Experience

Now that the issue with my family member had been settled, there was one more major issue that needed to be fixed. At the time, because I had virtually no income, I had been forced to move back with my parents. This was humiliating. It was horrible telling people that I lived with my parents. "How could an evangelist travel the world and still live with his parents?" I would wonder. That same wild night, as I continued on with my eight hours of praying in the Spirit, I could tell that I was praying about it. Suddenly, God got into that prayer with me. I actually felt like I had the money for my condo in hand, and had signed the papers. I was running and jumping and shouting at the front of the altar. I had it. I just knew it. Something had changed.

I forgot about this until a few weeks later when an opportunity arose out of nowhere. In just over a month of time from that night of prayer, I found myself in my own condo that was beyond what I ever thought I could have or afford at that time.

From that night on, my best friend became "Mr. Praying in Tongues." No other friend has had more to do with my forward progress as a child of God. Being the curious and inquisitive person that I am, I thought: *There is something to this praying in tongues business. What is it? Why is it doing this to me? And what else can it do?* Therefore, I made a life-changing decision: I decided to pray in tongues as much as I could, just to find out what else would happen.

CHAPTER THIRTY-THREE

Loving the Spin I'm In

"Never discourage someone from praying in tongues, suggesting that it has to be done in a solemn and boring room, else it doesn't count. It always counts."

Praying always with all prayer and supplication in the Spirit. (Ephesians 6:18 KJV)

Just as muscle mass transforms the social life of a skinny guy, praying in tongues began to revolutionize my spiritual walk. I noticed a phenomenal change in the way I ministered. I was no longer trapped and impaired by carnality. Preaching, I would hear things come from my lips and think, "Where in the world did that come from?" Scripture started connecting itself like a jigsaw puzzle, and I was seeing a greater image of God's Word.

Because I am a radical in whatever I do, I began to think, "I wonder how far I can go with praying in tongues? How far will this take me into God?"

One Friday, I received a call from my prayer mentor and he said, "How about we pray all day in the Holy Ghost? You know, like, twenty hours?"

I said, "Pastor, if we do twenty hours we might as well go twenty-four." This was my competitive side coming out. The only real motivation I had (besides knowing the results that it could produce) was that I could write it in a book one day and tell people I had done it.

By the time I arrived at the church it was 3:00 on a Saturday afternoon. Pastor Mack had already been going strong for several hours. He didn't plan to go all twenty-four hours because he had to preach on Sunday morning. But, because I was the evangelist without any meetings, I could go 24, 48, 72, 96 hours. I didn't have anything to do *except* pray.

It is good to be in that kind of position, however. The litmus test of faith comes when there are no Plan B's. It is easy for someone to preach faith when his back is not against the wall. They may be in faith, to a degree. Unfeigned faith, though, is birthed when it is time to do or die. Great legacies are produced from these kinds of experiences.

The first hour rolled by. The second hour rolled by, as did the third, fourth, and fifth. By 8:00 pm it was dark, and I was tired. Eight to nine hours of praying in the Spirit was an average Saturday for me. I had thoughts like, *Well, by 11:00 pm you can call it off and say that you had your normal Saturday of praying in tongues.*

The drive in me was so strong, however, I would immediately dismiss it. *Bless God,* I thought, *I am going the distance. Even if my tongue falls out and I have to pick it up and make it talk, I am praying twenty-four hours in the Holy Ghost.*

Passing the Hours of Prayer

I often get asked if I stay in one room and pray, or walk around. People want to know how I pass the time. Before I explain, I always share 1 Corinthians 14:14 (KJV), ***"For if I pray in an unknown tongue, my spirit prayeth, but my understanding is unfruitful."***

The process of praying in tongues contains two parts that must be understood in order to have a good comprehension of how it really works: 1.) Praying out *mysterion* and 2.) Receiving back *revelation*.

Praying Out *Mysterion*	Receiving Back *Revelation*
Truth goes up in mystery form	Truth comes back in revealed form
Mind is unfruitful	Mind is fruitful
Understanding not required (1 Corinthians 14:14)	Understanding required (Ephesians 1:18)
Awaiting edification/exhortation/comfort	Obtaining edification/exhortation/comfort

In these twenty-four hours of praying in tongues, I was only on step one in the process. I was giving God the material that He needed to send back the mysteries in a revealed manner. Unless a mystery came back to me as a revealed truth (which does sometimes happen while I am praying in tongues and meditating the Word), my mind would be off the clock. Knowing this now, I pray in tongues everywhere: airplanes, in the shower, driving, walking the mall, while fishing and, according to the cousin whom I used to live with, in my sleep.

I was explaining this once to a pastor and his family, and the pastor's daughter said, "Uh, yes, Chris, but you shouldn't babble in the Spirit."

Babble in the Spirit? Where is *that* in Scripture? The definition of babble means to utter imperfect sounds that contain no meaning. Even to suggest that the Spirit of God could take hold of us and pray out sounds that have no meaning is preposterous. God does not waste time, and He does not waste one word that you have ever spoken in the Holy Ghost, even if you did it while driving a go-cart or sky diving from an airplane. God doesn't care where you are and what you are doing. He is just excited that you are praying in the Holy Ghost.

There are times, however, when we need concentrated, focused times of prayer. When God wants to instruct us, lead us, teach us, and give us a word, we should give Him our fullest attention. During times of repentance, consecration, worship, and intercession, it is important that we are not doing anything else.

What I am talking about is different. This is another manner of prayer that doesn't work the same as the others. We don't need our minds in the process. God has designed it so that we can pray out mysteries anytime that we so desire. Next time you find yourself in a line or a traffic jam, bored and trying to pass the time, pray out some mysteries. You won't be babbling. You can't babble in the Spirit. The Spirit of God doesn't know anything about words without meaning. If babbling were possible, why didn't Paul warn against it? He didn't, because he understood that praying in the Spirit is *perfect prayer* regardless of what you are doing when you do it.

²__For he that speaketh in an unknown tongue__ speaketh not unto men, but unto God: for no man understandeth him; howbeit in the spirit he speaketh mysteries.

> *⁴He that speaketh in an unknown tongue edifieth himself.*
> *¹⁴For if I pray in an unknown tongue, my spirit prayeth, but my understanding is unfruitful.* (1 Corinthians 14:2, 4, 14 KJV)

Most of the time when I am speaking English, I am on my cell phone, or driving, or surfing the web, or walking, or ordering a meal in a restaurant. My communication is no less perfect than if I were sitting in the corner of my office, staring at the wall, trying to think about the pronunciation of every single word and syllable. When I am on my phone, if I sense something pertinent and immediate, I will shut off the TV, or close my web browser, and turn my entire attention to it. The same rule applies when I pray in tongues. I will stop and yield my *full* understanding.

I have grown to love praying in tongues so much I have become a blabber in the Spirit, speaking the mystery of everything Jesus Christ is in me, to me, and through me everywhere I go (Colossians 1:26). *Never discourage someone from praying in tongues out of a religious mindset that suggests it has to be done in a solemn and boring room, else it doesn't count. It always counts.*

Passing the time in this twenty-four hour period included everything from pacing the floor, to listening to sermons, to reading the Bible. There were times in which I grew solemn and offered to God my understanding and emotions, but not, however, every single moment.

I even got to the point where I went for a stroll in the middle of the night through the fluorescent-lit aisles of Wal-Mart. I figured if Paul could walk from Damascus to Jerusalem praying in tongues, I could at least go from frozen foods to the bike aisle. I remember passing through electronics, strolling through the furniture, and gallivanting by the toiletries. You know, they say that you can find some strange things in Wal-Mart at night. I am sure if anyone saw me walking around, whispering to myself they might have thought that I was half crazy. Even today I wonder if someone might have caught me on a cell phone and if I have a following on YouTube. Yet, it didn't matter to me at that point. I was on a mission to pray out the mysteries of God for a whole day straight.

The Spin Is Born

When I was driving back to the church, still praying in tongues, I thought: *Hmm, I have got to give this twenty-four-hour-time-of-praying-in-tongues a name. I am going to tell people I did it. Not only that I did it, but that I want them to do it. If I am going to be successful in motivating people, I need to come up with a name that puts it into perspective.*

I thought, and thought, and thought. (When you are praying a whole day in the Spirit, you have plenty of time to think, trust me.)

I was praying twenty-four hours, one whole turn of the earth. *While the earth was a-spinning, I was a-praying.* While the world was going near and far, to and fro, I was alone in the classroom of the Master Teacher, discussing the *mysterion* that our greatest scientists have yet to tap into.

Then it hit me: "A Spin. I will call it a Spin. That is brilliant. Thank you, Holy Ghost."

Today, I have had numerous people tell me: "Brother Palmer, I did a Spin just like you encouraged me to do, and I am so excited. Prayer is changing my life." When I hear that I just want to jump out of my skin. When I see sad, depressed Christians, I think: "Gosh, if I could just get them to go on 1/24 of a Spin. Just one hour of praying in tongues will fight that darkness and battle those emotions, and their lives will change. Spin, half-a-spin, a quarter spin, or whatever, just get those mysteries going up.

CHAPTER THIRTY-FOUR

Dying to Self

**"Increase? I'm not interested in you increasing right now.
I am interested in you *dying* right now."**

Little did I know that pacing back and forth and praying in tongues in that lonely, dark church was giving me an education in nearly every deficient area of my life. This was part of my journey down the path of righteousness. Although I was not fully aware of it at the time, tongues would cause me to shine brighter and brighter unto the perfect day.

Finally, 7 a.m. arrived, and the pastor was unlocking the door to get back into the church. I had made it past the most difficult time of doing a Spin, those early morning hours when it's hard to keep going.

Because the church was now being set up for service, I got in my Jeep (still praying in tongues) and made my way back home. As tired as my eyes were, I was going to go until 3 pm. Fighting heavy eyes and the fatigue of being up all night, I somehow made it to 2:30, growing more excited with every passing minute. I was actually going to get it done.

Boy, the ego can creep in when you least expect it. Just like that, my mind said something curious to the Lord. "OK, God. Look. I have done it. Twenty-four hours of praying in tongues." It was as though I were saying, "Search the land and see if there are any as righteous as Your servant, Chris." I said, "Since I have made this deep sacrifice, when are You going to *increase* my ministry?"

At that time, I was still the evangelist who had no church to preach in. Oh sure, I could go out and win souls on the streets, but I was called to preach in churches, too. I will never forget what I heard the Lord say. In twenty-four hours of praying in tongues, God said only one thing to me. *"Increase? I'm not interested in you increasing right now. I am interested in you __dying__ right now."* I was blown away by that response.

I could tell that this was the Father speaking to me. You know, when you get close to the Lord, you will begin to differentiate when it is the Father, or Jesus, or the Holy Ghost talking with you. The Father speaks to us like a loving father. His voice never lacks love, and it brings correction and wisdom.

When Jesus speaks, it is like the voice of a brother. Jesus Christ is *"the faithful witness, the first begotten of the dead, and the prince of the kings of the earth"* (Revelation 1:5 KJV).

He is the member of the Godhead who suffered with us, and:

> *⁷Made Himself of no reputation, taking the form of a bondservant, and coming in the likeness of men.*
> *⁸And being found in appearance as a man, He humbled Himself and became obedient to the point of death, even the death of the cross.* (Philippians 2:7-8 NKJV)

Of the three members of Jehovah, Jesus Christ understands our suffering, and identifies with it:

> *For we have not a high priest which __cannot be touched with the feeling of our infirmities…a man of sorrows, and acquainted with grief__* [**our grief**]. (Hebrews 4:15; Isaiah 53:3 KJV)

It is from this experience with our human grief that Jesus speaks. As a result, His voice will always carry the timbre of one who is our comrade and brother, having been in the earthly trenches with us.

When the Holy Ghost speaks to us it comes as a simple leading or a gentle sensation. He carries the tone of a friend who cares and desires the best in us.

Thirty minutes before my twenty-four hours were up, I knew it was the Father speaking to me, and I knew what He was saying. There were things in my life that needed to be eradicated in order for me to bear greater fruit.

There were weeds in my garden, if you will, that God needed to uproot in order to make room for what He desired to produce in my life.

Many times we think that prosperity means having an ample supply of what we need, and it can mean that. *It can also mean to subtract what we shouldn't have.*

> **And every branch that bears fruit He prunes [purges],**
> **that it may bear more fruit.** (John 15:2 NKJV)

God came along that Sunday afternoon with His pruning shears, and decided to do some pruning. What an honor. When God prunes us, it is because we *do* bear fruit, and He is interested in preparing us to produce more. But it comes through the death of those things that are weighing us down and not producing anything. God says: "Ok, here I come. That rotten bud that is growing in your life has to go. Help Me help you, and let Me purge it right out of you."

After God spoke, I finished my last 20 minutes. I had done it.

CHAPTER THIRTY-FIVE

The Helper Has Come to Cleanse and Purge

"Praying in the Holy Ghost, which delivers you to purging, has only one gear: forward."

God uses Paul as an example that nothing on earth and in hell can stop a child of God who has learned how to become solely dependent upon the Holy Ghost. This is why the Spirit of God charged me in my life to *instruct people how to develop a relationship with their Helper.* We may have thousands of notes and every book our pastor wrote, but unless we learn how to walk with the mighty Holy Spirit, we will find ourselves in constant defeat, because most of the time the answer is not more instruction. It is purging.

To purge means to get rid of that which is impure or undesirable. You are purging your house every time you take out the garbage. Imagine what it would be like if you never tended to this, but just let the trash continue to pile itself up in the corner of the room. You may be able to get by for a few days, but eventually it is going to be disgusting to live in your house.

"But, Chris, I thought you said that we are new creatures in Christ and that we have been perfected in Him. What trash do we have left?"

Purging is the constant, ceaseless process whereby God removes the dross and undesirable things of our mortality, bringing us one step closer unto glorification. The truth of the matter is that if God doesn't purge us, every year is going to look the same as every other, and we will be just as powerless in 2022 as we were in 2021. People circle the same mountain over and over again because they are not being purged. They believe the problem is in everything else *except* the weakness in their mortality.

Breakthrough comes when the Holy Ghost frees us from the limitations that our flesh keeps putting on us. *Many times it's not a breakthrough we need, it's a break from.* This comes through purging, our reward for producing fruit.

Praying In the Spirit Hunts Down Our Weaknesses

It is up to each of us to join with the Helper to get the job done. It is called praying out the mystery of Christ; speaking in tongues; praying in the Holy Spirit. Those are several terms for the same activity. Praying out the mystery of Christ Jesus in us literally puts our life under a microscope. Think about this for just a moment. You begin showing up to pray, night after night, giving hour after hour to the Holy Spirit to launch this mighty operation through you, privately, just you and Him. The more of this sacred time that ticks by, the more mystery of Christ you begin to pray out. The more you begin to pray it out in the form of *mysterion*, the more it comes back to you in the form of revelation. This becomes the supply you need to walk in the grace that God has called you to.

As you build up this supply in the Spirit, it is eventually going to track down the things in your life that are contrary to the Spirit's nature and look them squarely in the face. Praying out the mystery of Christ in you will mean that, at some point, you will pray out the mystery of peace, and it will find the fear in your life, and say, "Hello, Mr. Fear. I have a telegram for you that says that I am the new authority in town and you are, from this moment, unseated in this person's life." As joy is prayed forth in your life it will say, "Hey, there, Mr. Depression. It's time for you to pack up your stuff. Your lease has officially expired." Praying out the mysteries of the love of God will look the hatred in your life squarely in the face and say, "Sorry, Mr. Hatred, this town isn't big enough for the both of us."

This is what happened to me when I was harboring old anger toward my family member. Ambling around in a dark church, I prayed out the Mind of Christ regarding forgiveness and love, and it tracked down the bitterness, unforgiveness, and anger that I was holding, just as a hunter tracks down a twelve-point buck. As I prayed in the Spirit, unknown to me, a supply was beginning to be built up. The mystery of Christ entered the catacombs of my soul and found that rotten, diseased carcass of anger, roped it up, and began to slowly drag it to the surface of my renewed consciousness.

The further it came up, the more light was shed on it and, consequently, the more I began to hate myself for possessing it. This anger had been growing at a rate that it was beginning to scare me. I noticed that my confidence, instead of going up, began to go down. Praying in the Spirit started making me self-conscious. This created within me disgust, and I began to dislike the guy I was looking at in the mirror.

Oh, sure, I was born again. I was a child of God. I was an adopted son in the family of God. But, as any child can be ashamed of its behavior when it misses the mark that its father has expected, so too was I ashamed at missing the mark that my Heavenly Father had laid out through Jesus when He commanded, ***"Love one another; as I have loved you, that you also love one another"*** (John 13:34 NKJV).

That night while I was in that dark church, the Holy Ghost finally gave the order. "Bring that thing to the surface. Ease it on up." As I was praying and crying and groaning, the supply of everything Christ is came back from its hunt, carrying my bitterness and anger. I finally saw it for what it really was, no longer hidden in darkness, but *fully* brought to light.

This is the place God wants us to be. First, we must recognize the barriers impeding our path that shines more and more unto the perfect day. When this hateful thing came to light, I loathed it so badly that I wanted it out of my life, immediately. God was smiling, because His plan was working. I am sure He saw my tears and groanings, and was saying: "Good. I have been waiting for this. You now hate this thing the way I hate it, because you have been praying the mystery of Christ in your life. When you didn't mind it being in your life, or if you enjoyed it because you found relief in blaming another for your shortcomings, I could do nothing to help you. But we are now on the same page. You have yielded to me, and I now have the faith that I need from you to stick my hand down in there and eradicate it." And that is exactly what He did. I was free.

Peel Back the Flesh

This is the dynamic power of praying in tongues. This is what edifies every cell in the Body of Christ. This is what will remove those ugly barriers in your life, and give you the space you seek to house all that is true, honest, just, pure, lovely, and virtuous (Philippians 4:8). It is what gives you your supply to add to the Church: the revelation of the mystery of Christ in you, the hope of glory.

Since then, I have been purged all the more and have moved ever further into my walk with God. I didn't need a breakthrough. I didn't need an impartation from a man of God. I didn't need to jump and spin three times. What I needed was to be purged from the weaknesses that were acting like thorns in my feet, restricting my forward progress into what Jesus said I could be.

Compare this to darker things in your life that still need to be eradicated. Perhaps you are someone who is full of concealed pride. Concealed pride is arrogance that may not be visible in your actions, but it hibernates in your thoughts and steers your actions, causing you to commit sins of omission as opposed to sins of commission. Because of this pride you don't help others, or give in the offering, or volunteer at the church. On some hidden level you feel you are "too good" to do so.

Or maybe you are secretly jealous or disturbingly envious of someone. Perhaps you have fits of lusts that come and go like waves, causing you to brace yourself in seasons of peace for the next inevitable moment where lust swallows up your inhibitions and good judgment. Low self-esteem, stealing, unending gossiping, complaining, negativity, (the list goes on and on), are things that may be growing in your life like algae in a stagnant pond.

When the carnal man needs to be dealt with, it can be easier to give financially than to turn and face the real problem. There are cases where preachers come along and say that the way out of your problem is to send them money for their campaigns and programs. While it is beneficial to sow seed and to give cheerfully, if the problem is that there are layers of mortality that need to be peeled back, giving one million dollars isn't going to change that. Our responsibility is to face it, and allow the Holy Spirit to root the carnality from our hearts and minds.

Two Steps Forward, One Step Back?

The purging process is the reason why it *seems* that every time we take two steps forward in God, we suddenly take one step back. The frustrating part is that we may not have even done anything to take a step back. It just feels that way. Stay strong; it is part of the process, and the blessings will be like nothing you can imagine.

When I began giving myself over to the Holy Ghost I encountered this a lot. I remember after one season of seeking the Lord, I came to experience torment and fear like I had never known. This just came out of nowhere. I wasn't in any kind of sin and had been maintaining my usual time with the Lord, and even more, coming out of a time of seeking. It seemed like the harder I tried to break the thing, the worse it got. Probably the most difficult part was that I had a week's revival coming up in just a few days.

When I started that revival, I frankly did not feel like preaching. I was in an apathetic stupor. I almost felt like staying home and watching television. But when I stepped up to preach the first service, that dark depression suddenly broke. The glory of God fell on that place stronger than I had ever seen it at that point in my ministry. Because the miracles had gotten so strong, we extended the meetings. By the time we concluded, deaf and blind people had been healed, Type I diabetes had dissolved, a leg grew out about an inch back to normal size, arthritis disappeared, and congestive heart failure was cured, on top of numerous deliverances from demonic powers. People were testifying about the deliverances they had experienced from harassing entities and evil spirits. The Holy Ghost just blew the doors off the place.

I was left thinking, "What in the world just happened here?"

Little did I realize, I was being purged to enter into a greater dimension of faith, love, and peace. God was scraping the dross out of my life. It was this dross that would have kept me from stepping out in boldness and power during that revival. My ministry has not been the same since. It has never shrunk to what it was before. Though it might have seemed that I was taking a step back, I was actually taking several steps forward. Praying in the Holy Ghost, which delivers you to purging, has only one gear: Forward.

CHAPTER THIRTY-SIX

What Are We Doing When We Pray in Tongues?

"It became obvious that for this pattern to be so constant, something was unfailingly happening when I allowed the Holy Ghost to intercede for me."

As I began to wonder what praying in tongues was doing to me, I realized that it was taking me further and further away from the part that was awaiting glorification (the flesh), and was enabling me to walk more and more out of the part of me that had already experienced glorification, my new man. I would go into my prayer closet feeling carnal, and come out a different person. It was almost as if I were Clark Kent getting into the phone booth and coming out as Superman.

I was having experience after experience praying in the Holy Ghost, and it was becoming obvious in my life, ministry, and preaching. Even in my own personal life people were noticing that I was walking in greater love and patience. It was still somewhat of a mystery to me just exactly *what* I was doing. I knew in part, but I didn't know enough to explain it. I would just say, "Well, I am just praying in the Holy Ghost and letting Him pray for me." That answer satisfied me for a bit, but I knew deep down there was more to it than that. I knew I could find out if I wanted to.

Even more, I wanted to better explain it to people in hopes that they would start reporting to prayer. I knew too many believers who were at the end of their ropes and frustrated. They didn't realize that this frustration was, in part, due to the fact that they were waiting for their spiritual leaders to access the revelation that they, themselves, were responsible to access. If I could get them to cultivate a lifestyle of praying in tongues, they would start obtaining the revelation their heart was desiring, whether their leaders had it or not. This lifestyle of prayer makes it unnecessary for us to have to sit around and wait for *others* to discover what is *ours* to discover.

Because of praying in the Holy Ghost, I was accessing things from God's Word that were revolutionizing my life. Revelation was pouring in. I was busting through limitations. I was becoming authentic. And I was being transformed. I *had* to share it. But I first had to find out *what* exactly was going on.

A Fascinating Pattern

When I began praying in tongues, I started noticing a fascinating pattern.

1.) *I would start praying while I was feeling down and blue:* As I said, at this point in my life my battery was tapped out. Being at ground zero when I first began, this was every single time I reported to prayer. I always had to fight discouragement to keep praying.

2.) *I would end prayer feeling the same way:* Unless I fell into groanings or had a "peculiar experience" (which wasn't always so), I left feeling just as discouraged, if not more so. I remember driving home as the sun was coming up, thinking, "Gosh, I prayed all night, and I don't feel any better." I'd sigh and go to sleep as soon as I got home.

3.) *About two or three days later, though, I would sense a jolt in my spirit:* This jolt would come as a result of revelation. I would open up God's Word and see things that I had never noticed before. *More than that, I started seeing things that preachers were teaching that were not exactly correct.* These were preachers whom I loved and respected, but I started seeing that some of their teachings were done from tradition, or because their spiritual leaders had taught them so. *Avenues from the Word of God started opening up to me in ways I had always hoped for.* And I began to see what the Word was actually saying.

4.) *Every revelation invoked the presence of God:* Each time I received revelation, it felt like the Lord had grabbed me by the wrist and was walking me down the boulevards of His Word. Thankfulness, rejoicing, and contentment started showing up in ways I had never known.

5.) *I would suddenly notice I was one step further along than where I had been:* Although things in the natural didn't *always* change *immediately*, I noticed that I was developing as a child of God. It first became apparent to me, and then to others, that I was transforming.

This pattern happened time and time again. It became obvious that for this pattern to be so constant, something was unfailingly happening when I allowed the Holy Ghost to intercede for me. Paul lays it out in First Corinthians 14:2, 4, actually giving the order of what happens.

1.) *The person speaks to God in an unknown tongue:* This is the very beginning of the process. Some have questioned who is actually doing the praying, the human or the Holy Ghost. The Bible is clear about this: ***"For if I pray in an unknown tongue, <u>my spirit</u> prayeth, but my understanding is unfruitful. What is it then? I will pray with the* spirit, *and I will also pray with the understanding"*** (1 Corinthians 14:14-15 KJV).

When we are praying in the Holy Ghost, according to this verse *we* are doing the praying. To be even more specific, it is the *reborn man* who is praying. Part of the reason that praying in the Holy Ghost is so effective is because *the side of us that has now received glorification is praying.*

In this world, the spirit cannot speak and be heard *because* it is made up of spirit. In order for our prayers to be heard on this earth, *the spirit has to cooperate with the body for the sound to be formed.* Spirit is a heavenly material that our eternal man is made of. It currently dwells within the lining of physical man. When Paul said, "My spirit prays," he was simply pinpointing the *origin* of the prayer which is being spoken from out of the body.

In Acts 2:4 it says that the one hundred twenty *began to speak with other tongues.* It wasn't *the Holy Ghost* doing the actual speaking. *The one hundred twenty* were doing the speaking. But the verse adds, *"As the Spirit gave them utterance."* This is the Joint Helper assisting the one hundred twenty to pray by providing the utterance or language—content and dialect. The utterance that the disciples were being given was made up of the *mysterion*. That is proved by those who heard them, stating, ***"We hear them speaking in our own tongues <u>the wonderful works of God</u>"*** (Acts 2:11 NKJV).

Mysterion are hidden secrets from the mind of God that must be divinely revealed. They are inaccessible without the help of the Holy Spirit. These truths, unlocked by divine illumination, are the forces that accelerate the Kingdom of God on the Earth.

Here is how it works: The Holy Ghost comes along side of our reborn nature, the spirit man, and begins to feed that spirit with language containing *mysterion*. The spirit receives it and houses that language. At any moment that we desire, we can yield and give that language an audible sound by participating with our physical bodies by speaking.

When I began showing up at the church on Saturday nights, I was lending my spirit to a prayer language that was installed there by the Holy Ghost. My body was providing the sound that my spirit needed to give voice to the language that it had received from the Holy Ghost. It looks like this:

Holy Ghost + Prayer Language → spirit man → body/lips/tongue/ mouth → God.

2.) *The plans of God are prayed up in a mystery form:* Notice that when we are praying in tongues we are talking to God. We are *not* talking to the devil and warring with the Principalities, Powers, Rulers of Darkness, and Wicked Spirits in heavenly places found in Ephesians 6:12. "Going to war" is not what we are doing when we pray in the Spirit.

Consider something: Satan is *not* the opposite of God, although the whole world thinks he is. He is a created angelic being like Michael and Gabriel (Isaiah 14:12-14; Ezekiel 28:11-19). He is the opposite of Michael, Gabriel, and any other anointed cherub. This means Satan is not omnipotent (all powerful), not omnipresent (everywhere at all times), and not omniscient (all knowing). Granting these limitations, it is safe to say he is not personally familiar with *you*. Somewhere along the line his government is, but it is doubtful Satan himself knows. So, even if you were "warring," it wouldn't be with Satan. You would be "warring" with those under his chain of command. Yet Jesus said that Satan and every spirit that makes up the Kingdom of Darkness is defeated and subject to the believer (Luke 10:19-20; Matthew 28:18).

It is not the Gospel if we tell people we must go to war. The war has been fought, and Jesus was victorious. "***When he ascended on high, he led captivity captive, and gave gifts unto men***" (Ephesians 4:8 KJV).

"***And having spoiled principalities and powers, he made a shew of them openly, triumphing over them in it***" (Colossians 2:15 KJV).

There is nothing left to fight. Rather, God wants us to spend time praying in tongues, not to defeat Satan, but to *eliminate ignorance* concerning the victory that has been won by Christ. *Eventually, the mysterion will come down in an understood form called revelation.* Revelation will destroy ignorance and *result in edification*. Hence, the process looks like this:

1.) The person speaks to God in an unknown tongue

2.) The plans of God are prayed up in a mystery form

3.) Mysteries come down in an understood form called revelation

4.) Edification is received

If you have been consistently praying in tongues and sending those mysteries up, brace yourself, because revelation and edification is not far off. Therefore, steps three and four will be discussed in the next two chapters.

CHAPTER THIRTY-SEVEN

Praying in the Holy Ghost Reveals to Us Things Inside of God: *Mysterion* and Revelation

"It is now the Holy Ghost's job to take the knots that we have been given in the Word of God and untangle them for us. This is what we do when we pray in the Holy Ghost. We employ the help of the Spirit, and He starts the unraveling."

I was once in the airport headed to Johannesburg, South Africa, and I met a hunter who was leaving the United States for a week to hunt down wild game. As we talked I realized he was going by himself. "Isn't that going to be lonely?" I asked.

"Not really. To tell you the truth, I wanted to come by myself. I need to get away from everything for a while." In other words, this man was telling me that he needed more than just a few minutes out of his busy day to slip away into the world that is going on inside of him. We spent about twenty minutes talking as we awaited our flight. I heard a fragment of the things that were going on in him. Had I gotten a seat next to him, I would have had eighteen hours to hear more about that world. Even after landing in Africa I still would not have had a complete understanding of him. After baggage claim, he would have disappeared into a sea of people, mostly still a mystery.

The fact of the matter is that the world inside of us is known by us and to nobody else. The Scripture talks about this world inside of us: *"For what man knows the things of a man except the spirit of the man which is in him?"* (1 Corinthians 2:11a NKJV). Unless we communicate perfectly and the person hearing our communication receives it perfectly, there will always be parts of us that remain unknown.

Similar to you, there is a whole world going on inside of God. *"Even so [just like us] no one knows the things of God except the Spirit of God"* (1 Corinthians 2:11b NKJV). This world going on inside of God is referred to as the "things of God."

"Just what are those things?" Those things include (but are not limited to):

1.) The thoughts He thinks toward us (Jer. 29:11)
2.) His infinite/endless reservoir of knowledge & wisdom (Job 38-39; Proverbs 8:22-31)
3.) His future plans for the ages (Acts 1:7)
4.) His perfect understanding of what is going on in us (1 John 3:20)
5.) Everything Christ is in us, to us, and through us (Colossians 1:27)

Having no limit in their scope, these "things of God" cover every area of our redemption, this age, the past age, and the coming ages that shall go on into eternity (Ephesians 2:10). Even in the eternal perfect state we still will be learning from God. Just when we think we have learned it all, God will unveil another age that will require us to grow in our understanding. Although we know intellectually that this world is going on inside of God, Paul tells us that the details of this world are a mystery simply *because* we are on the outside, with no way of knowing what is going on in the inside.

A Nature That Understands

As long as mankind was in sin and had yet to enter in through the new birth, we were composed of a spirit that was not able to understand and comprehend God. Even the Old Testament saints and the children of Israel had to have special appearances of God because they couldn't know God through their spirit. The work of Christ had not yet been completed. *"But as it is written, Eye hath not seen, nor ear heard, neither have entered into the heart of man, the things which God hath prepared for them that love Him"* (1 Corinthians 2:9 KJV). Notice that the problem was not that God didn't *want* those things to enter. They *couldn't* enter because of the *heart*. It was diseased with sin and death. This verse is talking about the time where humankind was blinded by spiritual death.

When Christ finished His redemptive work on the cross, things changed. Through the second birth the whole composition of a man's spirit changes, and he receives a spirit *that can understand God*. Paul uses a metaphor and says that the veil of spiritual death is taken off the eyes of the heart, and it is able to see and understand. This new composition of spirit makes us fit candidates to delve into that world that is swirling around inside of God. Our reborn spirits have been granted clearance and all-access passes to enter into that realm where the knowledge of God can be known. This is a result of the second birth. ***"Now we have received, not the spirit of the world, <u>but the spirit which is of God</u>; that we might know the things that are freely given to us of God"*** (1 Corinthians 2:12 KJV).

This verse is telling us what the Holy Ghost now has to work with: our new natures. Our spirits had to be born again so that we could understand what the Holy Spirit would teach us and bring us into. This happened *after* the work of Christ and is why the Holy Spirit was sent *after* Christ ascended. Look at what happens to us now *after* having received this new nature: ***"That we might know the things that have been freely given to us by God"*** (1 Corinthians 2:12b KJV). The moment that we are saved we become enrolled into the school of God as pupils, able to learn as much as we are willing.

The Holy Ghost Teaches the New Nature

Having this reborn spirit that can now enter into the world that is swirling around inside of God, Paul tells us something phenomenal. *The Holy Ghost, as our great Teacher, has been designated to bring us into that place.* Every time you yield yourself to the mighty Teacher, it is His job to reveal more of that world to the part of you that can understand it, your reborn man. This is part of what the Holy Ghost does when He bears witness to you that you are a child of God (Romans 8:16). By running that world through your spirit, you begin to see more and more that you are indeed His child.

You may say, "Yes, but why do I need the Holy Ghost to do this for me? Why can't I just learn on my own?"

Well, you can *try* to learn on your own. Certainly you won't be the first, and you won't be the last. Yet, trying to learn God without the Holy Ghost is a form of pride, and is one of the great causes of deception, fanaticism, and false doctrine. Here is the reason: only the Spirit of God knows the world going on inside of God, just as only you know what is going on inside of you. The Holy Ghost is God, just as much as the Father and Jesus. He knows it all. The Scripture tells us that He has searched unto the deepest parts of the wisdom of the Godhead, and there is nothing to be known that He doesn't know. This makes for the perfect teacher and student relationship. *He has all the perfect content and wisdom, and you have the perfect ability to understand.*

"The Things We Also Speak"

Now, there is one thing that must take place for the Teacher to get this wisdom over to the student: communication. This is where Paul next takes his discourse in 1 Corinthians 2.

> **These things we also speak, <u>not in words which man's wisdom teaches</u> but which the Holy Spirit teaches, comparing spiritual things with spiritual.** (1 Corinthians 2:13 NKJV)

This verse, in the truest sense of its meaning, is not directly talking about praying in tongues. As long as I kept trying to fit tongues into this verse, the verse stayed locked up and was jammed. Instead the verse is sharing the *result* of praying in tongues.

The "things we also speak" is referring to the glorious gospel of Christ (2 Corinthians 4:4) and *"the glorious gospel of the blessed God"* (1 Timothy 1:11 KJV). Paul was in the middle of rebuking the Corinthians because they were trusting in human beings to bring them into that place where the world of God was swirling around (1 Corinthians 1:12-13).

Even though they were following men who had seen into that world, Paul was discouraging them from thinking that those men were the *source*.

In this verse he is saying: "Corinthians. Hear me now! You are so foolish walking around thinking that Peter, Apollos, and I got the things that we are speaking concerning the Gospel from the words of man. We didn't. No, we have another Teacher that knows the things of God. This Teacher has delved into the very depths of His wisdom and has been teaching us since He has come. He is the Holy Ghost. Stop following men around like they are the ones who originated the knowledge, and turn yourselves over to Him."

The whole point of the second chapter of First Corinthians is for Paul to reveal his source of knowledge that had been revealed to him. He recognized the spiritual hunger of the Corinthians, but he realized that they were looking to humans as their source. He pointed them in the right direction by saying, "The Holy Spirit teaches" (1 Corinthians 2:13 NKJV). A few chapters later, Paul made it clear *how* the Holy Spirit taught him, what he learned, and how He still teaches us today.

> *For he that speaketh in an unknown tongue speaketh not unto men, but unto God: for no man understandeth him; howbeit in the spirit he speaketh mysteries.* (1 Corinthians 14:2 KJV)

This verse is tied closely to 1 Corinthians 2:13. This verse above shows the cause, and 2:13 shows the result. "Yes, but *how* is that possible? How did praying in tongues provide the Apostle Paul with the things that he preached? How does praying in tongues provide me with the things that I want to speak?"

I am glad you asked. The key to understanding is found in the word "mysteries."

Mysterion and Parables

The word "mysteries" is the Greek word *mysterion*. The literal definition means, *"General mysteries confided only to the initiated and not to ordinary mortals."* It also can be defined as *"the secret counsels of God in dealing with the righteous."* Lastly, it can be said to mean, *"the hidden forces that accelerate the Kingdom of God."* When you consider the definition of this one word that is easily overlooked so many times, it becomes evident that the Apostle Paul is not talking about something small here.

It just so happens that this is not the first time that we see the word *mysterion* mentioned in Scripture. Jesus spoke about it in Mark's gospel.

> *¹⁰But when He was alone, those around Him with the twelve asked Him about the parable.*
> *¹¹And He said to them, "To you it has been given to know the <u>mystery</u> of the kingdom of God; but to those who are outside, all things come in <u>parables,</u>*
> *¹²so that 'Seeing they may see and not perceive, and hearing they may hear and not understand; Lest they should turn, And their sins be forgiven them.'"* (Mark 4:10-12 NKJV)

This is a very interesting passage of Scripture, considering what was going on. Jesus had come to the seaside, boarded a boat, and begun teaching the mass of people who had gathered on the beach, as was customary for Him to do. Jesus had a unique style of teaching that set Him above the rest. He taught in parables. Today, we take it for granted that Christ taught this way. The more and more I come to learn about Jesus and get to know Him, the more and more intrigued I become of Him. I have found the more and more I meditate the Gospels, the more I see things and wonder about them.

Once, I said, "Gosh. Why did Jesus teach like this? Why couldn't He just plain and simply tell people what He wanted to say?"

Then I began to compare how He taught to how I now teach. I said, "Gee, here I am, just giving information and communicating plain truth. And here is Jesus Christ of Nazareth: *concealing truth* in parables. Why did Jesus do that? Should I try to do that?" As I began to study, I found the answer.

I am not the only person who noticed the teaching style of Jesus. Unsurprisingly, His disciples asked Him about it, in Matthew 13:10 (NKJV): **And the disciples came and said to Him, "Why do You speak to them in parables?"** The answer that Jesus gave never seemed very impressive to me. I have come to realize something, however, after over ten years of studying the Bible. If Jesus says something that does not seem impressive, I am missing part of the story; there is something I need to find out to connect it to. One way to study the Bible is to find all the things that Jesus says that do not impress you or that don't make sense, write them down, and start digging for more of the story. You'll be amazed at what you find.

> *He answered and said to them, "Because it has been given to you to know the mysteries [mysterion] of the kingdom of heaven, but to them it has not been given."*
> (Matthew 13:11 NKJV)

A parable is a fictitious narrative by which truth(s) can be illustrated, but it works like a knot, a knot that requires unraveling. In fact, some of Jesus' parables were similar to riddles. Jesus did this because He was dealing with *mysterion*. His lips contained the most valuable commodity that the world had ever known: the manifold wisdom of God and the understanding of the ages. This wisdom made Him greater than any prophet or king that had ever risen up in Israel's history.

When Jesus taught the *mysterion*, there were two classes of people who were listening: those who would understand, and those who would not. Jesus played fairly and showed no favoritism, giving His teachings to all in the form of a large knot. The ones who could unravel them would understand, be converted, and be initiated into the Kingdom of God with an aptitude to learn more. Those who had dull ears and eyes that wouldn't see would be left with the knot in their hands, unable to enter into the Kingdom of God because of the state of their heart.

"So, what if there were some who were smarter than others? Does this mean that only those who were good at riddles could figure it out and be converted and initiated?" No. The ability to understand what Jesus is talking about is not hinged on human ability. It comes from a divine Joint Helper and a Master Teacher. It was human ability and pride that blinded people from understanding *mysterion*.

> *And the scribes who came down from Jerusalem said, "He has Beelzebub," and, "By the ruler of the demons He casts out demons."* (Mark 3:22 NKJV)

During the time of Christ's ministry the religious leaders, including the scribes, Pharisees, and Sadducees, would accuse Christ of having a devil. They believed that it was through Satan that Jesus worked miracles and taught. To these accusers, Jesus carefully warned:

> *28 "Assuredly, I say to you, all sins will be forgiven the sons of men, and whatever blasphemies they may utter;*
> *29 but he who blasphemes against the Holy Spirit never has forgiveness, but is subject to eternal condemnation."*
> (Mark 3:28-29 NKJV)

The only way that people would ever be able to understand what Jesus was talking about in His parable knots would be if the Holy Ghost, the Great Teacher, came along and opened up their hearts and eyes. The religious leaders were so incredibly blind by the time Jesus' ministry had begun, they could not tell the difference between the works of Satan and the works of the Holy Spirit. As a result they attributed the works of the Holy Ghost as the works of Satan, which is blaspheming the Holy Ghost. Seeing the blasphemy that was proceeding from their hearts, Jesus disguised the *mysterion* in parables as a judgment against the religious leaders. As long as they kept on blaspheming the Holy Ghost, *there would be no one to assist their understanding.*

The Holy Ghost is the great decipherer of the *mysterion*. The ultimate verdict that can be passed is to be denied His help. He helps us to get saved, to get delivered and healed, and to move forward in our progress with God by deciphering the mystery. Technically, it is not God that passes this judgment. He has laid out the way that we can access the Holy Ghost and draw upon His help. If we are denied His help, it is because our own hearts denied it. It is our own fault.

Jesus Describes the Teacher's Role

As Jesus' death approached, He told His disciples,

> *12 "I still have many things to say to you, but you cannot bear them now.*

¹³However, when He, the Spirit of truth, has come,
He will guide you into all truth; for He will not speak
on His own authority, but whatever He hears He will
speak; and He will tell you things to come." (John
16:12-13 NKJV)

Notice:

1.) *Jesus still had many things to say:* The many things that Jesus still
had to say are now contained in the New Testament in the form
of lively doctrine that was written by Paul, Peter, John, and other
apostolic writers who received the revelation of the *mysterion, after*
they had been through the new birth and had received the joint
help of the Holy Spirit.

2.) *The disciples could not bear what Jesus wanted to tell them:* Jesus was
indicating that they had not yet been given a reborn spirit that
could understand *fully* the things He wanted to share. More than
that, the Holy Ghost had not yet been sent *in fullness* to work with
that reborn spirit.

3.) *The Holy Ghost would guide the disciples into all truth:* The truth
that the Holy Ghost would guide them into would be the *mysterion.*
This revealing of it would make sense of Christ, who He was and
is, why He had come, and how His death, burial, and resurrection
fits into God's plan for humankind, changing the course of the
whole world. This was the side of the Holy Ghost called "the Spirit
of wisdom and revelation" (Ephesians 1:17-23; Ephesians 3:14-21).
The Spirit of wisdom and revelation wouldn't just reveal *further*
mysteries concerning the Kingdom of God; He would bring back
into *remembrance* the things that Jesus had previously taught, and
make sense of them as well (John 14:26).

It is now the Holy Ghost's job to take the knots that we have been
given in the Word of God and untangle them for us. This is what
we do when we pray in the Holy Ghost. We employ the help of the
Spirit, and He starts the unraveling, revealing to us that world that
is inside of God.

Mysterion **In Different Dialects**

Before He ascended, Jesus told the disciples that the Holy Ghost would come as soon as He ascended and to wait for Him before they did anything that pertained to ministry. They needed His supernatural help and would be powerless without Him. In Acts 2, the Holy Ghost came as Jesus promised. The very first thing that occurred was that everyone present in the upper room began to *"speak with other tongues, as the Spirit gave them utterance"* (Acts 2:4 KJV).

The witnesses who later heard them speak described these other tongues by saying: *"We do hear them speak in our tongues the wonderful works of God"* (Acts 2:11 KJV). Speaking forth the mysteries of God in an unknown tongue was the first thing that the Holy Spirit began to do through those who had received.

"Ah, yes, that would be nice to believe, Brother Palmer. I appreciate your zeal, you know, but you avoided the part that said, 'We do hear them speak in *our* tongue? Wouldn't that mean that they were just speaking in known human languages that they hadn't learned?"

Well, listen. Paul addressed this by saying, *"Though I speak with tongues of men and of angels"* (1 Corinthians 13:1 NKJV). He was not only speaking languages made up by humankind, but in the languages spoken by angelic hosts.

The important thing is to not to get stuck on what known or unknown dialect you are speaking: Hebrew, Greek, Spanish, English, Arabic, Russian, Angelic. What is important is to know that you are speaking a form of the *mysterion*. Though *your* understanding does not comprehend what is being said (1 Corinthians 14:14), those mysteries are still being spoken out of your mouth and are going up to God. This is how Paul received all of his revelation knowledge, through speaking these mysteries, day after day and night after night. *"I thank my God, I speak with tongues more than ye all"* (1 Corinthians 14:18 KJV).

If you are speaking to God in a mystery dialect, it will not remain a mystery long. The Holy Ghost will eventually reveal it to you as revelation. In return, that revelation will produce for you a massive amount of what you have been looking for: edification.

CHAPTER THIRTY-EIGHT

Prayer That Works, Prayer That Edifies

"If there is an explanation for something as goofy as a cell phone battery, surely God has an explanation for *why* praying in tongues edifies us."

A couple of days after my Spin, I was to meet with a facilitator who was assisting with a service I was hosting. My mind was busy figuring out what we would discuss, so, by the time I got to the restaurant, I wasn't too focused on the things of God.

As I got out of my vehicle and began walking through the parking lot, suddenly it felt like God came right up and tagged me with His glory, then left as quickly as He came. There I stood in the parking lot, a victim of God's drive-by glory. I immediately started to weep. I thought, *I can't go into the restaurant like this.* I whined, "God, I gave You a whole day. You could have made me cry in my bedroom, but You pick now when I am in full eyes of the world." I walked back to my vehicle, got myself together, and then went into the restaurant. During the meeting I kept thinking, "What *was* that? I feel changed." I couldn't wait to get back into prayer to figure out what had happened. Finally, the meeting ended, and I dashed back home. As I sought the Lord, I got my answer immediately. He showed me something about praying in tongues, and how it relates to the purging process, that I will never forget.

"Son, because you have willingly yielded yourself to the divine power of the Holy Ghost by praying out the mystery of everything Jesus Christ is in you, to you, and through you, the hope of glory, you have delivered yourself over to my purging. You have desired for Me to help your ministry increase. Well, I have. You see, I desire for your ministry to go the distance. I want you to accomplish everything I have created you for. But you would not have been able to do it unless I helped you overcome the mortality that is working in your flesh. Because you have turned yourself over to the Help of my Spirit, I went ahead of your ministry twenty years and located something in your life that would have completely destroyed you. I eradicated it. Now you are free. That crack in your foundation no longer exists."

I was dumbfounded. Here I was, concerned about the here and now, and there God was, covering me twenty years in advance. Oh, how He loves us. When God came by and tagged me with His glory, He ripped that thing out of my life, and I started crying because I was free. Someone asked, "Well, what was it that He removed?" I don't know, and I don't care. Because I dealt with it by the Spirit, I do not have to concern myself with it, ever.

Between this mind-boggling experience and the one that healed the anger against my family member, I could see that praying in tongues was demolishing great chunks of my personal debris, and was walking me into God's perfection. This is why Satan has done his very best to shift the Church away from tongues. He knows the effects it has in bringing us further and further down the road of righteousness. It is a road that we travel from being "newbies" in Christ, to being mature Christians, inheriting daily as heirs of God, based on deep, personal, ongoing experience in God. The difference is in the depth of richness we are willing to receive.

Prayer That *Works*

> *"Pray at all times (on every occasion, in every season) in the Spirit, with all [manner of] prayer and entreaty."*
> (Ephesians 6:18 AMP)

Paul, who wrote to the church at Ephesus about "all manner of prayer," was the same guy who wrote 1 Corinthians 14, where he explains about speaking in tongues. At the end of Ephesians, Paul mentions "all prayer." The Amplified Bible says, "all *manner* of prayer" (Ephesians 6:18). This particular use of the word "manner" means, "methods, kinds, and sorts." Paul urged the church to use all *kinds* and *sorts* of prayer.

The Church of the Lord Jesus Christ has missed the point in this area. How many times have you been with a person who prays the precise prayer every single time they pray for something? Have you ever been to a church where they pray the same prayer from the pulpit? People like to stick with what they think works. And yes, the best kind of prayer is the prayer that works (James 5:16), *but not every prayer is going to work.*

"How could you say that, Chris? That is an awful thing to suggest." Well, like it or not, it is true.

Sometimes, if we pray a certain way, on purpose or mistakenly, the prayer gets answered. If this happens it can create a rut, keeping us stuck by making us think that all prayer gets answered that way. For instance, praying the prayer of faith (James 5:15) may accomplish something tremendous in prayer. The next time, it may not require the prayer of faith. It may just need the prayer of agreement (Matthew 18:18-20). However, if people are not guided by the Spirit or praying by the Spirit, they will try to work up something themselves and risk not getting the answer.

If you are keen and spend enough time observing, you will notice people who pray and pray...and pray...and keep praying, and nothing happens. Then you will notice that there are believers who seem always to know the right lever to pull to release heaven's levees and cause a flood of answered prayer. My own observation has taught me why this happens: they pray the right manner of prayer.

"Well, how do I know the right manner of prayer to pray?" Often times you won't. The Holy Ghost will, however. Prayer, then, requires a genuine relationship with the Spirit so that you can pray with His help.

The highest mark of maturity in the believer's journey is being led by the Spirit, and this especially goes for the area of prayer. Learning the flow of the Spirit through daily fellowship will sharpen our understanding of prayer and help us to stay out of any ruts of religiosity or fanaticism, and pray exactly what is necessary. How can we become sensitive to the flow of the Spirit and always pray the perfect prayer, which will result in our edification? Paul tells us, *"He who speaks in a tongue edifies himself"* (1 Corinthians 14:4 NKJV).

"Charging Our Batteries?"

When I first began to pray in tongues, I was told that this was important because I was edifying myself. "Edify" means to uplift and build up. "Just go over there and pray in tongues," they said, "and you will edify yourself because the Holy Ghost will be interceding for you." Well, I believed it, and I took it by faith so much so that I began praying long hours in the Holy Ghost every night.

But this answer seemed vague. "Okay, but how come when we pray in the Holy Ghost we edify ourselves?" The normal answer was, "Well, we edify ourselves because we are building ourselves up on our most holy faith."

I'd think, "Well, that is wonderful. When I pray in the Holy Ghost I am building myself up on my most holy faith. Nice." So then I would go and pray more hours in the Holy Ghost, allowing Him to be my Joint Helper and intercede for me for a night.

Then another question arose in my mind, "Why am I building myself up on my most holy faith?" I started digging and asking around, and the deepest answer I got was, "You are building yourself up on your most holy faith because you are edifying yourself."

"Hmm," I would sigh. Seemed like a pointless merry-go-round.

Once, late at night, I was flipping around the television when I saw a preacher with a nice size congregation. The bottom label popped up and said, "Today's Message: The Benefits of Praying In Tongues." It is rare to hear television preachers preach on tongues today. I was excited, so I began to watch.

For ten minutes, I heard, "Praying in tongues edifies you. Praying in tongues builds you up." If that weren't enough, I heard the classic illustration, "How many people here have a cellular phone? Who has a battery in it? Whose battery gets low? Well, bless God, your battery gets low, too. And every time your spiritual battery gets low, you must plug that thing in." Everything he was saying I had heard before. What I was hoping to hear was, "*Why?*"

Picture me walking into an electronics store with my cell phone and the charger. I get the clerk's attention and say, "I noticed that after about a day of talking on my phone, my battery seems to get very low. As soon as

I plug it into the wall with this charger and wait about an hour and a half, the battery goes back up. Can you please tell me why?"

Do you think the man is going to say, "Because you are charging your phone"?

No. If he knew anything about it, he would say, "Why, yes, young man, allow me to explain. You see that charger in your left hand?"

"Yes."

"Well, you see, that charger has two metal prongs sticking out of it that connect to the outlet on the wall. Inside that wall is a current of electricity that steadily flows along, and is available for your use. This electricity is provided to your home by a greater power source, which is most likely powering the entire neighborhood. When you plug in the prongs and connect your cell phone to the other end, the power from the wall is harnessed into your phone. This causes the battery life to go back up to normal. All in all, it takes about an hour or an hour in a half."

Wow. What an explanation. I just got schooled in Battery Life 101. Now, I fully understand why I must plug the thing in if I want power. If there is an explanation for something as mundane as a cell phone battery, surely God has an explanation for *why* praying in tongues edifies us. The answer awaits in the next chapter...

CHAPTER THIRTY-NINE

Prayer Language: Everything that Pertains to Life and Godliness

"We are praying out, in a *mystery form*, every single detail that has to do with our personal blueprint and with our new life that is in *Him*."

When the Holy Ghost descended, He brought a prayer language that is a blueprint containing two things: everything that pertains to life, and everything that pertains to godliness.

> *As His divine power has given to us all things that pertain to life and godliness, through the knowledge of Him who called us by glory and virtue.* (2 Peter 1:3 NKJV)

A.) Everything that pertains to life: We need more than just doctrinal revelation from the Word of God to proceed forward as sons and daughters of God. We need revelation that pertains to each of us *individually*.

My only dilemma is that when I last checked the Bible concordance, there were Matthew, Mark, Luke and John. The Church Fathers seem to have left the Book of Chris Palmer out of the canon. This means that the Bible is *not* going to tell me the details of my life via the words on those pages. I needed to hear from God concerning my calling to ministry, what church to join, what college to attend, whom to marry—all the major watershed decisions of life that affect one's destiny.

Gladly, God has not stopped speaking. *"'Man shall not live by bread alone, but by every word that proceeds from the mouth of God'"*

(Matthew 4:4 NKJV). The word "proceeds" is a clue that lets us know that God is continually speaking. Once I asked the Lord in my heart about this and He said, *"Everything that has gone unheard has not gone unspoken."* The Lord wasn't just referring to revelation that is contained in Scripture.

God is continually speaking everything that pertains to life. It is up to us to tune in our ears. Everything that pertains to life is a reference to the born again life that we were born of when we received Jesus Christ as Lord and Savior by faith. Not only does that include the corporate and universal plan for those who are in Christ, but also it includes the specific details for our lives. He was specifically referring to the divine details in my life—and yours.

Single Person + Praying In Tongues = Preparing For Marriage

Speaking of life's details, I'd like to tell you about revelation I received during my first Spin. It concerned marriage. As you may remember, I was praying in tongues for 24 hours and had wandered the aisles of Wal-Mart, whispering in tongues. When I got back to the church I was alone. The pastor had gone home to tend to his family before he returned to preach that morning. But me, I was single and didn't have a family to be responsible for. In the dark church I kept thinking to myself:

> *32But I want you to be without care. He who is unmarried cares for the things of the Lord—how he may please the Lord.*
> *33But he who is married cares about the things of the world—how he may please his wife.* (1 Corinthians 7:32-33 NKJV)

I am convinced that Paul was saying that the single brothers and sisters in Corinth were to make full use of their time as single people, endeavoring to please God. It is not that when we get married we have an excuse to stop pleasing God. Rather, when we are married there is another ministry that we must give time to, that of our families. Paul described bishops, preachers, and those in ministry, saying:

> ⁴*One who rules his own house well, having his children in submission with all reverence*
> ⁵*(for if a man does not know how to rule his own house, how will he take care of the church of God?)* (1 Timothy 3:4-5 NKJV)

Have you ever seen a pastor or a preacher who was dynamic behind the pulpit and yet couldn't control his family? My heart goes out to these preachers, for they surely didn't will their kid to come down with a streak of rebellion, nor did they ask that their wife or husband threaten to divorce them. Although each case is different, no matter what place a family finds itself, it is safe to say that wisdom in ruling the family would be the antidote to fix any mess, and not just to fix the mess, but to prevent the mess from happening.

One of the reasons that preachers end up in these messes is because they begin their families without ever knowing how to govern them. They dive right into marriage because Paul said, **"But if they cannot contain, let them marry: for it is better to marry than to burn"** (1 Corinthians 7:9).

Go to Bible school, and every single person on campus knows this Scripture by heart. I heard it time and time again in the dorms, "Well, my girlfriend and I are trying to stay pure. But man, things are getting hot. I am going to propose next month, and we will get married over the summer."

Sometimes I would think, "Wow, that guy is blessed."

A few years down the road, a lot of these relationships crumbled. Maybe they all didn't end in divorce, but the same guy who once had passion in his voice began speaking like he was drained. "Palmer, I probably should have waited until I was further along in ministry, or had paid off more debt."

When Paul gave those instructions to the Church at Corinth there was an assumption on his part that the single men and women had met the prerequisite to entering a successful marriage: *they had taken full advantage of their single life.* I don't mean sowing wild oats. *What I mean is spending that time to acquire the knowledge and wisdom that it takes to enter marriage and to rule your house well.*

Here is what Paul was saying in 1 Corinthians 7:32-33: "*You, who are single and desire to be married, spend your single days seeking to please the*

Lord. For when you are married, you will have a responsibility, particularly the men, to please the wives and raise the children in the way of the Lord." You can do this by hungering for the mind of God, endeavoring to be filled with His wisdom. Seek His counsel. *Begin the acquisition of this knowledge when you have time as a single person.*

Any guesses how you can get the mind of God while you are single? *You pray out mysteries until they come back revealed.* I am not saying that the person who does this will never have problems once he or she marries. *I am saying that when there are problems, there will be a whole storehouse of wisdom to access right on the spot.* During your journey of prayer, should you desire marriage, you must pray out the mystery of your marriage and family. That is part of those things that pertain to life (2 Peter 1:3).

Singles spend all their time trying to hear God tell them who Mr. or Miss Right is. "I wonder who is 'the one'? Maybe he (or she) will pass by me today." All of that will come on its own, as you are obedient to the Lord. God's hand of provision has never failed the faithful.

Dear Single Person: Instead of being fanatical about finding "the one," spend your time praying in the Holy Ghost, and building up your supply of wisdom. Paul didn't waste his time trying to be the Apostolic Date Doctor. Paul never told the single person how to find the right one. He never talked about how we should go about dating. *Dating is not even mentioned in the Bible. Neither is courting.* In Jewish days, couples were betrothed.

Paul was more concerned that single people get the mystery of Christ, and all the wisdom that it supplies, into their hearts, so that when they do step into marriage they have a foundation of power and authority. Stop focusing on dating, courting, who's the one, when will the one come along, and where will I find the one.

Stop telling people you are dating Jesus. (He doesn't want to date you. Saying that says a lot about where your revelation knowledge is). Don't make any more announcements on Facebook that you are taking a break from the opposite sex. (Nobody believes you, anyway.) All that religious garble has much to do with nothing.

Turn yourself over to the Holy Ghost and pray in the Spirit until revelation knowledge begins to flood out your hurts, pains, insecurities, fears, rejections, and old memories, so that when the man or woman of God comes along, you can be free to love, forgive, communicate, and enjoy sex with them when you get married.

When we pray in the Holy Ghost, those unfamiliar words we speak are the raw materials containing precious and intricate specifics of our personal existence. Singles would be much better off if they spent their energy giving God these raw materials than spending their energy trying to find "the one," or to protest dating.

B.) Everything that pertains to godliness: Little did I know that all of this prayer time, including the Spin I was doing, was preparing me for marriage. I was not in a gym working on my physique. I was in a spiritual classroom, building up my spirit man for the things that God held for my future and developing godliness. Notice:

> **For bodily exercise profits a little: but <u>godliness</u> is profitable unto all things, having promise of the life that now is, and of that which is to come.** (1 Timothy 4:8 KJV)

Godliness is conduct that reflects God. *The mystery of godliness* is *the process* of *how* we *become* godly. The Greek word for godliness is *eusebeia*, meaning "reverence and respect for God," an attitude that will control our behavior. The mystery or *mysterion* concerning godliness is not conduct or deportment itself, but rather, *how* we were placed into the position where we can now stand as sons and daughters of our Father, and reverence Him with honor.

Look at the "mystery of godliness" as God's finest play in His playbook for mankind. When I was a youngster, I used to play football in my backyard with all of my neighborhood friends. We would draw up plays and keep them in a little binder and memorize them. They were "top secret." If the other guys saw them, they would know how to foil our strategy. When it came time for God to redeem mankind, He ran "the mystery of godliness." Within this play are the essential elements that needed to be executed to deliver victory to mankind. As children of God, the play that God ran and the specifics of it need to be written upon or hearts. This mystery of godliness is part of what we pray forth when we are speaking in an unknown tongue.

When the mystery of godliness is revealed to us by revelation, it supercharges our own personal lives and accelerates us into our destiny. This includes our lives in marriage. God is pleased with purity, no doubt. But don't just tell young people to stay pure. That is not enough to give them a reputable single life. Go a step further and teach them to prepare for marriage by getting into the classroom of the Holy Ghost until they are ready to say, "Till death do us part."

Purity is not the only thing we should bring to the altar. How wonderful would it be for two believers to come together at the altar, both knowing the mystery of godliness, who they are in Christ, their authority as children of God, and how to bring that together in a union to rule their family and children with all love and gravity and majesty? It would certainly make a great start for a lifetime together.

The mystery of godliness was revealed to Paul:

> **And without controversy great is the mystery of godliness: God was manifested in the flesh, justified in the spirit, seen of angels, preached unto the Gentiles, believed on in the world, received up into glory.** (1 Timothy 3:16 NKJV)

The mystery of godliness is actually outlining the trail that leads us into the new birth and which will one day bring us unto glorification.

1.) *God was manifest in the flesh:* This refers to the incarnation. But, more than that, it is the execution of the plan whereby the life of God came into the world to give man the opportunity to step into the new birth, as described in John 1.

2.) *Justified in the spirit:* This was the next step that led to our born again nature. As we have already read, the light that was in Jesus went out when He took upon Himself sin and experienced spiritual death. After man's penalty had been paid and the wrath of God had been satisfied, God justified Jesus and relit Him with life. **"For as the Father hath life in himself; so hath he given to the Son to have life in himself"** (John 5:26 KJV). Jesus, having received this life, can now pass it to all those who believe in Him.

3.) *Seen of angels:* Jesus was not alone when He vanquished death through the vindication of God. Angelic beings were present when God justified Jesus and relit Him with the light that now lights every human who believes. The angels forever serve testimony that all power in heaven and earth belong to Jesus. Not only did angelic beings witness this, but Jesus, after He arose from the dead, appeared to Peter, the other eleven disciples, James (the half-brother of Jesus), Paul, and over five hundred other brethren (1 Corinthians 15:4-8 NKJV). These brethren also became "angels" or "messengers" who witnessed that He was alive with the life of God.

4.) *Preached unto the Gentiles:* This preaching was the doctrine of everything Jesus Christ, the hope of glory, has now given to us. It was heralding the "the form of doctrine" that freed us from the power of sin, and set us into righteousness. It was backed by power and demonstration and produced the faith that was necessary to bring one through the second birth.

5.) *Believed on in the world:* Receiving the message changes a person's heart and gives access to Sonship. When one hears, faith is produced, the heart believes, and the mouth confesses with certainty. When this is done in faith, the person is translated from the power of darkness, and is initiated into the Kingdom of God. (Colossians 1:13) It sets him or her on the path of righteousness and gives the potential to start the forward journey as a child of God.

6.) *Received up into glory:* This represents the completion of our salvation, which is glorification. Like Christ and the many Old Testament saints that were taken up to heaven in glorified bodies, whether we die or are translated at the moment of the rapture, we too will put on that glory. *His* glorification stands as proof that *our* glorification now awaits us (Romans 8:23, 25).

Notice that the mystery of godliness is the born again encounter: God became flesh and came as Jesus Christ. He took sin and died spiritually; the heavenly and earthly realms witnessed this. He was, and still is, preached to the entire world. People believe on Him, are initiated into the Kingdom of God, and become His children, receiving the very life and nature of God in their spirit. Finally, glorification comes, and *"so shall we ever be with the Lord"* (1 Thessalonians 4:17 KJV).

Why We Are Edified

When we are praying in tongues, we are doing something that is much deeper than warring and beating up on devils that are already under our feet. It is a waste of time to beat a dead pig. Instead, we are praying out, in a *mystery form*, every single detail that has to do with our personal lives and the mystery of godliness.

"So, I am not talking to the devil? I am not putting him in check?" No. Jesus put him in check. I had better things to do on Saturday nights than to talk to the devil. Talking to the devil is not going to edify you. Keep your mind set on God.

I did not fully realize it back then, but on those Saturday nights I was walking around and praying out whole avenues of the mystery of godliness. The knots of mysterion, compliments of the Holy Ghost, were going up to God one by one in a language I didn't understand. My spirit was getting them from the Holy Spirit, and my body was providing them with the sound that they needed to make the process of prayer complete.

The last step in the process of tongues is when the edification that is a result of praying forth the mysteries of God arrives. 2 Peter 1:3 (KJV) tells us how:

> *As His divine power* **has given** *to us all things that pertain to* **life** *and* **godliness,** *through the <u>knowledge of Him</u> who called us by glory and virtue.*

His divine power is, of course, the power that comes from the Holy Ghost (Acts 1:8). Included in this power is our heavenly prayer language in which we pray out the mystery of those things that pertain to our life and the mystery of godliness. In order for the process to be totally beneficial to us, these mysteries must come back to us in a form of revelation knowledge that we can understand. Revelation often would occur *several days, sometimes weeks or months,* after I would pray long hours in the Holy

Ghost. While reading my Bible, things would begin to jump off the page to me and take up residence in my heart. The peculiar thing about this was that it was always some amount of time *after* praying. I began discovering that this interval of time was the time it was taking for the mystery to go up and the revelation to come down.

This led me to discover the reason that we are edified when we pray in tongues. We are first praying out the mysteries of life and godliness through the inspired utterance of the Holy Ghost. When these have been spoken before God, they return as revelation knowledge that sinks into our spirits, is received by our understanding, and *edifies* our whole man. The thing that we needed to produce forward spiritual motion in God was revelation knowledge. The process of praying out *mysterion* until it came back as revelation manufactured it for us.

Yes, we may be "charging our batteries" when we pray in tongues, but this process that Paul and Peter illuminate for us tells us why. Mysteries are going up and revelation is coming down. As they say, *"What goes up must come down."*

CHAPTER FORTY

The Different Uses of Tongues

"Paul took for granted that the Corinthians understood what we now should understand: tongues function the same as any other language."

Once, I was preaching in another country for a week of revival. The pastor I was with is a wonderful gentleman and full of the Spirit of God. The very first service fell on a Sunday night, and I talked about the power of praying in tongues. The church got excited about it and you could see that people were soaking it in like a sponge. After the service, the pastor explained to me that he had halted anyone in the church from any kinds of tongues *during the service.* "Brother, I only encourage them to do it in their private time. Is this wrong?"

The humility of this pastor astounded me. He sincerely wanted to get it right. As a matter of fact, the tone in his voice told me that he knew he was wrong, but couldn't figure out from Scripture how he could make it right. This occurs when people don't pick up that there are different ways that tongues are used, including publically and privately. Fortunately, by the time that week of revival was over, the pastor and I had implemented the correction and got the congregation back to praying in tongues, both in their own prayer time *and* in service, using 1 Corinthians 14 as a guide to teach them how to be orderly.

We Are Stewards Over Our Use of Tongues

A fire hydrant is a vessel with an unseen, underground pipeline that provides it with an endless flow of water anytime it is needed. The pipeline, however, doesn't turn the fire hydrant on. The steward over the fire hydrant turns it on. In the same way, we decide when we want to speak in tongues, and when we don't.

Knowing this, Paul put up traffic lights to govern the traffic of inspired utterances. Confusion arises when tongues is not treated as a language that can be used exactly as any other language. Just as you can be disorderly with your native tongue, you can be the same way with heavenly tongues. "Are you saying that the Holy Ghost is disorderly?" Nope. If you are disorderly with tongues, *you* are being disorderly.

We have been made stewards over this language, and it is the only gift of the spirit that we can consciously use anytime that we want. Paul addresses this when he says, ***"And the spirits of the prophets are subject to the prophets"*** (1 Corinthians 14:32 NKJV). This is not only referring to prophets, but to anyone who is using inspired utterance from the Spirit of God. He is the source, and we are the vessel.

Seeking to put order into the mystic church at Corinth, Paul gave rules to monitor the use of spiritual gifts among the congregation. Even among people who speak in tongues, there is confusion as to how to enforce what Paul is saying. This chapter, 1 Corinthians 14, is one of the most argued chapters in the New Testament because Paul touches on a number of different aspects and usages of tongues without stopping to clarify them. This chapter starts to make sense when we realize that Paul took for granted that the Corinthians understood what we now should understand: tongues function the same as any other language.

Just like your native tongue, your heavenly tongue can be used to:

A.) *Pray privately* (1 Corinthians 14:2, 14): Speaking of the private function of tongues as a language that we pray with, Paul said we speak mysteries and edify (educate and enlighten) ourselves. This is not referring to a public use of tongues because when we are speaking in tongues privately and praying out the *mysterion,* we "speak into the air" (1 Corinthians 14:9). Those hearing us don't understand. The edification that will arrive in the form of revelation knowledge comes to the one doing the praying. It is beneficial to the one praying, but not to the one listening, without interpretation.

B.) Speak publicly (1 Corinthians 14:4-5): Just as we can speak in tongues privately, we can do it publicly. Speaking publicly in tongues means to *give a message* to the Church in an unknown language. This *must* be followed with an interpretation for the Church to receive edification. A message in an unknown tongue plus an inspired interpretation of what was uttered equals edification for those who are present to hear. This is exactly the same thing that happens during the private use of tongues: an inspired utterance eventually comes back understood and provides edification for the one praying. Hence, this process can happen publically in the matter of a few minutes or privately over the course of another length of time.

Those who provide inspired utterance in an unknown tongue and those who interpret publically in a known tongue are those who have been *gifted* or *graced* to do so. Not everyone in the Body of Christ will be used in this manner (1 Corinthians 12:30). Yet everyone who desires a *private* prayer language can have one, as was Paul's desire for the Corinthians (1 Corinthians 14:5).

Speaking publicly in tongues to give a message should not be confused with praying privately in tongues in a public setting. This is where my pastor friend had gotten hung up. When corporate prayer is made in the Church, there is nothing wrong with believers praying in tongues in unison. For instance, if during a prayer meeting someone is leading out in prayer in a known language, it does no harm for those joining in to pray in a known language *or* an unknown language. It does no damage for them to speak in whatever native tongue is spoken and say, "Yes, Jesus. Amen. Hallelujah. Right now, Lord. Yes!" That is just adding agreement to the prayer. Similarly, praying in tongues does no more harm. The person praying in tongues is adding their agreement in an unknown language.

Should someone who was praying in a known language get too loud and try to take over the prayer meeting, they would be out of order. The same applies to someone praying in tongues who gets out of line and becomes overbearing, to where everyone is distracted by them and can't follow the individual appointed to lead the prayer.

C.) *Sing privately or publicly* (1 Corinthians 14:15): As with any other language, we can sing with tongues. Doing so, obviously, is tongues with an inspired accompanying melody. I have been in services when someone sings in tongues and it is interpreted. I have also been in services when the worship leader is singing in English and suddenly begins singing in tongues, where it is left uninterpreted.

Once, someone asked me about this and said, "How can she do that? That's against what Paul said."

At first I thought, *Well, he does have a point.* But then I thought: *Gosh, I was blessed, though. Watching that person sing in tongues was beautiful.*

I gave it some prayer, and I discovered something. When Paul gave his list of rules for organizing inspired utterance in a service, his concern was *order.*

Now, a worship leader shouldn't make it habit of starting off in tongues while the people's attention is still on him or her (unless an interpretation is provided to produce understanding). The worship leader needs to get people engaged into God's presence, and it takes words of understanding to do this. Words of life bear witness to something in people's hearts and produce an excitement and love for God that will lead them into God's presence.

As I thought back on the service, there were at least a couple thousand people in that service with their hands in the air and their eyes closed, worshipping God. Many of the same people were worshipping God in tongues.

Then it dawned on me. Though we worship corporately, worship never ceases to be a personal, one-on-one interaction with God. If the corporate worship is successful, you may be in a place with thousands of people, but everything else will fade away, and it will be you and Jesus, alone in the midst of the crowd. That can lead you to enter privately into praising and lifting up Jesus with your heavenly language.

The failure was not that the worship leader was singing in tongues; most of the congregation was worshipping in tongues in their own hearts. *The failure was on the part of my friend who noticed. His own self-righteousness and religiosity kept him from entering into that place of private devotion to God.*

Just as we can sing publicly in tongues, we can sing privately in tongues. I remember one morning I woke up and, from the moment my eyes opened, I was full of joy and excitement toward God. All during the time I was in the shower and getting dressed, I was singing in the Spirit *and* singing in English. It is a good combination. I was full of spiritual exuberance. Ideas and visions were flowing into my spirit, and I could feel faith rising the more I sang. I thought: *Gosh. I haven't even had my coffee yet. This isn't a caffeine kick. God is moving in my belly.*

When things settled down in me, I desired an answer. I said in my heart, "God, those songs I was singing in the Spirit and in English, they sounded so beautiful." Without saying more or asking God a question concerning it, the Holy Ghost quickened a verse to me.

> **The Lord thy God in the midst of thee is mighty; he will save, he will rejoice over thee with joy; he will rest in his love, he will rejoice over thee with singing.** (Ephesians 3:17 KJV)

Immediately, a memory flashed in my mind, taking me back to when I was a boy about four or five years old. There was a storm going on in the middle of the night. I woke up in my bed, and I was petrified. I called for my parents in terror and gnawed on my bedpost as I waited for one of them to come reassure me that everything was all right. My dad came and picked me up. He held me while the lighting and thunder crashed, and I could hear him singing some kind of melody that brought so much peace and comfort that it put me right back to sleep.

Then, my memory flashed forward. During a difficult time in college, I found myself actually singing the song that my dad had sung when I was scared of the storm. That song had buried itself into my understanding and had become a source of edification and elevation for me. As I remembered all these things, I could hear myself singing the song.

Here is the lesson: *I realized that the Lord was teaching me one more thing about this father/son relationship.* The Lord said to me: "Son, when you wake up with a song in your heart it is because your spirit has picked up on the song that I was singing over you while you were sleeping. These songs contain my thoughts toward you. They are songs of healing, joy, peace, and they describe the world that is going on inside of Me. When you sing them out, they release victory in your life." When I discovered this I made it a point never to hold back a song from God. I may not be the greatest singer, but I am always singing in my heart.

> *¹⁸Be filled with the Spirit,*
> *¹⁹speaking to one another in psalms and hymns and*
> *spiritual songs, singing and making melody in your*
> *heart to the Lord.* (Ephesians 5:18-19 NKJV)

When these songs are inspired in your native tongue, write them down. New songs that are sung in churches often come as a result of a song that was heard privately. If the song first comes in an unknown tongue, sing it out. At some point (while you are singing or afterwards) ask God for the interpretation of it. This will enable more than just your spirit to be fruitful, as the interpretation will enrich your understanding. Then you can share this song with others so that it can be a blessing to them as well.

D.) *Bless a meal privately* (1 Corinthians 14:16): This Scripture says we should not pray in tongues to bless our meal *with others present.* The concern was that the others present could not understand what was being said, plus they wouldn't know when the prayer was over so they could say Amen. (That sounds like a joke, but it isn't. Look it up.)

Someone usually asks at this point, "So when I am by myself can I pray in tongues to bless my food?" Of course, you can. If you bless a meal in tongues it works. Just be mindful not to do it when others are around. Paul went on to say, *"For you indeed give thanks <u>well,</u> but <u>the other [person] is not edified</u>"* (1 Corinthians 14:17 NKJV). Because tongues are generally an unknown utterance, the use of them at dinner with others present would require an interpreter for them to be beneficial, and it is inappropriate.

E.) *Convict an unbeliever of Jesus* (1 Corinthians 14:22): This operation of tongues can happen when an unbeliever is present who speaks a different language from that which is being spoken. ***"Wherefore tongues are for a sign, not to them that believe, but to them that believe not"*** (1 Corinthians 14:22 KJV). A believer, under the unction—or prompting—of the Holy Ghost, would speak forth in a tongue that is unknown to him, but known to the unbeliever present. For instance, if the believer speaks English and knows no other language, by unction of the Spirit, he may supernaturally start speaking Russian. It might happen that an unbeliever who speaks Russian would be present and hear him, knowing full well that the speaker doesn't know Russian.

"Yes, Chris, but what would he be saying?" you might ask. According to Scripture, under this usage of divine utterance, the speaker could be doing two things:

1.) *Preaching the Gospel:* ***"We do hear them speak in our tongues the wonderful works of God"*** (Acts 2:11 KJV*).*
2.) *Giving a word of knowledge concerning something in the person's life that could not have been known except for by a divine revelation:* ***"And thus the secrets of his [the unbeliever's] heart are revealed"*** (1 Corinthians 14:25 NKJV).

F.) *Privately edify a believer* (1 Corinthians 14:13): I have noticed that in my personal life that revelation and edification arrive in three ways:

1.) *A spark of revelation from the Word of God* (Romans 16:25): After I pray privately in tongues, the Word of God seems to animate itself in a way that is very strong. It has been so strong at times that my mind cannot keep up with the revelation that is being pumped into my spirit. The peculiar and astonishing thing about this is that often the revelation is a shade different than what I previously held onto. The animation from certain Scriptures does not match what I thought they meant in the past.

The Holy Ghost told me: "Son, let me teach you. If you allow your preconceived ideas concerning this Scripture to block the revelation that I am sending you, then the truths will remain locked."

The first thing that the Holy Ghost starts dealing with when you pray in tongues is your doctrine. Nothing assists meditation more than praying in the Spirit. Praying in the Spirit will launch richer meditation that will break you free from any error you may have picked up from well-intentioned teachers. This error, whether you knew it or not, happens to be one of the greatest limitations that stunted your forward progress in God.

At first, the greatest challenge I encountered was letting go of what I previously thought a verse meant. Because the Holy Ghost was teaching me the longer I held onto the wrong meaning of a verse, the stronger the unction became to let go of it.

What is unction? It is a prompting that carries with it a knowing. It is simply intuition, accompanied often times with grieving, gut aggravation, and earnestness. So the Holy Ghost was *strongly* prompting me to let go of my error.

As soon as I let go, revelation would come from that verse and provide great power to my walk with God.

2.) *A private interpretation of tongues:* I have found that when I need immediate edification, exhortation, or comfort, there is grace in the form of unction to interpret the tongues that I am praying out. In this interpretation, God reveals specific plans concerning my life and the assignment that I now have as a minister of reconciliation, born of the new birth.

Interpretation of tongues could be one of the most under-used gifts available in the Church today. Pastors would benefit their congregations by patiently encouraging them to begin interpreting tongues in their own private times. Privately praying and interpreting tongues help to strengthen the working of the utterance gifts in our life, and builds our confidence while we are operating in them.

This kind of operation never fails to produce clarity regarding some matter. You will notice that when a true manifestation of tongues and interpretation is brought forth, carrying the revelation of some mystery, it will always leave a solemn residue of worship and reverence. These are marks that testify that God has just spoken and has released to you some of His mind.

When making key decisions, private tongues and interpretation can be relied on as a help. I have made some great decisions because I first took the time to get quiet before God, pray in tongues, allow the interpretation, and follow it through.

> *3.) A vision or flashing image:* Revelation through visions, tongues and interpretation, and reading the Word are all methods whereby God *reveals* His Word to us. All too often believers get stuck on the *means* by which God releases His mind to us. *What is important is that we are receiving His mind, not how it comes.*

Visions are a way that we can receive revelation knowledge that drives us forward down our path as children of God. Visions are great when they come from God. Unfortunately, many Christians have gone to great lengths to conjure up visions because they can then be perceived as being "deep" and "mystical."

Although there are several different kinds of visions, the one that occurs the most is like a flash that goes off on the inside. The flash instantly imprints a picture inside of my spirit and then disappears. This not only happens when I am reading and studying the Word of God but, many times, when I am not even being mindful of spiritual things.

"Why do you think that is, Chris?"

Our prayer lives are not relegated to the hours that we set apart to talk to God. Prayer, in its simplest definition, is communication with God. True fellowship makes it possible for God to speak to us at any moment He chooses. When I have a flash of revelation from my Heavenly Father there is no difference than if my earthly father decided to send me a text message. There is a continual fellowship that is not limited by time. *Part of what makes a great relationship is the element of spontaneity. Religion has come in and tried to do away with any kind of spontaneity because religion desires to control, and spontaneity cannot be tamed.*

Once I was driving in my truck with the windows rolled down, and I was having a conversation with the Lord in my heart. "Lord, why do you often talk in pictures to me? It seems as though whenever I ask you something you answer with an image that I haven't seen or known before. What's the reason for this?"

Do you know what came after that? An image. As odd as it may seem, in a split second, I saw a basketball rim flash before me. And I had the answer!

Allow me to explain. Within that flashing image, I noticed that the rim was orange. It wasn't just any kind of orange, though. It was the shade of orange that one sees on professional basketball rims. Then an understanding came into my heart that explained everything to me. My spirit got the answer from God in *image form*.

In order to explain it, my mind has to give words to the image because humans cannot communicate by sending images back and forth to each other. This is what the conversation sounded like between God and me in *word form*.

God: "Son, what color is that rim?"

Me: "Orange."

God: "What kind of orange?"

Me: "The kind of orange used on a basketball rim."

God: "If you were trying to describe this orange to someone who has never seen a basketball rim, how would you describe it?"

Me: "I wouldn't be able to, Lord."

God: "Now you see why I send images. Imagery is the highest form of communication. Words are used to produce images, usually unsatisfactorily. I am not limited to words. I can send the image."

When God put it that way I was blown away. Some of the greatest things I have ever heard God say to me have come in *image form*. This is not to say that God doesn't speak in words, however. It just goes to show that God is not limited to them, or by them.

G) *Groan:* The most powerful use of tongues in all of Scripture is groanings. This is the use of tongues mentioned in Romans 8:26 (KJV):

> *Likewise the Spirit also helpeth our infirmities: for we know not what we should pray for as we ought: but the Spirit itself maketh intercession for us with groanings which cannot be uttered.*

Groanings are a form of praying in the Spirit that can be classified with all the other operations because it is being done with the Holy Ghost's help. The word literally means, "to sigh with grief." For as long as I have been praying in the Spirit, I have noticed that groanings do not happen as frequently as the other functions. Up to this point in my life, I have only groaned four or five times.

"Well, what is the purpose of these groanings?" you might ask.

The true definition of the word tells us. Groanings occur as a result of grief that comes alongside of praying in the Spirit. The real question, then, is not what is causing the groan, but what is causing the grief. When you are groaning, the mystical part about it is that, although you are experiencing the grief, what is *causing* the grief is usually hidden. I have observed that it is not until *after* I am done groaning that the cause of grief is revealed to me. A few things that could cause grief are:

1.) *Travail:* Travail is the pain that comes because of childbirth. When you are praying this, the intensity of it can throw you into groanings just like a woman who is giving birth to her child. When travail in prayer comes, this means that something is being born by the Spirit. This is one reason why groanings are such a high form of prayer. *The manifestation of the thing that you are praying is right at the tip of the womb. The crown of the head is pushing from the realm of the spirit into the natural. It is the final push toward the birth of what God wants to get over to you.*

Churches and ministries have exploded from being small into huge growth after a night of travail. Financial breakthroughs have come, and debts have been paid because of travail. I believe that one of the quickest ways to grow in any venture that God tells you to undertake (a business pursuit, ministry, etc.) is to have committed prayer partners who actually know how to pray and can recognize travail when it comes. My ministry grew a huge step when God sent me two women who *know* how to pray and have had experience with travailing.

Notice this about travail:

> a.) *A woman doesn't give birth to a baby every day:* People who claim to travail every day cause me to raise an eyebrow. Travailing occurs only as the Spirit wills. I know this because, unlike praying in tongues for edification, I can't steward into it whenever I want to.
>
> b.) *Travail needs to be carried out to the end:* It doesn't do you any good to travail halfway through. God awards no points to a person who just travails until they think it is time to stop. Travailing is not the end; it is a means to the end. When the baby is born, travail will cease. You will know when travail comes over you, and you will know when it leaves. Because you are praying by the Spirit, you will not have to work yourself into it or get out of it. Your only job is to yield yourself to it.
>
> c.) *Joy comes when travail is over:* Although travail begins with grief and sorrow, it always ends with joy. Whether or not you understand what you were giving birth to, you will have just as much joy knowing that it has finally been born. Travail will leave you exhausted and tired, but you will rejoice with exceeding joy when the Lord places the end result in your arms.

2.) *Intercession:* To intercede means to act on the behalf of someone who is troubled. It also means to act as mediator in reconciliation between two parties. Intercession is different from just praying for people. The word gets tossed around and has become so vague that it has lost the sharpness of its meaning.

When I am praying to the Lord and asking the Lord to bless someone, prosper and increase him or her, I am *supplicating* for them (Ephesians 6:18). To supplicate means to ask by humble entreaty. I am asking God to do something for someone who is probably not in severe trouble. Yes, they may need something, but there is no severe suffering on the horizon if something doesn't change quickly.

However, when intercession hits, the praying person is now acting on behalf of someone who is *in danger.*

These dangers include:

> a.) *Going to hell:* True intercession comes when God's people are continually praying for the lost and unsaved to come into the Kingdom. Churches do not meet enough to pray for the unsaved. There needs to be a reawakening in the Church that intercession on the behalf of the unsaved will break the powers of darkness that are blinding them and deliver them into the hands of the Kingdom of Light.

Though preaching finalizes the work, the intercession behind the preaching is what prepares the hearts of those who hear, and softens the soil so that the seed of God's Word can be received. I have dozens of stories about people who have suddenly been compelled to pray for someone who is lost. This compelling comes in many forms, including dreams of the lost person being in hell, or a sudden impulse to pray for someone, or a constant bugging to *keep* praying for someone, day after day after day.

One time, our church had a Friday night prayer meeting to pray for our country, state, city, and church body. As was usual with protocol, the staff ministers took turns leading out the prayer, while the congregation prayed in the Holy Ghost or however the Spirit led them. My bishop motioned to me to go up on stage and start praying. As I was walking up to the stage I didn't feel anything at all. And that was okay. I was going to lead out in fervent prayer regardless of how I felt.

Not five minutes into prayer something came over me so strongly that I hunched over and could hardly speak. The Spirit of God was kicking in. The whole time I was on stage, I was groaning and crying and weeping. I was experiencing grief. This was supernatural prayer. *Usually, the kind of emotions that you feel while you are groaning will indicate to you what you are praying for.* Because of the kind of praying that the congregation was doing, I am certain that I was groaning on the behalf of those who are lost in the world, particularly other countries and nations. I felt helpless and lost. It was a miserable feeling. This is because I was taking the place of the lost and was praying on their behalf.

Later, in my heart I asked the Lord why the groanings came on me so quickly. It was interesting what the Lord shared. He said, "I was using you to give birth to the thing that the church had been corporately praying out for hours." This again proved to me that although we are stewards over praying in tongues, we cannot be stewards over groanings. They come only as the Spirit wills.

> b.) *In harm's way:* Being in harm's way is another aspect of intercession that will produce grief and cause one to groan. Because someone can be in danger at any moment, the Spirit of intercession may come on you when you least expect it. It can, in fact, get so strong it could launch you into groanings. If anyone has ever had groanings, they will tell you that they are not desirable unless you consider the outcome they produce. The times I have sensed them coming on, I have thought, *Here we go.* Should this happen, you can kiss your plans for the night goodbye. This is our duty as the Body of Christ, though.

When I say intercession, intercede, or intercessor, people often think of the lady at church who waves pastel flags while spinning herself into circles. Whatever impression you have in your mind concerning what "intercession" is, put it on the shelf for a second.

Intercession carries a stigma. People think it means to pray for a long, long, long, long, long time without a break. As a kid, when I went to church they'd announce, "Well, come out on Sunday nights an hour before church for intercessory prayer." I never liked going. The senior pastor would pace up and down, drawing out his "Oh, hallelujah," with a deep baritone voice twenty or thirty times. Then, there always seemed to be the "chief intercessor." It was *always* a woman. The lead dog never runs alone, however. She would have two other women with her, and they'd come in and kick up quite the prayer storm. I purposely tried avoiding these ladies because they always tried to look through me to see what sin I was hiding.

While everyone was walking around with solemn faces, I'd be thinking, "Gosh, I sure am hungry. Maybe dad will take us out to eat tonight." I'd look over at my brother, and he'd be doodling a stick figure on the church bulletin. This was my first impression of "intercessory" prayer.

Sadly, I am sure there are many people who can relate to this. If that is you, let it go right now. I desire to bring you into the real meaning of intercession, and I promise you it won't be anything similar.

To intercede also means to act on the behalf of someone who is in trouble, with a petition or pleading. It is a humbling responsibility.

The very definition implies a few things:

i.) At least two parties must be involved
ii.) One party is in trouble
iii.) The other party or parties are not

At the end of 2007, I learned a hard lesson concerning intercession. To this day it remains a lesson that I wish I could have learned the easy way. To understand exactly what happened, we must go back to 2005 while I was sitting in my dorm room. Like any college student, I had plans. I wanted to go out for the night to improve my social standing as a college junior. As I was getting ready, a sense of hopelessness came over me. I felt something was wrong. I took a quick inventory of my life and thought: *Hmm, nope, nothing wrong. Not in sin. Not in unforgiveness. Everything is great.*

Then it dawned on me, "Uh oh. Someone else isn't great." I didn't want to start praying though. I had just finished putting gel in my hair. I couldn't blatantly ignore God, though. So I did what we all do at times; I tried to convince myself it wasn't God.

"Oh, no, Chris," I said to myself, "This isn't God. This is your hormones and your mood that is making you feel this way. It is a full moon outside tonight. You know what they say about that. The gravitational pull affects how you feel." I look back on this and cannot believe all that I conjured up to soothe my conscience so I could go out and have fun.

Well, as soon as I got in that night, the Father was waiting for me. "Son," He said in a gentle tone, "that was Me speaking to you tonight. Someone was in trouble and my Spirit was looking for someone to pray. I seek intercessors because I love my children and I don't want any danger to befall them." I was humiliated. "Chris, it is okay. I found another intercessor. However, the next time I speak to you concerning someone who needs intercession, stop whatever you are doing and pray." That was all that I heard the Lord say.

I fell to my knees and repented, and asked the Lord to forgive me. I stood up and took out a new red pen and the brand new Bible I had just bought. I wrote on the cover page of my Bible, "When God tells you to intercede for someone, stop what you are doing and pray right then." I committed to God and to myself that I would never again make this mistake. One day, I might be the one who needs the intercession, and I would desire someone to sacrifice their evening to intercede for me, even if it meant that they spent the night groaning instead of eating sushi with their friends.

About two years later, I had a similar encounter. The difference was that in this instance, my previous failure had taught me a valuable lesson, or at least, it *should* have taught me a valuable lesson.

It was a Friday afternoon, and I was off work. I had plans for the evening and was tidying my room before I went out for the night. At this point in my life I was a full time minister working sometimes sixty hours a week, doing one-on-one ministry with hurting people. It was a challenge not to be selfish during my days off. As I was putting the comforter back on my bed, I thought of an old friend from my sophomore year in college. I thought, *Wow, I haven't thought of Rick since I graduated.* Then I began to think about how Rick and I used to lift weights together in our dorm and how he tried to teach me to play the guitar.

Being spiritual, I then realized: "Why would I just randomly think of Rick? This is the Spirit of God talking to me. I need to pray for Rick." You would think that the next thing I did was to get on my knees and start interceding on his behalf, right? Wrong. I finished folding my comforter, took a shower, and ventured off for an evening of leisure. I reasoned: "Why would God ask *me* to pray for Rick? I am doing sixty hours a week of ministry. I can only pray for so many people in a week. It probably wasn't even God. He should find someone else if Rick needs prayer." Yet, "someone else" didn't have a Bible with a red-inked commitment to pray the moment God told him to. I had made that commitment. Surely, if serious business was going on, God could trust me. Right?

Friday night came and went, as did Saturday. As usual, I got up at 5:00 a.m. on Sunday morning to get ready for church. I suddenly had a hunch to check my Facebook. Now, I never check my Facebook before service; I rarely have time to put on my belt, let alone see the latest status updates. The little red icon notified me that I had a message. I eagerly opened it up to discover that it was from someone I wasn't expecting. "Why is Barry Manchester Facebooking me? I haven't talked to that guy in a couple of years."

As my eyes scrolled through the message they became as wide as saucers, and my legs turned to rubber as I read these words: "Palmer, I found out this afternoon that Rick was killed two nights ago in a car accident. Sorry to tell you this way, but I thought you might want to know. Funeral is Monday in Oregon. Be praying for his wife and family."

I was devastated. It was surreal. This was the first friend I had ever lost. My heart broke for his wife, his family, and for him. When the initial shock ended, through the fog appeared the words, *"two nights ago."* Two nights ago I was putting the comforter on my bed and preparing for a night of fun. When feeling came back into my hands, I was holding something. It was the Bible where I had imprinted my commitment to God in red pen just a few years before.

Although I don't blame myself for Rick's death, I do know this: I believe my intercession could have prevented it. On November 18th, 2007, I learned a hard lesson about prayer. A lesson I will never need to be taught again.

When we signed up for God's Army, His expectations and requirements were no different from the United States Army: your whole life. In order for us to stay on the path of life and continue going down the straight and narrow, we need other believers to pray by the Spirit and intercede for us. The wiles, schemes, and plans of the devil make this absolutely necessary. We cannot afford *not* to pray for our brothers and sisters when we sense danger gathering around their lives.

> *H.) Help our infirmities (weaknesses)* (Romans 8:26): I still find this amazing each time I consider it. After writing all that he did on our victory over sin through Christ, righteousness, and the new nature, Paul *still* had the audacity and gall to tell us that we have some form of an infirmity (weakness).

Hyper grace doctrines don't like to consider this aspect of God's Word. They would rather sweep it under the rug and think that everything is just peachy. But Paul made it a point to insert it into his writing to let us know that even after receiving Sonship, we need help.

"Well, Brother Chris, what do you mean? I give in the offering plate. I was in my Christmas production at church. I don't swear or drink. Why on earth would I need help?"

Because you have a mortal shell that has death working in it. God Himself said that you need help with it. That is why He gave you the Holy Ghost. If you are a tightwad (or are in financial fear) and only put a few bucks into the offering plate every so often, He has come to break you of that. If you are afraid of flying, He has come to help you overcome the fear. If you just went through a break-up and don't know if you can live without that special someone, He has been given to strip you of the emotion that is messing up your perception.

Here is how it works. There you are, walking the path of righteousness, evolving as a child of God. You are going to church and hearing the Word, which is producing faith in your life. You are staying pretty consistent in your Bible study time and are learning to share your faith with confidence. All of this is producing revelation and is powering your forward motion.

Then, all of a sudden, the problem of a lifetime comes along. You turn to the concordance in your Bible, but you don't find a topic that says, "I lost my job." Your pastor gives you a list of "prosperity scriptures," and you start confessing them every day while you sit at your kitchen table, while no revenue comes in. The hours turn to days, the days turn to months, and the months turn into a year, and you still have no job. Your "prosperity scriptures" collected too much food on them, and you threw them out three months ago. You think, "What did I do wrong? Why don't I have a job yet? This stuff doesn't work."

Here is the real problem: you have an infirmity (weakness). The infirmities/weaknesses are the limitations that have been imposed upon you by your mortality and which are dominating your thinking. Like a volcano that spews molten lava, your brain is spitting up negativity. It is withering your emotions and caking them in unbelief. The only difference between the guy who *just* got his pink slip and the guy who lost his job *a year ago* is the thickness of the unbelief.

Instead of enjoying the preaching, you now are annoyed with it. This is partly because 1.) It worked for the preacher (as far as you know), and it isn't working for you, 2.) You still know that it is true.

So this leads you to the one thought that cripples your pride: *I* must have done something wrong. Yes, *you* did. In the middle of all that time and all those confessions, did you employ the Helper? Was it *you* trying to make the Word work? Or were you turning yourself over to the Holy Ghost and allowing *Him* to make it work for you?

"How can I know?" Very simple: When the Holy Ghost begins to get under the hood and *intercedes* on your behalf, He works internally, inside of you. Notice the verse tells us that He intercedes *against the infirmity, not the circumstance. The Holy Ghost isn't going to change the circumstance.* You are still currently out of a job. People sit on their hands and wait for their blessing to show up, and it never does. It isn't the thousands of places that won't hire you. It isn't your educational background. It isn't because you are white or black. It isn't because you are too young or too old.

It is because you have an infirmity in your flesh that needs to be eradicated, and you've refused to employ the Helper to rip it out.

In this case, the jam is *unbelief* that someone will hire you. The Holy Ghost works on the jam inside us, caused by our mortality, that is keeping the circumstance from changing. "How come my confessions didn't work?" Confessions don't do a thing for God. He would move on your behalf the first time you confessed something, *if you truly believed* it. But you began confessing with *a root of unbelief.* As long as that root gives life to your confession, the more you avow, the more unbelief muddies your emotions. What you need is *help.* You need a spiritual gardener to come along, stick His hands in there, and jerk that root right out of your life.

One time, I was having a difficulty that I couldn't overcome myself. As I was meditating I saw a vision of what looked to be a guy in an oily mechanic's coverall. He wore a grimy hat and work boots, and there was a dirty red rag sticking out of his back pocket. He was looking through a set of blueprints. I looked at him, and he smiled and said, "Hey, I was thinking you should let me help you. What I have here is the set of blueprints to your life. I actually have identified the problem, and I am willing to fix it for you, free of charge. It will only take a second. What do you say?"

I started laughing. I immediately realized Who this dirty mechanic was who had come to assist and intercede for me. "You're hired!" I said. With that, I began praying in the Holy Ghost.

CHAPTER FORTY-ONE

Our Place in the Body

"If I am ever tempted to get an inflamed head about my title and position, this experience acts like a needle, deflating my ego and reminding me what being a "minister" really is."

The marvelous book of Ephesians sheds a colossal light on the Church of Jesus Christ corporately, and on the individual believer who is a part of that Body. This chapter is key because you will recognize yourself in one of the ministries that Paul defines and, hopefully, learn how to magnify your gifts and talents to the Body of Christ.

While the books of Romans and Galatians happen to be different shades of the same revelation—the righteousness of faith—Ephesians sets forth revelatory truths for the organization of the Church, the Body of Christ. This is the heart of the leadership set up to guide the Church of Jesus Christ:

> *⁸Wherefore he saith, When he ascended up on high, he led captivity captive, and gave gifts unto men.*
>
> *¹¹And he gave some, apostles; and some, prophets; and some, evangelists; and some, pastors and teachers.*
> (Ephesians 4:8, 11 KJV)

In Ephesians, Paul gives the titles of these ministries: apostles, prophets, evangelists, pastors, and teachers. In 1 Corinthians 12:28, Paul reiterates them; including other ministries that he did not mention in the list in Ephesians.

> *²⁷Now ye are the body of Christ, and members in particular.*
> *²⁸And God hath set some in the church, first apostles, secondarily, prophets, thirdly teachers, after that miracles, then gifts of healings, helps, governments, diversities of tongues.* (1 Corinthians 12:27-28 KJV)

After we are born again, we will eventually enter into one or more of these ministries to assist the Body of Christ. God does not want His people to be passive. Instead, He desires for us to begin filling these positions. Every one of us can expect that God has selected us by His grace to at least one of these, as we will see (Romans 12:6). Fulfilling what God has called us to is based upon our cooperation with our Helper. To the degree that we fulfill, or fail to fulfill, what God has elected us to will determine our heavenly reward (Romans 14:12). Therefore it is necessary to discover what ministry we are called to fulfill and figure out how to enter into it.

Variety of Gifts

Apostles: An apostle is a special ambassador of the Gospel. Apostles are an envoy or delegate especially appointed by the King, sent forth with orders to carry out. The authority that an apostle carries is not in word only. Rather it is demonstrated in patience, signs, wonders, and mighty deeds (2 Corinthians 12:12). Patience, because apostles are given difficult assignments and have to endure much; signs, because apostles are to present infallible proof that Jesus is alive; wonders, to confound the wisdom of those who challenge their message; and mighty deeds, to give validity that what they are preaching is, indeed, the Truth.

Apostolic authority comes one way: from having been with Jesus. There is no other way to get it. Notice:

> *Now when they saw the boldness of Peter and John, and perceived that they were unlearned and ignorant men, they marveled; and they took knowledge of them, that they had been with Jesus.* (Acts 4:13 KJV)

> *After that, he [Jesus] was seen of James; then of all the*
> *apostles.* (1 Corinthians 15:7 KJV)

If the election of grace has chosen one to the apostolic office, one will have deeper encounters with Jesus Christ that result in a tremendous amount of authority that cannot be hidden. This authority will be the fuel that guides one to start works, train ministers, disciple the Body of Christ, and influence people of importance.

Prophets: Prophets are the mouthpieces of God. They are moved by the Spirit of God and speak that which *currently* is on the mind of God. Their inspired utterances carry behind them a weight that does more than inform and provide instruction. Their words pierce the hearts of men and create change. The result is a shift in the atmosphere.

God sends these specially anointed oracles to demonstrate the nearness and reality of His Kingdom. Because prophets declare the mind of God, they are graced to foretell future happenings and disclose past events. When a prophet is finished doing that which God has graced him or her to do, their ministry leaves a residue of the fear of God. When I have witnessed the prophetic ministry in motion, there was more than just foretelling going on. People began returning to their first love again, as the ministry of the prophet installed back into them a true reverence for the Lord. The prophetic ministry is like a blacksmith's fire that purifies the vessels that it reaches. Notice the following Scripture that gives insight into the ministry of the prophet:

> *23And it shall come to pass, that every soul, which will*
> *not hear that prophet, shall be destroyed from among*
> *the people.*
> *24Yea, and all the prophets from Samuel and those that*
> *follow after, as many as have spoken, have likewise*
> *foretold of these days.* (Acts 3:23-24 KJV)

In this verse we see the prophets' ministry speaking forth the mind of God, urging people to realign with God's ways, and foretelling future events. Though death is oftentimes unlikely the result of failure to hear a prophet, if one gives a warning and it is ignored, there are usually consequences, sometimes severe. Thank God for this ministry, as it serves as eyes, ears, and mouth to help the Body of Christ along the journey.

Evangelists: Paul does not cite evangelists and pastors by name, but defines them by description. Notice the textbook example of Philip: this is what an evangelist looks like from Scripture. Philip was the only one in the entire Bible specifically called an evangelist. Paul told Timothy to **"*do the work* of an evangelist"** (2 Timothy 4:5 KJV), but there is a difference between the *work* of an evangelist and a bona fide evangelist. Philip is bona fide:

> *On the next day we who were Paul's companions departed and came to Caesarea, and entered the house of <u>Philip the evangelist</u>.* (Acts 21:8 NKJV)

Philip was called an evangelist because, more than simply *doing the work* of an evangelist, he stood in that office within God's government. As a result of his office and his willingness to yield to this office, notice what happened in his ministry:

> *⁵Then Philip went down to the city of Samaria and preached Christ to them.*
> *⁶And the multitudes with one accord heeded the things spoken by Philip, hearing and seeing the miracles which he did.*
> *⁷For unclean spirits, crying with a loud voice, came out of many who were possessed; and many who were paralyzed and lame were healed.* (Acts 8:5-7 NKJV)

One more story is given concerning Philip the evangelist and an Ethiopian eunuch, a man of great power who held all authority over his queen's treasury. The eunuch had come to Jerusalem to worship, yet was confused. He was just sitting in his chariot, reading the Book of Isaiah, and scratching his head as to the meaning. And God took this moment to send Philip, the evangelist, to preach Jesus to the eunuch:

> *³⁵Then Philip opened his mouth, and beginning at this Scripture, preached Jesus to him*
> *³⁶Now as they went down the road, they came to some water. And the eunuch said, "See, here is water. What hinders me from being baptized?"*
> *³⁷Then Philip said, "If you believe with all your heart, you may." And he answered and said, "I believe that Jesus Christ is the Son of God."*
> *³⁸So he commanded the chariot to stand still. And both Philip and the eunuch went down into the water, and he baptized him.*
> *³⁹Now when they came up out of the water, the Spirit of the Lord caught Philip away, so that the eunuch saw him no more; and he went on his way rejoicing.* (Acts 8:35-39 NKJV)

Scripturally, a bona fide evangelistic ministry is not *just* about exhorting people to be saved. That is the ministry of exhortation or an exhorter (Romans 12:8).

A true evangelist preaches Jesus, *and* he or she has a steady pipeline of miracles, signs, wonders, and marvels that deliver people from bondage, prepare the soil for the Word to be planted in a deeper measure, advance the Kingdom, and break up the darkness over a particular region. When Paul mentions "miracles" in 1 Corinthians 12:28, he was giving the entry-level characteristic that designates a true evangelist from one just doing the *work* of the evangelist, occasionally.

Perhaps an illustration would bring understanding. Consider a farmer. Each day he works in his field and is an expert at agriculture and cultivation. His expertise is so extensive he could teach the ins and outs of his trade to anyone who wanted to learn.

Should, however, someone help the farmer irrigate his field for a day, it would not designate the helper to be a farmer. He would just have done the *work* of a farmer for that particular moment, or maybe even for a season.

Bringing good tidings and preaching Jesus, *through the supernatural power of God*, is the ultimate work and end of the evangelist. But it can be performed by those who are not evangelists, according to 2 Timothy 4:5

(remember that Timothy was a pastor), hence making it the *work* of an evangelist. One simply doing the work of an evangelist heralds the gospel and sees intermittent miracles. *A true evangelist has a regular flow of miracles and can teach and lead others into doing the work of the evangelist.*

Pastors and Teachers: Pastor and teacher is another designation that Paul doesn't mention by name in 1 Corinthians 12:28. Rather, he describes another entry-level qualification of the pastor/teacher office: *gifts of healings.*

James is the greatest example of a New Testament pastor and teacher that we have in Scripture. He was the half-brother of Jesus, and pastor of the church in Jerusalem. He also knew something about healing. He said, *"Is anyone among you sick? Let him call for the elders of the church, and let them pray over him, anointing him with oil in the name of the Lord. And the prayer of faith will save the sick, and the Lord will raise him up"* (James 5:14-15 NKJV). One thing is for certain: James didn't fight against gifts of healings as many denominational pastors do today. As a matter of fact, he preached, taught, and practiced healing.

Once, in the spirit of false humility, a pastor/teacher of a big church confided to me, "I've had awful experiences in praying for sick people. I tell my congregants that it is better for them to stay away from me, because they are more likely to die than get healed if I pray for them." Then he chuckled, and continued on with his academic discourse about how to conduct a ministry. The whole time he talked I was thinking: "This guy has got to be kidding. Who would say such a thing? That is exactly why nobody gets healed when he prays for them; he doesn't believe." I would never recommend that anyone sit under a pastor/teacher who has not learned healing and how it works.

Although *gifts of healing* work in all the offices, it is beyond doubt an entry-level gift that allows a pastor/teacher to function in his or her responsibilities, *especially since a pastor/teacher has the greatest contact with people.* I believe that when God calls a pastor/teacher, he or she will be graced to function with this specific gift. God's desire is that this gift should not come and go. He gave it, and He desires for it to stay and work consistently.

Many believers think that is selfish to be concerned about healing. Well, a lot of those believers pay good money for medication, too. Maybe the next time they get sick, they should sell their medicine and give the proceeds to the poor, since it is selfish to want to be well.

"Are you saying that every pastor/teacher should operate in gifts of healings?"

To my ear that sounds like, "Are you saying that every doctor should know something about medicine, and work to get people well?"

James, the great pastor/teacher, believed healing so much that his ministerial staff was trained, not just in healing, but also in *expecting* to see healing manifested when they prayed the prayer of faith. More pastors/teachers today need to have this same spirit of faith that the apostles carried and walked in (2 Corinthians 4:13). Think of all the people who come into church as visitors, knowing nothing about Jesus, and needing healing. Think about all the elders who need a touch from God as they age. Think of people in the pain of dysfunctional relationships who need inner healing. *Though the gifts of healings certainly can function in the membership, it will function in a greater way if it first begins to function in the pastor/teacher.*

With this new perspective, as we read 1 Corinthians 12:28 we now notice the mention of apostles, prophets, evangelists, pastors and teachers, as well as three other ministries of the body that are not given in Ephesians 4. These are *governments*, *helps*, and *diversities of tongues*.

Governments: This refers to guidance and steering through administration. This organizational aptitude qualifies a person for leadership. "Governments" is a word used for individuals who have been given wisdom and judgment to manage the Body of Christ. This is not an office; it is a description of something that works within an office, like gifts of healings. It is seen in the apostle, prophet, evangelist, and pastor/teacher. Even before one enters these offices, governments begin developing in them while they are learning the foundation of ministry as a deacon, elder, minister, and/or preacher—four functions that oftentimes come before one takes upon him or herself one of the offices listed in Ephesians 4.

Deacons and Elders, Ministers and Preachers

1.) **Deacons and Elders**: The first deacons were appointed in Acts 6 to solve an administration issue. The Greek believers were murmuring against the Jews because the Greek widows were being neglected in the daily distribution of goods (Acts 2:44-45). So, seven deacons, *"full of the Holy Spirit and wisdom"* were *"appoint*[ed] *over this business"* (Acts 6:3 KJV). Notice that deacons were "appointed" over their responsibility, which was "business."

What is the difference between a deacon (Acts 6:3; Philippians 1:1; 1 Timothy 3:8-12) and an elder (Acts 20:17; 1Timothy 5:17; Titus 1:5; James 5:14)?

Deacons primarily are involved in the *business* of ministry, and elders are primarily involved in the actual *ministerial duties* of the ministry, although both are seen in Scripture as having supernatural power from the Holy Ghost. Paul appointed and ordained deacons and elders wherever he went, as soon as they had been tested and proved (1 Timothy 3:10). Not only did he do it himself, Paul urged his pastors to do so, as well.

Many churches never grow because the pastor is not interested in the appointment of congregants to these offices. Every pastor should seek out the potential of, not just a few, but *all* who could be ordained to some particular area of church governance, as soon as they are proven through the Ministry of Helps (1 Timothy 3:6).

Paul shared his key to an effective ministry, giving Titus a model that always works: appointing these offices in every church.

> *For this reason I left you in Crete, that you should set in order the things that are lacking, and <u>appoint elders in every city as I commanded you.</u>* (Titus 1:5 NKJV)

In Acts 20:17, Paul sent for the elders who had already been appointed in the Church of Ephesus, while he was in Miletus (thirty miles south of Ephesus, in modern-day Turkey). He clues us in on how they became elders: through *impartation*.

¹⁸You know, from the first day that I came into Asia, in what manner I have always [in all seasons] lived among you.

²⁰how I kept back nothing that was helpful, but proclaimed it to you, and taught you publicly and from house to house. (Acts 20:18, 20 NKJV)

To prepare the elders, Paul spent time pouring into them. More than a classroom, Paul took them by word, precept, and action, the way a father would teach his child through a lifetime of experience. He knew his time was short, and he had to give and impart everything they would need to manage on their own.

Paul warned his elders that he was headed for Jerusalem and that great affliction awaited him there. He knew he would never see his elders again (Acts 20:22-25). I am sure there was weeping and sorrow accompanying his announcement. I can't imagine how I would feel if my spiritual father pulled all of us together and reminded us of the work that he had accomplished in us, and told us that he would be leaving (counting his life nothing), and that we would never see his face or hear his voice again.

Despite the sorrow, Paul gave them a charge. In the charge, he indicates the role of the elders.

Take heed therefore unto yourselves, and to all the flock, over the which the Holy Ghost hath made you overseers, to feed the church of God, which he hath purchased with his own blood. (Acts 20:28 KJV)

If we combine the above Scriptures, we can see that elders are appointed by pastors to rule and govern to the degree of authority that they are given. Elders are ministers, *"nourished up in the <u>words of faith</u> and of <u>good doctrine</u>"* (1 Timothy 4:6 KJV). Elders believe in healing (James 5:14), and they practice it while carrying out the ministerial role and duties of the ministry. They are prepared by spending time with spiritual authority, learning how to be *"an example of the believers, in word,* *in conversation, in charity, in spirit, in faith, in purity"* (1 Timothy 4:12 KJV).

As a young pastor, I saw a perfect example of how elders and deacons operate in a ministry. Being on the ministerial staff of the largest church in Michigan, I had been appointed by the Bishop; he personally trained me and the other staff ministers, even before we were appointed. Every day, we were busy teaching, preaching, being with the people and helping them in whatever role they needed—*on the ministerial side of things.*

The deacons were different. Though appointed by the Bishop as well, they didn't busy themselves with ministry duties. Instead they oversaw and helped govern the tithes, offerings, and other *business aspects* of the ministry. Both of these arms, the elders and deacons, worked together administering, and they helped the ministry operate as a healthy local body. Both elders and deacons are governance gifts that require wisdom and virtue and should be appointed in every church.

2.) **Ministers and Preachers**: When individuals venture out into ministry, they often make the mistake of spending 100% of their time developing as a preacher, and 0% of their time developing as a minister. But, as my good pastor friend told me once, and I'll never forget, "There is a difference between preaching and ministering to people." I didn't understand this when he said it, but it soon convicted me as a true statement. I later discovered this to be true from 1 Peter 4:11 (KJV):

> *If any man speak, <u>let him speak as the oracles of God</u>; If any man <u>minister</u>, let him do it as of the ability which God giveth: that God in all things may be glorified through Jesus Christ, to whom be praise and dominion for ever and ever. Amen.*

When an individual focuses *only* on time in the pulpit as an oracle and mouthpiece for God, neglecting the second half of the responsibility (being a minister as well), they will end up sitting at the dining table expecting God's people to serve *them.* "After all," they think, "I am the oracle. I am God's man for this hour. They owe it to me." Ah, hubris. While preachers should be honored and respected, they absolutely should not carry this kind of you-owe-me-something, arrogant attitude. Though they might be a blessing as a preacher, they stink as a minister.

Preacher is seen four times in the New Testament and shares the same Greek word, *keryx,* meaning *"a herald or messenger."* Oracle means a divine answer to a particular question. *It also refers to the agent giving the particular speech.* When under the influence of the Spirit of God, any preacher is an oracle speaking forth the divine wisdom of God.

The word *minister* is the Greek word *diakoneo* and it means, "to wait upon." It goes so far as to suggest that it means to wait upon tables, offering food and drink. In college, I had two jobs as a waiter, so I can relate. I was trained to take care of each table's needs efficiently, effectively, and precisely so that the guests could have an enjoyable and refreshing dining experience. Similarly, it is the designation of a minister working for Jesus Christ to wait upon God's people efficiently, effectively, and precisely so that they can experience all the blessings that are in Christ Jesus.

The title of *"minister"* is found in other places in Scripture, particularly Romans 15:16 (KJV): ***"That I should be the minister of Jesus Christ to the Gentiles, ministering the gospel of God."*** This word in Greek is *leitourgos.*

Leitourgos simply means "a public servant." It refers to those who were public servants of the time. As a soldier, police officer, congressman, and fireman are now here to serve today's community, so Paul was saying that he was a public servant to the Gentiles to bring them Jesus Christ. As a preacher brings forth the oracles of God, so a minister serves the people of God.

Effective preaching is easy to develop. One can learn how to preach by spending time with God in fervent prayer and intercession for others. The fervent prayer will teach you how to reach and hear God, and the intercession will teach you how to identify with the hurts and pains of others. Combine these two, and you have effective preaching.

For a true minister, *it is more of the essence to develop the inner fortitude that makes one a good public servant of Jesus Christ.*

As I look back on the path that the Lord has been walking me down now for almost two decades, hindsight lends me the ability to recognize how God was leading and developing me all along. As a minister in training attending Bible College, I remember watching others moving past me faster, getting opportunities that I would have loved, and doing things that were bigger and better, so it seemed. Students would go on summer mission trips and preach to crowds of people and come back to school in the fall, full of stories. Of course, there is no problem with this. It just wasn't what God was using to develop me to *"be a good minister of Jesus Christ, nourished in the words of faith and of the good doctrine"* (1 Timothy 4:6 NKJV).

I thought about my options in my dorm one day. The Lord said, "Nope. This summer I want you to go back home to Michigan, get a job to support yourself, and serve your bishop." It wasn't as glamorous as flying to preach in Italy or Japan, but I knew it was what the Lord asked me to do.

Then I thought, *I don't even know my bishop personally. What do you want me to do for him?* As I reflected, I thought about how the church facility was immaculate. My church is a ministry of order and excellence, and I couldn't think of one thing that it needed. I went home to visit before summer break, and I was sitting in service when the Lord spoke to me about how He wanted me to spend my summer.

"Clean the bolts that hold the seats down to the floor." When the Lord told me this, my face turned pale. Everything in the church was clean except for these little bolts that held 5,000 seats to the floor. I examined each seat and saw that each chair's restraints consisted of four 1/8" bolts. That's 20,000 bolts. "God. I am not going to Bible College to be a custodian."

I think God may have smiled because He knew that in my heart I was excited about doing this task. Whenever you hear God's voice, no matter what He asks you to do (dangerous or crazy as it may seem), there will always be excitement.

God was recruiting me into the Ministry of Helps. I would be supporting, succoring, and aiding my church, as small a job as it may seem. After receiving approval to clean the seats in the sanctuary, I went to the drug store and bought three brand new toothbrushes. They would be the best tools to get in between the crevices of the metal and eliminate the dirt from the bolts. And so it began. I worked at a furniture store, hauling pieces of heavy furniture off trucks from 6:15 a.m. to 4:00 p.m. every day. At 4:00 p.m., I punched out, got a snack at the gas station, arrived at my church around 5:00 p.m., and cleaned bolts until around 7:00 p.m. As tough as it seems, I was anointed to do it. I was so full of the peace of God. These were some of my very best days.

"How could that be? You weren't making any money. You had no time to yourself. You were alone." Yes. But I was in the will of God, and I knew I was running as fast as I could down the path of the just. With every bolt I cleaned, I took one more step into everything Jesus said I could be. I would laugh, "God has anointed me to clean these bolts on the floor. There are great theologians, great preachers, and great pastors, but I am the greatest of all bolt cleaners."

I spent a lot of time listening to sermons and confessing the Word of God when I was in between the rows of chairs, cleaning. Once, I got bold and did something I had wanted to do since day one of bolt cleaning. I walked to the front of the sanctuary with my Bible and stared at all the empty chairs. I first thought, *Golly. This is what it looks like when the Bishop is preaching to all these people.*

Then I remembered the verse:

> *¹⁰Of which salvation the prophets have enquired and searched diligently, who prophesied of the grace that should come unto you:*
> *¹²Unto whom it was revealed, that not unto themselves, but unto us they did minister the things, which are now reported unto you by them that have preached the gospel unto you with the Holy Ghost sent down from heaven; <u>which things angels desire to look into</u>.* (1 Peter 1:10, 12 KJV)

I thought, *Angels are interested in the Gospel plan? Well, bless God, I am going to call them in here and preach it to them."* I said: *"All right, angels. I have room for five thousand of you. Come in and hear a lecture in the Gospel.* Although I couldn't see them, I was convinced I preached to a packed house.

I spent a couple of months toiling with the bolts. By the time I was supposed to head back to college in Minneapolis, I had completed two sections. *Well,* I thought, *I guess I'll have to make trips home from school to clean these bolts.*

One weekend in September, I flew home to clean them. I remembered the exact row I left off on. I was excited, because I had just a few rows to go before I could begin a new section. And the very first seat to clean in that new section was none other than the Bishop's seat.

I finished the section and was eager to throw some detergent on what I considered to be the highest seat in the house. That is when the Spirit of God stopped me with some bone-chilling news, "Don't clean that seat."

What? I thought. *Don't clean this seat? Why wouldn't I clean this seat?*

Then the Lord said to me: "You are now done with your assignment. Take the brushes and bucket back to the custodial closet. Your assignment is now complete."

"But, Lord!" I chimed back. "I have 4,500 seats left to clean."

"No. You have cleaned enough. Go home and enjoy your family. I don't want you flying home to clean these bolts anymore. This assignment is over."

When I scanned the entire sanctuary, that lonely dark sanctuary, I realized for the first time how daunting a task this really was. I couldn't believe I hadn't realized it sooner. But, you see, the anointing had left me for performing that task. Now, it would have been toil and labor, instead of a pleasure. Had I kept cleaning in an attempt to be religious, I would have struggled endlessly to clean the 4,500 seats that remained, and probably would never have heard God's Voice as I did while I cleaned the first 500 seats.

A year later I was honored to be placed on staff at that Church. I received healthcare benefits, a great starting salary, a company car, and was now part of one of the greatest churches in the USA. It was a position that would last two years and four months. In this time I received training that was priceless, experience that I could have nowhere else, and I was shaped and molded by the Bishop himself. During my first few weeks on staff, we were in the sanctuary during a Sunday morning's praise and worship. As I looked down, I noticed the clean bolts on my seat. This was the section I spent the most time cleaning, and the last section I cleaned before the Lord told me to stop. Then I heard His voice again concerning this whole bolt-cleaning job. I hadn't heard Him talk about this for a whole year. He said, "Son, remember when I had you clean the bolts in this sanctuary?"

Was this a joke? I thought. *God, do I remember? If I was ever tempted to forget I have the worn-out cartilage on my knees to remind me.*

That is when God finally revealed something to me that I will never forget. It was a missing puzzle piece that helped me to understand why He assigned me such an unusual task. It also helped me to understand how promotion comes within the Kingdom of God.

The seats that God had me clean were, for the most part, the section that the Bishop's ministerial staff sits in. *"Son, before you could be promoted to sit in one of these seats, I had to test your heart to make sure that you would be willing to first clean them."*

Wow. That is the reason why He didn't want me to clean the Bishop's seat. I didn't have to. I cleaned five hundred seats, just so I could clean the section where I would one day be sitting as a preacher. This experience of serving built in me something more than just being an oracle and a preacher. *It taught me the form of ministry and the essence of service.*

If I am ever tempted to get an inflamed head about my title and position, this experience acts like a needle, deflating my ego and reminding me what being a "minister" really is. Ministry is done on our knees. To this day when I go into churches to preach at conferences and seminars, I am not too proud to get on my knees, before or after I am done being an oracle, to clean the bolts. Yes, I am a successful preacher now, but only because I learned how to be a minister *first*.

The Ministry Of Helps: *Helps* is another function in the Body of Christ listed in 1 Corinthians 12:28, and it means, literally, "to lay hold of." Often, this function is given so little attention that the benefits God designed for it go unrealized. Consider the mammoth undertaking for the New Testament Church at its inception. And, even now, two thousand years later, it remains no small thing to have an organized church body and to see that it runs correctly.

Too often, the Ministry of Helps is dismissed as being of a lower importance in the Church. These are people who set up chairs and clean the fellowship hall after service, or weed the prayer garden, or do any one of the million things that must be done around the church. Some think they are "too good" to be part of this ministry.

When I was in college studying to be a preacher, many of the students who sat next to me in class filled up their itineraries, and spent summers preaching to youth groups. A majority of them are no longer active in ministry. There is no doubt that they were called. But they got sidetracked, and were not found faithful for the work of the ministry. They never developed roots early on. They'd come into the dorm, talking about all the places where they'd preached.

I'd think, "Well, maybe I should go out and preach. Maybe I should work out an itinerary of summer engagements." But I would always get a witness that just said, "No."

Instead, the Lord told me to join the "zest team" at church. "Zest team" is another way of saying "scrub-the-toilets-after-service-team." I scrubbed those toilets and sprayed air freshener over the bathrooms, and I'd think: "God, it is an honor to do this for You. Maybe someone will see how clean this bathroom is, and join this church, and their life will change the way mine did when I got under this teaching."

Instead of allowing me to become an applauded preacher in my early years, God was cementing a foundation of humility, faithfulness, and a love for service. This would guarantee that I would last. Somehow, every time I cleaned a toilet, I felt as though the "novice" in me was dying a bit more.

As I have preached from church to church, I have never been to a church or event where I did not see the Ministry of Helps functioning. I'm startled how many people do not realize that their Ministry of Helps determines how the whole ministry excels. The Ministry of Helps was acknowledged, and greatly appreciated, by the Apostle Paul in virtually all of the letters he wrote. Notice one example: ***Greet Priscilla and Aquila my helpers in Christ Jesus*** (Romans 16:3 KJV).

The devout couple, Priscilla and Aquila, provides a textbook example of how God's Government (administration) can develop in our lives as believers. When Paul came to Corinth, as was his *modus operandi,* he would go into the synagogues and reason with the Jews. Though nothing is said about how Aquila and Priscilla were converted, it can be safely assumed that they were Paul's converts from his ministry in the synagogue at Corinth.

Aquila and Priscilla were Roman Jews who relocated to Corinth when Claudius Caesar forced all the Jews to leave (Acts 18:2). After their conversion, they discovered that Paul had the same trade as theirs, tent making, and they welcomed Paul into their home. This gesture of hospitality is part of the Ministry of Helps.

I have had the privilege of speaking numerous times in one church near Chicago, Illinois, where one of the couples reminds me of Aquila and Priscilla. They joyfully open their home to visiting guest ministers. It is a lovely dwelling, but, more than that, they have a true home. Every morning, I wake up to a gourmet breakfast. And they always have my favorite sodas, desserts, and even home cooking for me. I can't think of a better ministry.

Although Aquila and Priscilla may not have had pastries and espresso ready for Paul each morning, they took care of his needs while he was in Corinth so that he could fully preach the Word of God. They "helped" him and, in doing so, helped God's Word break into modern day Greece. Yet, this Ministry of Helps led to more than just thanks and a pat on the back. Paul promoted this couple and made them his travel companions. Either he couldn't go without Priscilla's cooking, or he began to see the call of God maturing in their lives.

> *And Paul after this tarried there yet a good while, and then took his leave of the brethren, and sailed thence into Syria, and with him Priscilla and Aquila.* (Acts 18:18 KJV)

Being Paul's travel companions, Aquila and Priscilla spent constant time in the presence of the greatest apostle of the New Testament Church for a whole season of their lives. God usually does it that way. A spiritual father only needs to give you constant time and attention *for a season* until you have become absorbed into his spiritual DNA.

Eagles don't spend their whole lives sitting in the nest, being fed worms by their parents. If you have a true heart to learn and a pliable and humble spirit, truly desiring to walk in what your spiritual father walks in, the intensity of your observation will require you to need only a *short season* around them. After that, they will be in you everywhere you go, having shared their DNA.

After Paul left Aquila and Priscilla in Ephesus, an articulate preacher by the name of Apollos, who was mighty in the New Testament Scriptures, arrived. What happens next is extremely interesting. Apollos goes into the same synagogue where Paul had been preaching during his stay at Ephesus, and starts preaching. As eloquent and educated as Apollos was, the couple that walked with Paul pulled him aside and *taught him!*

> *So he [Apollos] began to speak boldly in the synagogue. When Aquila and Priscilla heard him, they took him aside and* <u>*explained to him the way of God more accurately*</u>*. [expounded unto him the way of God more perfectly]*. (Acts 18:26 NKJV)

Do you think that this couple ever dreamed that they would be in Ephesus (all the way across the Aegean sea from their home in Corinth) teaching a preacher about the Scriptures? Paul and Aquila and Priscilla were now working together to mature the Church. Though separated by distance, they still worked as one unit. Here were a couple of little old tentmakers doing the same work as the mighty Apostle to whom they'd opened their dwelling.

The last we see of Priscilla and Aquila, they have been promoted to pastors (1 Corinthians 16:19). How did this come about? The test of time had been won because Priscilla and Aquila first opened their home to Paul and faithfully allowed themselves to be used in this Ministry of Helps.

The wonderful thing about the Ministry of Helps is that everything we invest in helping the work of the Lord is always returned back to us abundantly. *Much of that return occurs because of the transformation that the Ministry of Helps produces in us.* The blessing that God has laid up for those who allow Him to use them in the Ministry of Helps will always surpass all that we could ever ask, think, or imagine.

Diversities of Tongues: The last designation that we see the Apostle Paul mention in 1 Corinthians 12:28 is "diversities of tongues." To be honest, I have wished that the Apostle Paul had left out this part of this chapter, only because it has—and still does—cause so much confusion.

I have spent services preaching on the power of the Holy Ghost and the importance of praying in tongues. Afterward someone will come up to me and say, "Yes, Brother Palmer, you say we must all speak in other tongues to pray out the mind of Christ, however, that is not what Paul taught."

Usually I just sigh inside because I know where they are headed. *"Are all apostles?"* Of course not. *"Are all prophets?"* Certainly not. *"Are all teachers?"* It would be absurd to think so. *"Are all workers of miracles?"* Not a chance. *"Have all gifts of healing?"* No.

After getting me to say "no" five times, they get ready to set the hook with their final question, *"Do all pray in tongues?"* As they wait for me to say "no," I remind them of what Paul said in 1 Corinthians 14:5 (KJV), just nineteen verses later, ***"I would that ye all spoke with tongues."***

"Perhaps we are at a stalemate in our conversation because in just nineteen verses Paul has contradicted himself, right?" Of course not. Paul knew exactly what he was talking about. The problem comes when people take portions of Scripture *out of context* to back up preconceived ideas. Taken in context, what Paul is saying makes complete sense.

In 1 Corinthians 12:28-30, Paul is talking about offices and giftings that are done in *public*. Apostle, prophet, teacher, pastor, evangelist, helps, government [administration], and the *public* use of tongues are what he is referring to here. Notice that immediately afterward, Paul says, *"Do all interpret?"* Interpret what? The tongues.

So Paul was asking, "Do all speak in tongues as a *public* oracle?" Of course not. "Do all interpret tongues as a *public* oracle?" Certainly not.

So, in case the people thought they could get off the hook without coming into the ability to pray in tongues, Paul clears that up by saying, just nineteen verses later, ***"I wish you all spoke with tongues*** (1 Corinthians 14:5 NKJV), and just thirteen verses after that, ***"I thank my God I speak with tongues more than you all"*** (1 Corinthians 14:18 NKJV).

In these two verses, Paul expresses his desire for all those in Corinth to speak in tongues privately, and acknowledges that a great percentage of them *did* speak in tongues privately.

With this fact in mind, we can see what Paul meant when he laid out rules for the Corinthian Church. So look at the list that we have here:

Apostles
Prophets
Teachers
Miracles (Evangelists)
Gifts of Healings (Pastors)
Governments (Deacons and Elders, Ministers and Preachers)
Helps
Diversities of Tongues (Public use, including an interpreter)

All of these operations that have been placed into the Body of Christ work toward *a singleness of purpose*. Paul gave us that purpose in Ephesians 4:12 (KJV):

For the perfecting of the saints, for the work of the ministry, for the edifying of _the body of Christ_.

Christ gave the Ministry Gifts to be used in the entire Body of Christ to bring about the corporate completion of the saints. They are corporate graces that work toward the common good for the Body of Christ. In them the Church of the Lord Jesus Christ grows up into maturity, completes the work cut out for it, and nourishes itself up. God will not allow us to go long on our journey without encountering them, and eventually, becoming them.

CHAPTER FORTY-TWO

Fruit of the Ministry Gifts

"Biblical edification is not a narcissistic process that results in the glorification of self."

It is vital to fathom what Christ intended the purpose of the giftings to be. Then we can more fully cooperate with the Holy Ghost in how to use our gifting and be a blessing to the Body of Christ. I'll bet that you have been examining your own heart to determine what your gifting is (if you don't already know), and what the Holy Ghost would have you do next to prepare for stepping into it.

Ephesians 4:12 gives the *fruit* that the *offices* produce:

Perfecting of the Saints: The Greek Word for *perfecting* is *katartismos*. This simply means "furnishing." To furnish means to provide and supply, particularly those things that are necessary. When we furnish our house, we obviously have already laid the foundation. To furnish means that you are completing the workmanship that has been started by the architect. Christ is the chief architect of the Body of Christ (1 Corinthians 3:9). The Godhead drew up the blueprint (Ephesians 1:4-5), designed the plan (Hebrews12:2), and laid the foundation for the Church to be erected upon (Ephesians 1:22; Colossians 1:18; Hebrews 6:1).

Jesus, however, ascended before the completion of the Church and gave the "Ascension Gifts" to furnish the Body of Christ through the power of the Holy Ghost, until the Church is brought to the perfection of completion. They are referred to as "Ascension Gifts" because they are *the* gifts that Jesus gave when He ascended into Heaven. These Ascension Gifts are Apostles, Prophets, Evangelists, Pastors and Teachers—as seen in

Ephesians 4:11. They are the *only offices* that "furnish" the Body of Christ. The other offices produce different fruit, which will be seen later.

Some say, "Ah yes, but that cannot be so. What power and authority do you have to give to such titles?" Those who think this way have probably never met a true apostle, prophet, evangelist, pastor, or teacher. Just because one *says* that they are one, does not mean that they are. It is the fruit their ministry produces that will vouch for them. I have met authentic Ministry Gifts in each office, and I can say with certainty that men and women who operate with their kind of authority, positioned all over the world, are sufficient to bring the Church to its compete furnishing until Jesus Christ comes.

This is not so for the jokers and self-deluded swindlers that I have run across, who bear a self-given title without any power to furnish.

Work of the Ministry: The work of the Ministry is another result of the designations found in 1 Corinthians 12:28. The word *work* is the Greek word *ergon*. This means, "to toil, labor, and act." It is congruent with the idea of doing business, enterprise, or accomplishing anything by hand. Although the Ascension Gifts must work to accomplish that which they are called to do by God (Acts 13:2; 2 Timothy 4:5), this specific designation of "the work of the ministry" refers to the *whole* work of the *whole* ministry.

The brunt of the toil, labor, business, and enterprise should not fall on the backs of the Ascension Gifts. They have enough work of their own, hearing from the Lord and furnishing it to the people of God. Rather, the majority of the workload should fall upon Governments and Helps. In any given ministry, the number of Helps workers, deacons and elders, ministers and preachers will (or at least should) outnumber the Ascension Gifts. The "work of the ministry" is a result produced by the Governments, the elders and deacons, ministers and preachers, and by Helps, all of whom are appointed by the Ascension Gifts, who are appointed by Christ.

Edifying of the Body of Christ: This is the last public result produced by the offices found in 1 Corinthians 12:28.

Biblical edification is not a narcissistic process that results in the glorification of self. Rather it is the ancient procedure of surrender to the

Spirit of God, set in order by the Godhead, an evolution of the inner man set into motion through praying in tongues. Edification leads to humility as it removes the carnal barriers that stand between the believer and God, including pride.

When we study Paul's letters, it is important to keep in mind that all of the letters were like fruit that springs from one great vine. Paul had a great vine of revelation and, from it, came all his letters. Had Paul written more letters (which I am certain that he did; we just do not have them) we would discover that they are harmonious with everything that he wrote in his New Testament letters that we do have. The subject matter varies, the issues differ, but Paul's wisdom and revelation do not.

No other writer in the entire Bible is more misconstrued than Paul. This is why most heresies through the ages come from an imperfect rendering of Paul's writings. *Partly, the mistake has been made from readers dividing Paul's revelation into separate books that he wrote.* By this, I mean reading Galatians with the mistaken idea that he is talking about something else in Romans; reading Ephesians thinking that it is completely different than 2 Corinthians; reading Titus and believing it is far from what is discussed in 2 Timothy.

When Paul said, *"the **edifying** of the Body of Christ"* in Ephesians 4:11 (KJV), it was also what he meant in 1 Corinthians 14:5 (KJV): *"that the **church** may receive **edifying**."* And 1 Corinthians 14:28, 30 (KJV): *diversities of tongues...do all speak with tongues [publicly]? Do all interpret [publicly]?"* This is the public designation of those used by God to *bring forth a Word from God, corporately in tongues; and God's designation for an individual to interpret those tongues to bring about edification.* This *ministry* of edification in tongues and interpretation is so important in the Body of Christ that it has its own category.

"Chris, are you saying that the Ascension Gifts, elders, deacons, ministers, preachers, and Helps, cannot be used to bring edification?"

While it may be true that a lot of what these saints do (preaching, teaching, helping, laboring) brings edification in the sense that it "uplifts," it cannot replace the *special kind* of edification released by tongues, plus the interpretation, in a public setting.

When the ministry operations are firing on all cylinders, notice the corporate result:

¹³till we all come to the unity of the faith and the knowledge of the Son of God, to a perfect man, to the measure of the stature of the fullness of Christ;
¹⁴that we should no longer be children, tossed to and fro and carried about with every wind of doctrine, by the trickery of men, in the cunning craftiness of deceitful plotting.
¹⁵but, speaking the truth in love, may grow up in all things into Him who is the head—Christ—
¹⁶from whom the whole body, joined and knit together by what every joint supplies, according to the effective working by which every part does its share, causes growth of the body for the edifying of itself in love.
(Ephesians 4:13-16 NKJV)

The Body of Christ develops in unity, knowledge, perfection, stature, fullness, maturity, stability, gracious speech, and love. Yet, for as much as God seeks to champion His Church corporately through the *public* operations in 1 Corinthians 12:28, He desires to champion us *personally, when we are by ourselves.*

Where Can We Pick Up Our Supply?

Although the whole discussion of Ephesians 4 is about *the whole Body*, Paul quickly mentions *each individual* member of that Body when he says, **"Knit together by what <u>every</u> joint supplies, according to the effective working by which <u>every</u> part does its share"** (Ephesians 4:16 NKJV).

Every one of us, as individuals, plays a part. Not only do we "play a part," but each of us is integral, and intended to be working effectually, adding a supply. *Where do we get that supply?* If we are called to the office of an apostle, where can we look for the supply to be an apostle? If we are called to be an evangelist, where can we go pick up our allocation? Where can we get the resources when we are called to be in the Helps Ministry or a deacon, or an elder, or a minister, or a preacher, or one who can give tongues publically or interpret them? You cannot be an apostle, prophet, evangelist, pastor and teacher, deacon, elder, minister, preacher or Helps minister *privately*. They do no good for anyone, personally. They are giftings to help others.

Of the *public* operations, *only one of them has the ability to work outside of a public setting and supply us with the building material that we need to build the office that God has designated us to in our personal blueprint: tongues*.

Paul let the Corinthians know this when he differentiated between public and private tongues: *"I thank my God, I speak with tongues more than ye all: Yet in the church...."* (1 Corinthians 14:18-19 KJV). It was apparent that Paul had his own prayer language outside of the Church, on his own. It was this prayer life that supplied him with enough of the Mind of God to fulfill his grueling call as the Apostle to the Gentiles. Though his calling was *by grace*, Paul *responded to that grace* by praying in the Holy Ghost, enabling that working of grace to come to fruition.

Perhaps an illustration will help. An architect may come to me and say, 'Rev. Chris, I want to build you a house. My company has been examining you and we have drawn up what we know will be the perfect house for you and your family. We are going to do all of the work required to build it. All we are asking of you is to take us down to the Depot and supply us with the building material that we need: 2x4's, nails, pipes, marble, dry wall, etc. It has all been paid for, we just need your cooperation as we put it all together." Am I going to cooperate? You bet, I am!

In like manner, the Godhead has drawn up a blueprint for your life before you asked Him. Included within the plans is the designation(s) to the ministry He has called you to do as your part of being in the Body of Christ. This is *grace*. All He wants from you is to *respond* to that grace and *cooperate*. When you pray in tongues, you are driving down to the Depot and giving God the material that He needs to start turning those blueprints into a tangible reality.

Praying in the Spirit accomplishes this because it gets us one on one with the Holy Ghost, personally. To me it is baffling that people want to fight this. Who wouldn't want to meet one on one with the Spirit of God? When you pray in the Spirit, the Holy Spirit will do for you, *personally* and *privately*, what the operation of 1 Corinthians 12:28 does for the Body of Christ *corporately*. Praying in the Spirit in our own private lives will do for us all of the things mentioned in Ephesians 4:13-16, in a very personal way.

1.) Keeps us in the unity of the faith (Ephesians 4:3)
2.) Releases the knowledge and mind of God to us (1 Corinthians 2:13-16)
3.) Grounds us in doctrinal truth (1 John 2:20, 27)
4.) Keeps us in the love of God (Jude 21)
5.) Causes maturity (1 Corinthians 2:12-16; Galatians 1:15-2:2)

When I yielded myself over to the Holy Ghost early in my ministry, praying night after night in the dark, lonely church, the Spirit of God was releasing the mind of Christ in me. After that, the Holy Spirit gave me the ongoing supply I needed to perform the work I was called to do. The wisdom and revelation shooting up out of the pages of the Word of God astounded me. There was a change in the way I preached. There was a new authority in the way that I ministered. The building material was showing up and the edifice was taking form!

In fact, at one particular meeting, the minister I was preaching for reprimanded me. He said, "Well, the problem is not that you *haven't* been spending time in your prayer closet, that is for sure. Actually, it seems as though you have been spending *too much* time in your prayer closet. The revelation that you brought was too, oh, how do I say it, *intense.*"

After thinking about the service, I realized I may have jumped and shouted and gotten a bit overly excited, like a water cannon that spews water all over the place without a precise aim. However, I could never apologize for being too on fire. During that meeting, I spoke a word into those young students, concerning Satan's operation to isolate the anointed and pick them off. I warned them that most students of ministry don't make it through. Sure enough, I have received reports of the many in that class who have fallen to it. (Perhaps we should encourage more intense messages, and less feel-good messages.)

I began noticing that this edification, coming through my private time of praying in tongues, began yielding a difference when I laid hands on people. It literally felt different, like power flowing; there was a connection. Before this, it had been hit or miss. The power increased. In the next meeting, the altar was full of people wanting a touch from God. A tremendous Presence showed up that was thick enough to cut with a knife. I started laying hands on people, and they began getting healed.

There was also a very strong flow of deliverance that freed people from demonic oppression, instantly. I had gone from *just* teaching and preaching information to seeing power and demonstration (1 Corinthians 2:4). I was assaulting the Kingdom of Darkness! This had never happened in such magnitude before I prayed those long hours in the Spirit. After this meeting I went back to my room, got into the shower, and humbly thanked the Lord, knowing that I had reached a new level in the Spirit. What could possibly be next after this?

CHAPTER FORTY-THREE

The Kingdom of Darkness is Like a Serpent

**"Do not be fearful.
You are in Christ and thus have the tools necessary
to combat this realm."**

I fell into a depression. This was not the kind of depression that comes as the result of the cares of this world, the deceitfulness of riches, or the lusts of other things. No, this was an indescribable heaviness that seemed to hang over my head. It felt like an entity was following me and harassing me at will. During this time, I would think, *Why is this happening? I just entered into a new level in the Spirit. How can this be the result? What is causing this?*

Ignorance is bliss, until you are ruined by it. The Holy Spirit's job is to dispel any ignorance that blankets our understanding. Ever faithful, the Spirit of the Lord began to give me tremendous insight into something that I had not yet discovered up to this point: *the enemy's operation in the world today, particularly in the lives of believers.*

It seems that there are ministries that rise almost overnight. The anointed vessel that is being used by God finds a wave of grace and begins riding that wave into tremendous endeavors that go toward advancing the Kingdom of God. A minister may punch his hands through to the next level, and find such an awesome healing anointing in those hands that multitudes of ill people recover when he touches them. Another may get her head through the next level and find that her speech becomes richer and heavier, as God uses her mouth to turn the masses toward repentance. Some get their understanding through to the next level and receive such rich truths about Christ that they, almost single-handedly, begin, through their materials, to grow the Body of Christ. Should this ever happen in your ministry or if you observe it in another's, ***"Be sober, be vigilant; because your adversary the devil walks about like a roaring lion, seeking whom he may devour"*** (1 Peter 5:8 NKJV).

Snakes are the most sagacious creatures alive (Matthew 10:6). Their acute mental capabilities lend them advantage over their prey. *A snake will never announce that it has arrived.* It stays quiet, unsuspected, all while blending in with the surroundings. You may walk past a snake dozens of times and never realize it is there, camouflaged and hidden, *observing you and making notes.*

Cutting my lawn one summer, I lifted a large planter that had been turned over for some time. Under it was an enormous black snake coiled up and looking at me with its big, black, beady eyes. I was caught completely off guard, so taken by surprise that I jumped and ran. Now, don't get me wrong, I am not afraid of snakes. My reaction was due to the fact that I was 100% surprised. Fortunately, it was not a venomous snake or I might have been bitten when my hand was on the planter.

Humorous as it now seems, the snake just sat there and watched me freak out. I finally got myself together and went into the garage to get a spade. *Off with his head,* I thought. To the snake's credit, when I returned with my weapon of choice I saw he had made a break for it. I searched and found the last part of his black tail going down into a small fissure where he was perfectly sheltered from my vengeance. That snake knew its surroundings so well that it had marked places of refuge where it could escape if threatened.

More important than knowing when to hide is knowing when to strike. If all a snake knew how to do were to hide, it would starve itself to death. *Snakes are masters of timing.* They will let prey run around them hundreds of times before they attack. If you have ever watched a documentary about snakes, you know what I mean. A busy little mouse, so ignorant and unprepared for what is about to happen, scurries about until, out of nowhere, it is being pumped full of venom. I always think, *I wonder if it even had time to realize what was happening.* It doesn't matter; it is dead.

The Kingdom of Darkness (every being of deception and light which comprises it) is skillful in human affairs because it has been watching humanity for over 6,000 years. *While humankind is busy laboring for success and promotion, Rulers of Darkness blend in, stay quiet and unsuspected, never announcing to you that they have come to develop a plan for your ultimate demise.* Veiled by the busyness of your ambition and ignorance, they go unnoticed during their demonic planning and strategizing. Like Mr. Snake, whom I accidently discovered in my yard, you have walked passed them countless times without it ever occurring to you that you are being watched.

Before Paul was struck by the presence of an entity, the Kingdom of Darkness was no doubt *watching him.*

> *¹³Then some of the itinerant Jewish exorcists took it upon themselves to call the name of the Lord Jesus over those who had evil spirits, saying, "We exorcise you by the Jesus whom Paul preaches."*
> *¹⁴Also there were seven sons of Sceva, a Jewish chief priest, who did so.*
> *¹⁵And the <u>evil spirit</u> answered and said, "Jesus I know, and <u>Paul I know</u>; but who are you?"* (Acts 19:13-15 NKJV)

The New American Standard Bible translates verse 15 like this: *"I recognize Jesus, and I know about Paul, but who are you?"* How did these evil spirits know about Paul? Obviously, there is communication that goes on in the spirit world. We forget that the unseen realm of the spirit is similar to ours. Why wouldn't communication go on?

"Well, who is communicating?" you ask. Leave it to the Great Apostle to tell us.

Classes of Darkness

> *For we wrestle not against flesh and blood, but against <u>principalities</u>, against <u>powers</u>, against the <u>rulers</u> of the darkness of this world, against <u>spiritual wickedness</u> in high places.* (Ephesians 6:12 KJV)

The greater revelation we come into about the ongoing warfare that those in Christ have been under since the Church's inception, the more clearly we will come to realize that *there are really no coincidences or simple misfortunes.* Ministries don't just collapse. Preachers don't just have moral failures. Finances don't just dry up. Pastors don't just quit. *The serpent kingdom has struck, following a well-planned, meticulous reconnaissance to blockade any further progress down the path of righteousness.*

Should the purging of old attitudes be effective and the believer no longer finds himself being tripped up by the flesh or the soul, the enemy is going to notice. Now that your own flesh is not preventing your progress in God, the powers of darkness feel they must get involved to stop you. Otherwise, you may hit a level of understanding in Christ that may break open a portal of heaven and release tremendous revival in your area or community. This is what happened during the Azusa Street Revival that began in 1901. Don't think the enemy doesn't remember. A ray of light broke through his canopy of darkness that enveloped the world, causing a great loss of territory for him.

Therefore, I want to explain to you how the Kingdom of Darkness works, so that you may be alert for its attacks and know how to counter them.

> *Do not be fearful. You are in Christ and Christ is in you, and thus you have the tools necessary to combat this realm.*

How It Works

Classes are an earmark of any kingdom with a government and an organized body of people. Ephesians 6:12 details the caste system of the realm of darkness.

A caste structure is defined as a hierarchal system of social division that regulates position, based upon vocation and other hereditary elements. In the pyramidal caste system of India that prevailed for centuries, there were Brahmins (priests) at the peak. Under Brahmins were Kshatriyas (warriors), followed by Vaisyas (skilled traders, merchants, and minor officials). Beneath the Vaisyas were unskilled workers, called Sudras. At the lowest level and base of the pyramid were the outcasts of society, the Pariah.

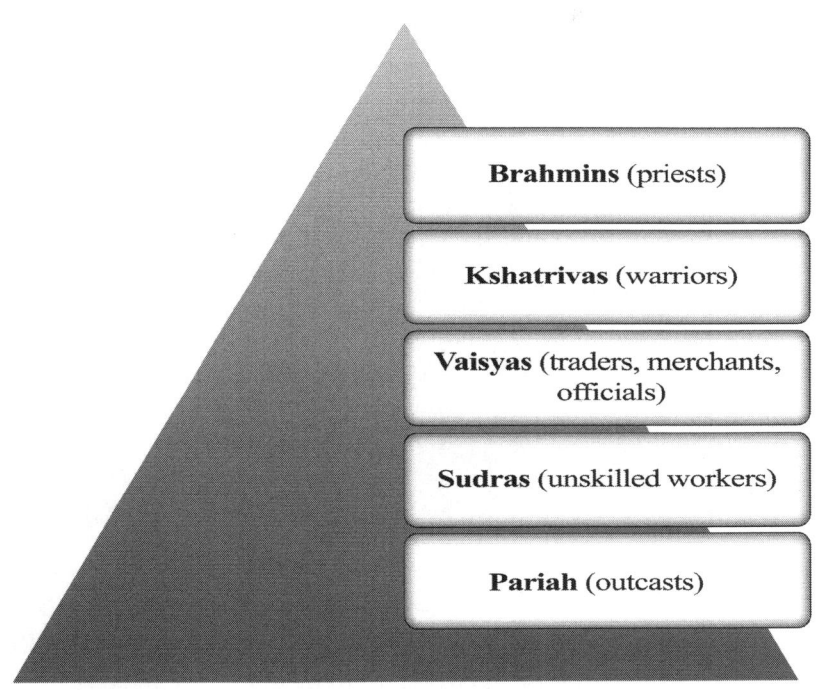

The Kingdom of Darkness, ruled by its supreme authority, Satan, maintains the following order:

1.) *Principalities*: indoctrinating influences that govern the masses (Daniel10)
2.) *Powers*: mystical agencies that convincingly deceive through demonstrations of power (Acts 8:9-24)
3.) *Rulers of Darkness:* defensive beings that suppress mankind through blocking the light of Christ (Matthew 4:16)
4.) *Wicked Spirits:* demon spirits that harass, torment, tempt, depress and oppress humans with sin, sickness, disease, confusion, etc. (Mark 5:1-20)

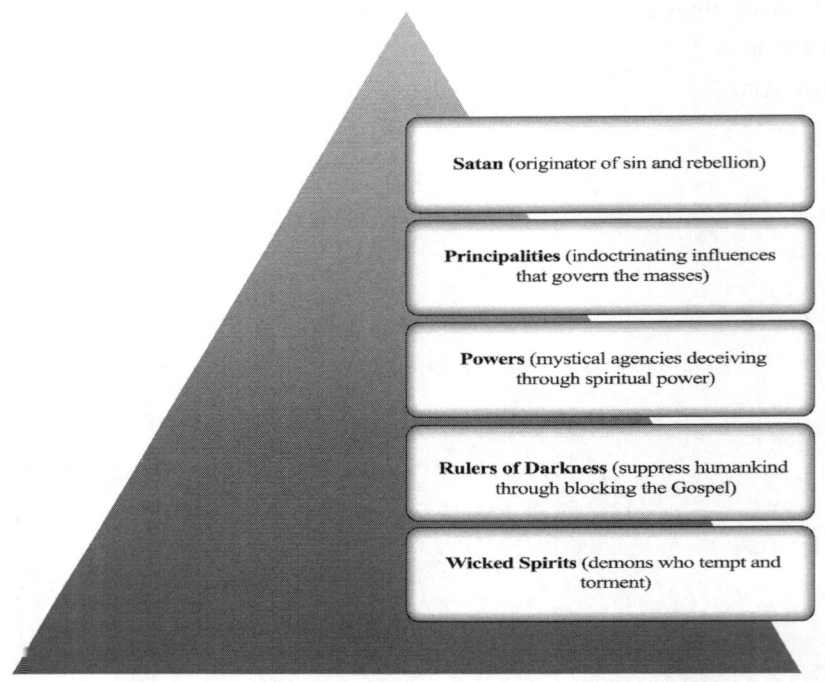

More than having distinct classes, the Kingdom of Darkness is a well-oiled military machine. Paul's explanation would have reminded the Ephesians in Asia Minor of the Roman military. Rome conquered much of the known world because of the strength and cunning of its military arm. As exact and precise as the Roman forces that were subduing their enemies, Paul warned that there was an unseen military, standing face to face against the Church of Jesus Christ. Let's examine each division, beginning at the base.

Wicked Spirits

Often someone pleads, "Oh, Chris, please pray for me. The devil is attacking me left and right." Although they might think it is the devil attacking, it is not. Satan is *not* omniscient (all knowing,) *not* omnipotent (all powerful,) and *not* omnipresent (always present). Unlike God, Satan is a *limited* being. Considering that there are over seven billion people in this world on seven continents, chances are Satan doesn't even know who Joe Anybody is.

There are only three instances in Scripture where Satan *himself* is personally responsible for tempting an individual: David (2 Sam. 21:1), Job (Job 1:6), and Jesus (Matthew 4). (One more instance occurred in Scripture where Satan contended with the archangel Michael over the body of Moses (Jude 9), but we will not count this one because we are talking about human beings.)

Each of these men was extremely important in God's plan for man, so there was good reason for the devil to be personally involved with them. It is safe to say that they were not the average person. Even to suggest that it is Satan personally attacking us would be putting us right up in league with David, Job, and Jesus. Satan has a kingdom to run and a plan to execute. Unless you are a major player in that, or have begun to create some sizeable waves, he has only his legions watching you. It is commonly a Wicked Spirit doing what it can to restrict your progress in God.

Wicked Spirits are low-level devils and demons that are involved with the day-to-day affairs of humans. As a full time minister now, I have seen many cases of people under the influences of Wicked Spirits. This does not mean that these individuals are possessed, although I have seen that before. More than fully possessing people, these demons can oppress, depress, enflame, and pervert. Note the differences:

1.) *Possession*: Possession means that a demon or demons has gained complete control over the trifold aspect of a human being (spirit, soul, and body). Christians *cannot* be possessed by demons. An understanding of what happens to us when we are born from above is enough to prove this. A devil could never gain control over a believer's spirit, for it has been reconciled to God, has received the life of God, and is under the Lordship of Jesus Christ.

Those in the world, however, are a different story. While possessed, an individual may lose complete control over all of his or her free will while the spirit(s) operates and channels through them as an earthly vessel. Witchcraft, voodoo, idol worship, mysticism, new age practices, and continued rebellion through sin are roads that take people down this path.

2.) *Oppression:* Oppress means to exercise burdensome authority and power over. Christians *can* be oppressed by demons. In oppression, demonic powers load up and burden the believer with anything and everything that can slow him or her down. Many times I have dealt with people who are oppressed, with no external circumstances to blame. Instead, it is the unseen fiery darts of the wicked one (Ephesians 6:16) weighing down their faith toward God.

Oppression mainly comes in the life of thought, tuning the believer's mind to lies, suggestions, and deceptions of the enemy—illusions that seem more authentic than reality. Every time the mind explores one of these illusions, the oppression grows. Only a spiritual eye is capable of recognizing the imp in the corner, firing the darts of deceit.

3.) *Depression*: Depression is on the other end of the spectrum from oppression. Oppression means to burden down; depression means to weaken, to make dull, to suck dry. Depression turns people inward, instead of outward. Depressed people become self-absorbed, and their affections are swallowed up in a black hole of hopeless misery. These people become a dead sea; nothing can flow out from them, and everything slowly begins to die. Behind this affliction is usually a Wicked Spirit hiding the believer's eyes from the reality of God's goodness, all the while sucking the joy and laughter right out of them. Oppressed people are carrying the weight of the world; depressed people have nothing left to give.

4.) *Enflame and pervert*: Wicked Spirits also come along to enflame and pervert people's passion. The sex drive has been given to us by God to be used in love, decently and in order with the instructions God gave us. Wicked Spirits will attempt to enflame it by igniting it with temptation. This is not the ordinary kind of temptation where you can subdue it through self-control. Instead, it is a moment where you feel so engulfed by passion that you ask yourself, "What has come over me?" Many people can attest to experiences where one minute they were going about their normal day, and in a second their sex drive went up in flames and they were driven to look at pornography or to fornicate. This is the presence of a Wicked Spirit.

Beyond the enflaming of our passions comes the perverting of our passions. Where "to enflame" means to heighten and accelerate, "to pervert" means to distort and corrupt the normal course of something. If a Wicked Spirit comes to pervert the sex drive, the individual may be led into homosexuality, lesbianism, pedophilia, and sexual addictions. The spirit's influence has shifted the normal course.

The sex drive isn't the only thing that can be affected. Anger can be ignited and turned into rage. Anger can be perverted into murder or a reason to commit suicide. Common disappointment can swamp us into insecurity.

Wicked Spirits are known to cause sickness and diseases of all sorts (Matthew 4:23-34; 9:32-33). This does not mean that every sickness is the presence of a Wicked Spirit. But there are certain diseases that medical science will never find a cure for, because the cause is a wicked being that is unaffected by medicine.

These low level devils at the base of Satan's pyramidal system are responsible for provoking countless sins and disobedience toward God. Their main objective is to do whatever they can to deter, mislead, and hinder a human's personal progress on his or her journey into everything God has called His children to inherit—body, soul, and spirit. They can be resisted (Ephesians 4:27) and overcome through the Word of God, the power of the Holy Ghost (John 14:17), and the armor of God (Ephesians 6:11).

Remember this; it is critical: *Do not be afraid. You can overcome through the power of the Holy Spirit.*

Rulers Of Darkness

Rulers of Darkness are unlike Wicked Spirits. "Rulers of Darkness" is not a specific name given to one particular being: it is a descriptive term depicting their task. I imagine the innumerable beings that make up this class have their own separate celestial names. (Remember, the spirit world is not much different from ours.)

Rulers of Darkness have a specific assignment. We fail in our understanding when we think that there are evil spirits running amok without consistency or reason. It is quite the contrary. I would believe that since they have been operating for thousands of years they are more organized than the US military.

Ruler is a term that means potentate. Potentates are monarchs endowed with authority over specific jurisdictions, to maintain order and to govern their subjects. The fact that Paul calls them "rulers" (having a plural form) indicates that there are literal jurisdictional boundaries in the spirit realm. *Each Ruler's jurisdiction has Wicked Spirits assigned to fulfill the purpose of holding that area in darkness.* The idea here is that the Kingdom of Darkness forms a canopy around the earth. This canopy blocks the light of the Gospel from shining into humanity, keeping mortal man blinded from the truth of Jesus Christ. *Rulers of Darkness oversee this.* Ephesians 2:1-3 (NKJV) describes this canopy:

> *[1]And you He made alive, who were dead in trespasses and sins,*
> *[2]in which you once walked according to <u>the course of this world, according to the prince of the power of the air, the spirit who now works in the sons of disobedience,</u>*
> *[3]among whom also we all once conducted ourselves.*

To keep the world dead in sins and walking the course of darkness, each Ruler of Darkness governs his respective jurisdiction in an attempt to keep light from breaking through the covering of spiritual darkness that Satan has worked thousands of years to erect. John alludes to their efforts by saying, *"We know that we are of God, and the whole world lies under the sway of the wicked one"* (1 John 5:19 NKJV).

This canopy is again mentioned in Genesis 6:5 (KJV), *"And God saw that the wickedness of man was great in the earth, and that every imagination of the thoughts of his heart was only evil continually."* Satan's kingdom was so active in Noah's day that evil had become the culture and custom. Light was so rare that Noah and his family remained the only flicker of hope for humanity to go on existing. Whereas the Wicked Spirits increase darkness and are *offensive* spirits, Rulers of Darkness are *defensive* spirits and see to it that no light can pierce through the darkness that has been fixed over the earth.

Powers

Higher than the Rulers of Darkness are *Powers*. Just as soon as you bust through the canopy of bondage into freedom, Powers are the spirits that come to challenge you. *Powers are mystical spirits that seemingly have the same kind of supernatural power that God has.*

These Powers are referred to in Luke's gospel:

> *¹⁸And He said unto them, "I saw Satan fall like lightning from heaven.*
> *¹⁹Behold, <u>I give you the authority</u> to trample on serpents and scorpions, and <u>over all the power of the enemy</u>, and nothing shall by any means hurt you.*
> *²⁰Nevertheless do not rejoice in this, that the spirits are subject to you, but rather rejoice because your names are written in heaven."* (Luke 10:18-20 NKJV)

To be successful in earthly ministry, the disciples needed dominance over the *power* of the enemy. The "power of the enemy" is more than just a mystical *energy* that the Kingdom of Darkness possesses. Jesus is referring to Wicked Spirits (literal entities and personalities) that are deployed in battle against the saints. These have now become *subject to us through the authority of the highest name on earth.*

In Luke, Jesus was giving His disciples the *authority* they needed to defeat the Powers and liberate their captives. When the disciples would be confronted with these opposing mystical forces, they had the highest authority on the earth to overrun and unseat them, the authority of and backing of Jesus Christ.

Jesus, in sending His disciples forth to set the children of Israel free, is a fulfillment of what was typified in the story of Moses. God gave Moses a staff and told him to cast it down in front of Pharaoh and demand that he let Israel go (Ex. 7:1-13). "Pharaoh," said Moses, "let God's people go." Moses threw down his staff, a symbol for a type of Christ, and the staff turned into a snake.

"Not so fast, Moses," said Pharaoh. "Hey, wise men and sorcerers. We have power that we have come up against. Come in here and show your stuff." Then the contest began. The next thing Moses knew, the diviners had thrown down their staffs, which also turned into snakes. As two opposing Powers stood on the front line of battle and stared each other in the face, Moses' power proved greater. In a heartbeat, Moses' rod (snake) ate the diviners' rods (snakes).

The power demonstrated in Moses was the power that came from God, a forerunner of Christ who would come and swallow up the deceptive serpent power of the enemy that held Israel in captivity to spiritual darkness. This same power of God is still available today, liberating the rest of the world from these demon entities.

Principalities

Right under Satan are his generals, Principalities. A couple of Principalities are mentioned in Daniel 10, and are given the names "Prince of Persia" and "Prince of Grecia." They were so strong that they fought an actual struggle in the heavenlies with two of God's archangels, Michael and Gabriel. Principalities were part of the rebellion of one-third of the angels, just as Powers and Rulers of Darkness were. The Principalities battled such a struggle with God's archangels that it is more than possible they were high-level angels themselves before their rebellion.

Interestingly, Paul uses the word *arche* in the Greek to introduce them, a word that politically means, "magistrate." Another indication of their might and authority is indicated in the fact that they're named after whole territories and kingdoms, Greece and Persia. This indicates that Principalities, too, have jurisdiction, although much greater than Rulers of Darkness and Powers. Because of the brevity of their influence, these Principalities report to Satan directly.

These ruling workers of darkness do not cause people to roll on the ground and shriek and foam at the mouth. *They are set over large regions, and take their orders from Satan as to where to steer culture, based upon the blueprints of his plan. When Satan releases further insight concerning society's demise, these Principalities get to work on indoctrinating humankind to follow suit.* In order to affect society, Principalities must first get their grip on people and things of influence. Political bodies and organizations, top businesses, and the entertainment industry are places that Principalities target to bring about a change in the way a society thinks, navigating it further toward its downfall.

Satan's System at Work

Satan's whole kingdom and system of spirits are always at work, enforcing his agenda. These spirits never sleep and traffic back and forth, busied with their tasks. When Satan decides on his next move he chooses the geography where he wants to carry it out and summons the Principality over that jurisdiction. The Principality then summons the Powers, which, in turn, transfer it to the Rulers of Darkness they have under them. The Rulers of Darkness finish the chain by giving orders to the Wicked Spirits.

Satan's tactics are not always the same in each region. Look at the different types of wickedness in the world and you can see the different jurisdictions of this canopy at work. Places in the deep of Africa, the Caribbean, and certain parts of Asia are steeped in witchcraft, voodoo, and mysticism. Enthroned in the Middle East is Islam, a religion that was birthed when a Principality visited a man by the name of Muhammad and led him into the greatest deception the world has ever known, responsible for the souls of billions. Western countries are entrenched with atheism and agnosticism. Places like San Francisco and Minneapolis are affected greatly by homosexuality. Detroit deals with crime. Miami is the capital of sexual fever and lustful pleasure. A jurisdiction in Nevada, called Las Vegas, is taken with greed.

The prevalent sin and prevailing beliefs of the region indicate what kind of dark jurisdiction it is. At work behind all wickedness is a kingdom whose efficiency cannot be measured by any earthly standard.

When Paul began to take his journey into the depths of Christ, a journey that would release a tremendous amount of light into this canopy of darkness, it didn't go unnoticed. It suddenly dawned on me that all of this praying in tongues had brought me higher in the Spirit and *I* was being noticed. How about you, have *you* been noticed?

CHAPTER FORTY-FOUR

Hello, Mr. Strongman

"Although there are strongmen that hamper us in our journey, none can resist the believer who has learned how to cooperate with the Holy Ghost."

As we walk down our journey we will encounter all kinds of strongmen (any class of being that denies us getting to the next level) that will try to neutralize our progress in God. I have found that when I am about to reach another level, a strongman usually meets me. Typically, they come so deceptively that we don't even realize that it is a spirit that we are dealing with. Overcoming begins when we realize that we are dealing with an unseen demon spirit that came forth out of Satan's hierarchy, carrying an order to destroy.

Below is a list of common strongmen. It isn't always a spirit that causes these sorts of issues; however, many times it can be. As you grow spiritually you will know when the Kingdom of Darkness is challenging you, and when you are dealing with an unsanctified emotion or thought. And you will always have the tools necessary to combat either.

Mr. Condemnation: Condemnation is not from God (Romans 8:1). When we sin, the condemnation is typically from our own reborn man, telling our flesh or soul that what it just did was *against* the life of Christ working in it (1 John 3:20-21).

But what about when we don't miss the mark and still feel condemned? The strongman of condemnation is an accusing voice that tries to penetrate our emotions by first gaining access to our minds. The thoughts it produces are accusatory, and the emotion birthed is guilt. Nothing has the ability to shut you down quicker than guilt born out of condemnation. Its effects are devastating, because it will result in a deformed perception of yourself and disable the working of your righteous standing in Christ. It can't make you unrighteous, but rather, it makes you *perceive* that you are unrighteous. Prayer no longer becomes a fellowship with God, but turns out to be a time of endless introspection and repetitive repentance until, frustrated, we decide not to advance further, and quit.

Mr. Intimidation: When Mr. Intimidation arrives on the scene, insecurity sets in. This insecurity shapes a false perception, not just of us, but others. No matter the case, when this spirit influences us, we discover that we will never measure up to anyone. And that is the problem. Intimidation creates a voracious appetite in us to compare ourselves, until our peace and joy have been strangled to death. Intimidation quenches boldness as it fosters an extreme sense of self-consciousness, turning our focus off of Christ in us, the hope of glory. This subtle influence has a proclivity to focus our attention upon what we *don't* have, and blind us from what we *do*.

Mr. Torment and Fear: Mr. Torment and Fear is a vague spirit that comes in all shapes and sizes. A couple of years into my ministry I had a season where I would wake up between 4:30-5:30 every morning, and lose my breath as I heard myself thinking thoughts of regret, fear, failure, all tormenting me. My emotions can be usually reined in a few days through the Word of God. But this was beyond emotion. Rather this was an influence that ignited my life with fear. I didn't realize that it was Mr. Torment and Fear that was waking me up so early in the morning and beating me down.

I have dealt with this one on a few occasions. Every time I overcame it, however, I noticed that I was on a higher level of ministry when I preached and prayed for the sick. The faith and confidence I possessed would be stronger, and the miracles would be greater. Yet before that happened, I had to wrestle with this guy.

I am not suggesting that everyone will; however, not everyone won't.

Mr. Discouragement: I texted someone the other day, "We all get discouraged at times. It happens." Common discouragement is not what I am referring to.

There is a strongman of discouragement that acts like monsoon rain, incessantly, relentlessly beating on the roof of your mind. People can have seasons of discouragement that last for years, until they finally throw up their arms and quit. This spirit aims at and hinders *patience*, one of the greatest weapons of God that vouchsafes victory. I once had a vision of the spirit of discouragement: he walked up to a man whom I knew represented patience, and started choking him until he collapsed.

Patience is the consistent force that will bring to pass every good and perfect thing in Christ. The moment that we get the Holy Ghost in the fight, He will begin to reinforce our patience which, when robust and resilient, will drive this strongman away.

Mr. Sadness: Though the Word of God makes clear that there are times to be sad (Romans 12:15; Eccl. 3:4), the strongman of sadness desires for you to see your last day of joy. Joy is the key to strength and boldness. Much of the confidence that comes for praying over the sick and working the works of God is from the joy that comes from seeing God's Word in action. Sadness prevents revelation from exploding in our hearts, and muddies up our perception of the Word so that it seems bland, rendering it uninteresting and ineffective in our lives. Like a cold front that comes over a city and swirls round and round creating gloom, so sadness comes to hang over your journey so that it no longer is enjoyable.

Mr. Confusion: Mr. Confusion has a clear strategy. Like a catfish enjoying the depths of a murky pond, Mr. Confusion swims furtively around Bible Colleges and churches. He knows that if there is nothing to muddy, he cannot confuse. Therefore, this spirit waits until enough of the Word of God has been measured out to the believer he wants to isolate. Then, he thrashes in and confuses it.

There is a difference between changing a belief through the help of the Holy Spirit and changing a belief through the spirit of confusion. The Holy Ghost has been given to change our belief system, where it *needs* to be tweaked. The Spirit of God will draw us through the uncertainty of things that we have once held onto that are incorrect, and lead us into further revelation and truth. And, when God brings you further into a truth, you won't despise those who, either inadvertently or on purpose, kept you from it. You will still honor them, have compassion for them, desire to pray for them, and give humble thanks that Holy Spirit has let you see the truth.

Not so, for the person blocked by confusion. Watch the *attitude*. It is the confirmation that the negative power of confusion is thwarting someone: everything they ever appreciated is undermined, and the teachers whom they used to hold in high esteem become villains who sold them a lie. It won't be long until truth becomes relative, and confusion's victim feels hypocritical for saying anything that may have substance. Confusion makes us back-pedal and wonder if truth can be found.

The believer who yields to the spirit of confusion is like one who breaks his spine. At the onset, this spirit tells the person that they are missing out on great teachings found elsewhere and, through curiosity, gets them digging in other places. The material they discover becomes damaging, but not as damaging as the resentment festering toward previous mentors. False humility sets in, and the individual makes himself seem more enlightened around his former coterie, all the while feeling vexed at heart.

If the strongman has his way, he will lead the person into giving up the pursuit of truth, or he will carry the person into heresy. If the person gives up, he or she will never be effective for the Kingdom. If they keep going and enter into false doctrines, they will lead others astray. The only two destinies that this strongman leaves its victim are that of a poor steward or that of a false teacher (if confusion runs its whole course).

Although there are other strongmen that hamper us in our journey, none can resist the believer who has learned how to cooperate with the Holy Ghost. Paul realized this. That is exactly the reason he mentions the Spirit's ministry in Romans 8:26 as *the* effective weapon for the reborn child of God to grow in maturity and overcome every force that would slow down or stop the forward progress into God. Though praying in tongues and uncovering the mystery of Christ will get you noticed by the Kingdom of Darkness, it is *exactly* the thing that will bring you through to the other side, victoriously. When we pray in tongues, it will supply enough of the mind of God to get us right out of the darkness that comes upon us, against our will. It will strengthen us in the love of God and make us a target that hell cannot hit. He has done it all for us. All we need to do is to keep going.

CHAPTER FORTY-FIVE

All Paths Lead to Love

"We will notice that He has the same body that we do. In this body will be the scars on His hands and feet, which He chose to keep, so that you and I could know that He understands our suffering."

Along the believer's journey, we have seen the astounding power of praying in tongues. Unquestionably we have observed the Holy Spirit's power to purge us and cleanse us. We've learned about our offices and functions in the Body of Christ. And even more, we have learned how to overcome the pressures of this life and have been equipped to spot the enemy and put him under our feet, where he now belongs. Is there anything greater that awaits us beyond *this*?

Paul told us that there is: ***"And yet I shew unto you a more excellent way"*** (1 Corinthians 12:31 KJV).

The book of 1 Corinthians is *not* deep. It was written to people whom Paul considered to be spiritual babes (1 Corinthians 3:1). When people think that they have discovered something super deep from this book, I remind them that it was written to immature believers who could not get their act together. Because of their immaturity, Paul had to write sixteen chapters, giving basic instructions to correct the faulty congregation.

Here is a brief summary of the major contents in First Corinthians:

Chapter 1—Greetings
Chapter 2—Paul's source of revelation knowledge
Chapter 3—The foundation of every believer: Christ
Chapter 4—Persecution
Chapter 5—Instructions concerning immorality in the church

Chapter 6—Instructions concerning saints going to court with one another

Chapter 7—Instructions concerning marriage

Chapter 8—Instructions concerning idols

Chapter 9—Instructions concerning giving

Chapter 10—Instructions concerning Christian liberties

Chapter 11—Instructions concerning communion

Chapter 12—Spiritual gifts and ministry offices

Chapter 13—Love

Chapter 14—Tongues

Chapter 15—The resurrection and glorification of the body

Chapter 16—Closing

Just about all of these subjects are *basic* and *uncomplicated* truths. Paul's frustration was that the Corinthians took pride in themselves for things that were, in the scope of eternity, temporal. Instead of developing in maturity, the church at Corinth was full of individuals who were braggadocio teachers, carnal believers, and self-appointed experts. Because they had an abundance of spiritual gifts and a desire to grow in them, they felt they could justify their shortcomings.

In 1 Corinthians 12:31-1 Corinthians 13:3, the book takes an unexpected turn. Before introducing the greatest path of all, love, Paul reviews *seven other paths* that the Corinthian church had already walked along prior to this point. Notice how each of these seven things provide much of the contents in First Corinthians:

Paths	Chapters
Spiritual Gifts (12:31)	1 Corinthians 12
Tongues of men and angels (13:1)	1 Corinthians 14
Gift of prophecy (13:2)	1 Corinthians 12
Understanding of mysteries and knowledge (13:2)	1 Corinthians 2

Faith that moves mountains (13:2)	1 Corinthians 12
Giving (13:3)	1 Corinthians 9 and 16
Martyrdom (13:3)	1 Corinthians 4

He calls the majority of these paths that he gave to the Corinthians unprofitable without the virtue of love (1 Corinthians 13:3). *In the short run*, these things produce splendid results. But Paul was never overly concerned about the short run, as we should certainly know by now. These things are *unprofitable in the long run*. Paul wasn't *discouraging* these things in and of themselves. He was *discouraging* the hyper-emphasis that the church at Corinth was placing upon these things and treating them as an *end*, and not a *means* to a greater end.

Along our journey, we must keep it in our minds that everything that we have learned to employ above are *not* the goals, alone. They are things that *deliver* us to that goal. Though tongues, ministry offices, supernatural power and authority and purging are paths that we take, they all lead to a greater path that is eternal in scope: *the love of God*.

I once got to a place in my journey where everything seemed to be going smoothly. My flesh was under control, the enemy wasn't pushing up against me, miracle power was flowing in my ministry, and my finances were doing quite well. Suddenly, I had a thought, "Now what?" This was another opportunity for the Lord to teach me something I had missed along the way: *The end cannot be substituted by the things that lead us to the end.* Plain and simply put: *The things that make that love known to us cannot replace the love of God.*

How God Loves Us

⁴Charity suffereth long, and is kind; charity envieth not; charity vaunteth not itself, is not puffed up,
⁵Doth not behave itself unseemly, seeketh not her own, is not easily provoked, thinketh no evil; ⁶Rejoiceth not in iniquity, but rejoiceth in the truth;

307

> ***⁷Beareth all things, believeth all things, hopeth all things, endureth all things.*** (1 Corinthians 13:4-7 KJV)

We see this verse so frequently that its meaning becomes shaded. This verse was originally given to describe *how God loves us.* Too often, people think it is *only* how we should love one another. Yet, we cannot love one another until we experience how much love He now has toward us.

An *experience* with this love is what the Holy Spirit is working us towards in all of His different protocols. The Holy Spirit is not necessarily working us toward spiritual gifts; He *uses* spiritual gifts. He is not working us toward our heavenly prayer language; He *uses* our heavenly prayer language. He is not working us toward purging; He *uses* purging. These are all utilized to bring us to the path of God's love. Along this path we come to know His astounding love and to show to others the dimension of that love we have experienced.

For those Corinthians who thought otherwise, the Apostle Paul delivered a stunning truth that toppled their theological sand castles.

> ***"Charity never faileth."*** (1 Corinthians 13:8a KJV)

Often this verse is thought to mean that if our spouse is heckling us, all we need to do is show them love and we will win the fight. Well, yes, showing love is always the best route to take, but that is not exactly what this verse is saying. "Faileth" means, "pass away." Paul was telling the Corinthians that the love of God would never see a day in which it would vanish.

Contrariwise, *the paths* that the Spirit of God was using to bring them to that love *would* end.

> ***But whether there be prophecies, they shall fail; whether there be tongues, they shall cease; whether there be knowledge, it shall vanish away.*** (1 Corinthians 13:8b KJV)

Everything that the Corinthians were priding themselves on would come to an end. *Along the journey, we must recognize that the tools that the*

Spirit of God has equipped us with will be put down as soon as this journey is over. Like a worker building a house, once the last nail is driven, those tools get put away.

This day is coming very soon.

> **For when that which is perfect is come, then that which is in part shall be done away.** (1 Corinthians 13:10 KJV)

The "perfect" thing that is being referred to here is *our perfect understanding of God's love.* The tools that we have been given provide us *glimpses* of that love. Gifts of healing prove to us, through healing, that God loves us. Working of miracles proves to us, through the miraculous, that God is with us. The gift of prophecy proves to us, through utterance, that God desires to speak to us. The same holds true with every gift. Yet, no matter what experience we have ever had with the love of God through these means, our understanding of that love is still incomplete because, according to the verse above, they can only show us God's love "in part."

We Shall Know as We Are Known

In spite of all the manifestations of God's love in this age, Paul likens our understanding of it to the understanding of a child.

> **When I was a child, I spake as a child, I understood as a child, I thought as a child.** (1 Corinthians 13:11a KJV)

What a blow to the Corinthian church and to all those who pride themselves on their giftings, graces, and good works. None of these can ever bring one into a place of total maturity. They can only help us until we get to that place.

> **11but when I became a man, I put away childish things. 12For now we see through a glass, darkly; but then face to face: for now I know in part; but then I shall know even as also I am known.** (1 Corinthians 13:11b-12 KJV)

Eventually, we will become full-grown adults in God and put away the childish things that we *used* before we became grown. This occurs when we put off this mortal body and take up our glorified bodies. It is at that moment that we will no longer need to depend on another path to take us into God's love. Instead, we will be present with the Lord.

In front of us we will see the Shekinah glory of God: a cloud full of light and sound that no man has ever seen or heard before. As intimidating as that cloud would be for any individual, there will be no fear. For out of that cloud will come the fullness of the Godhead bodily: Jesus Christ (Col 2:9). We will notice that He has the same body that we do. In this body will be the scars on His hands and feet, which He chose to keep so that you and I could know that He understands our suffering (Hebrews 4:15). The glorified Christ will look you and me in the eyes, and we will know perfectly the love that the One who died and gave Himself for us has had from the moment we were conceived in His thinking—the love that He has been trying to demonstrate to us this whole time.

There will be no more questions that ask, "Why didn't God heal me while I was on the earth?" "Why did God let my family member suffer?" "Why did God allow me to be molested as a young girl?" The love that you and I will know fully at that moment will prove to us that the whole time He was doing everything He could to deliver us from the situation. Nevertheless, it will not matter then. Mankind will be with the Lord for the rest of eternity, abiding in His unending love.

In eternity, should one of us get an assignment from God to go to a distant and far off galaxy and meet a civilization of angelic hosts who inquire about the love that they see in us, we would say, "Ah, yes. Let me tell you about this love that you have observed in me. It all began one day when the Holy Spirit got a hold of my heart and helped make the love of God known to me, through various means. It put me upon a path. And with His help, I took that path all the way past death, into eternity, where I now stand today."

Yes, the path of love is the path that has no end. It takes us straight into the Presence of Jesus Christ where we will know Him and all that He is. This is the end that everything is bringing us to. *Until that day our knowledge of His love will be incomplete*. Fortunately for us, He gave us His Word. In it we can get a glimpse of the Love that we are soon to meet.

CHAPTER FORTY-SIX

The Spiritual Darkroom

"Meditation, with the Help of the Spirit, enables you to develop the image that is already there."

"Your word is a lamp to walk by, and a light to illumine my path." (Ps. 119:105 NET)

Something transpired at the instant of our salvation. We became pilgrims. The idea of a traveler on a journey is employed throughout the Word of God.

> *²²Since you have purified your souls in obeying the truth through the Spirit in sincere love of the brethren, love one another fervently with a pure heart,*
> *²³having been born again, not of corruptible seed but incorruptible, through the word of God which lives and abides forever.*
>
> *⁹But you are a chosen generation, a royal priesthood, a holy nation, His own special people, that you may proclaim the praises of Him who called you out of darkness into His marvelous light.*
>
> *¹¹Beloved, I beg you as <u>sojourners and pilgrims</u>.* (1 Peter 1:22,23; 2:9,11 NKJV)

The word *pilgrim* in the Greek is *parepidemos,* meaning, "one who comes from a foreign country into a city or land to reside there by the side of the natives." It also means to "sojourn in a strange place." A sojourn is nothing more than a temporary stay. If you have ever traveled out of country, you've probably tasted what this feels like. Strange languages, strange accents, strange foods, and strange customs are just a few of the alien things that endlessly remind you, "Pilgrim, you are far from home."

The difference between a pilgrim and a citizen is that a citizen is already home, and a pilgrim must take a journey home. In foreign countries, I always meet citizens whom I grow to love and enjoy. I've spent up to three weeks with them, every day, non-stop preaching and teaching God's Word. But there comes the time when I must say, "See you soon." I hit the trail home (on an Airbus or Boeing, of course) because I am a sojourner, just passing through. As believers, we are strangers and foreigners on this planet, having our citizenship in heaven. We are just passing through, as we reconcile the world to God (2 Corinthians 5:18-21).

Our heavenly Father placed us on a path the moment we became His children, and it is in daily walking this path that we are propelled, ever closer, home to our Father. God has called believers down this path, but it is up to us to decide how far we want to go. Some believers have gone so far that they consider this life absolutely nothing. Others don't even know that there is anything beyond getting saved.

Oddly, some believers are unable to recognize that they are on this path. They don't see themselves as peculiar, or as a stranger. They are carnal believers. The difference between a spiritual believer and a carnal believer is that a spiritual believer is receiving illumination from the Word of God. This illumination causes them to see clearly what we have become in Christ, and draws a line of differentiation between the world and us.

This is not so with a carnal believer. Carnal believers will justify the world, including worldly entertainment, godless political stances, and unsanctified behavior. They may attempt to rationalize why there is nothing wrong with what they are doing. I am not going to say these people are unsaved. This is not my job. What is clear, however, is that there is less illumination from the Word of God penetrating their inward man than in the spiritual believer who has wholeheartedly opened arms, mind, heart, body and soul to Christ.

The Word of God *and* Praying In Tongues: Two Legs For the Traveler

The reason I travel everywhere, teaching and preaching about praying in tongues, is not so that people can brag about how many hours they do it. That is *not* the point. Praying in tongues is a *means* to an *end*: the *end* being the total illumination of love that lights up our path and enables us to take one more step into God.

Our Bible, the Word of God, is the agent responsible for illuminating our path, and is the most important entity in our development as pilgrims through this life. An *abundance* of the Word of God will accelerate us down the path of love and righteousness. A *lack* of the Word of God will keep us treading in place, most of the times slogging around in circles.

"Well, I thought you said it was praying in the Holy Ghost." *Praying in the Holy Ghost does not replace meditating the Word of God.* Rather, it assists the Word of God into doing what it acutely desires: to illuminate us. They are two legs needed to walk down the path that leads us all the way into God.

Every time I return home from preaching, I check my Facebook page. There are always requests from people with all kinds of direct questions. Whether on social media or in person, I am always asked, "How do I grow in God?" What they are really saying is, "How can I go further down this road? I am tired of being where I am. I want to go further in."

I enjoy this question, because I can look back on my own experience and answer it with absolute certainty. Like a doctor, I can prescribe the things I have done and still do, and guarantee that the prescription *will* take them from being a carnal or immature believer and begin to grow *them* into mature sons and daughters of God.

Immersed in The Word of God

You have the Bible sitting on your nightstand. Many times you have been compelled with excitement to open it. Yet, just as soon as that excitement arises, it is met with the sobering thought, *Look how enormous that book is. Remember what happened last time you tried to read it? You didn't understand all that heavy and confusing speech. Besides, you have to go to college to learn this book. Why not leave it to the preachers? But then again, they all have their own interpretation of it anyway. I should just watch TV tonight, and forget it.*

So television is what you do. This happens night after night until you grow discouraged, and you think, "Lord, if I could only figure out a way to get what is on these pages into my life. But I don't know how." Been there before? So have I.

Let me share a few things about approaching the Word of God. There are a few ways to pursue an understanding of the Bible. They are all useful, and none of them will hurt you. However, based on my experience, the best method is listed *last*.

1.) **Reading:** Reading the Bible is where we all start. Reading primarily familiarizes us with the text. As soon as you learn to read, you can begin doing this. It is simply picking up the Bible and going through it like any other book, newspaper, or magazine (with far less pictures). You will encounter stories, poetry, nuggets and proverbs, history, prophecy, songs, psalms, letters, parables, and much more.

Christians and non-Christians read the Bible regularly. A businessperson reads it in the airport. A soccer mom reads it in a coffee shop. Students and professors read the Bible at the local university. *Reading the Bible doesn't promise to produce any life changing results, except you will become accustomed to its contents.*

2.) **Memorizing:** If any of us have been through catechism, Sunday school, or any other Bible study, we have gone through the memorization stage. I encourage memorizing and have spent ample time doing it myself. I got serious about memorizing scripture when I was a freshman in college.

Back in 2002, we didn't have smart phones and apps to help us out, so I bought a pocket Bible. I carried it everywhere. Each day, I would highlight a new verse that I wanted to memorize. Instead of doodling stick figures in a boring class, I would write out the verse over and over again. Then,

I would see if I could write it without looking at the text. If I could, I'd wait a few hours to see if I could still write it perfectly. If I was able to do so, then I had successfully memorized the verse, and I could add it to my Word Excel database. Every night I went over the verses I had memorized that week, and on Sunday night, I would go over all of the verses in my database. It was quite the memorization strategy.

If you want to be a good preacher, I recommended you memorize Scripture. Nothing is better than a brain that always has a Scripture in the chamber. Memorization not only familiarizes you with the text, but it enables it to stick in your consciousness. However, memorization is purely a mental thing. You are more than just a mental being.

Memorization is *not* what opens up the text to you, and pours in the revelation, and illuminates your path. You need something more.

3.) **Studying:** Every believer should study God's Word, as it is this study that will enable us to be approved by God (2 Timothy 2:15). Studying God's word is a grand enterprise in and of itself. Study is best defined as, "Research or a detailed examination and analysis of a subject." The Bible presents such a plethora of topics that you could spend a lifetime of study and not encompass its entirety. Take up a study in the Word of God, and you could find yourself studying archaeology, history, character studies, geography, the meaning of Hebrew, Greek, or Aramaic words, past civilizations and their customs, cultures, and worship, as well as the lessons, teachings, and knowledge that are spread all through the Bible.

The most common study of the Word of God is a topical study. This includes picking a subject and examining it through the different places it is found in the Bible. For example, choose the topic of selfishness, and examine selfishness as it is presented in the stories, characters, and text of the Scriptures.

Another common way of studying is an expository study of the Word of God. This is taking a particular text and examining it piece by piece to discover its meaning.

Secular people can also study the Bible. Some study the Bible to prove it wrong, find contradictions, or point out error. They apply their mental capabilities to discredit the content of God's Word.

For as much as study can help, it can also damage us, especially if we study with the wrong motive or intention. Study is not always divine and spiritual. It can, at times, be carnal. I have been around many teachers of God's Word who study more than their fair share, yet their own lives come up short, and they miss the mark and live defeated. I don't question the state of their heart; I am sure they truly love God. Yet, for all their study, don't you think they would be able to get the victory in certain areas?

On the other hand, I have been around preachers who are fine students of the Word of God, yet they use all their acquired information to put their congregations to sleep. (How can anyone make God *boring*?)

4.) Meditation: We see that studying God's Word is beneficial and should be done constantly, but study is not the end. *There is one more thing, a catalyst to throw open the windows of knowledge and cause light to shine upon our path, so that we can march down it with the power of a trained soldier: meditation.*

Meditation is different from reading, memorizing, or studying the Word. In Joshua 1:8, *meditate* is the Hebrew word *haga*. It means, *"to murmur, to ponder, to imagine."* Though the word "meditate" is used fourteen times in the Bible, the word *haga* is used twenty-four times in the Old Testament alone, having other English words designated to it. Notice some of the places where *haga* is used:

> **But his delight is in the law of the Lord; and in his law doth he meditate (haga) day and night.** (Psalms 1:2 KJV)

> **Why do the heathen rage, and the people imagine (haga) a vain thing?** (Psalms 2:1 KJV)

> **I remember the days of old; I meditate (haga) on all thy works; I muse (haga) on the work of thy hands.** (Psalms 143:5 KJV)

In all of these passages, notice how it would be impossible to substitute read, memorize, or study for *haga*. It is this meditating that opens up the door for the Holy Spirit of God to bring forth the illumination that we need on a certain topic or Scripture.

Reading, memorizing, and studying *aid* this kind of contemplative meditation, and give us what we need to go deeper. Familiarity with the text and information regarding dates, times, and characters help to deepen meditation. It gives it more avenues to explore. But when the above are done *without* meditation, the majority of what God desires to get over to us is not realized. Here is why:

Meditation is the process whereby the Holy Ghost comes alongside of us and begins to bring us into the text, all the while revealing the mind of God to us, illuminating the truths that God desired for us so deeply that He sent His Word to us, and preserved it for us.

The Bible that you and I hold in our hands is God-breathed and inspired by God (2 Timothy 3:16). God took mere human words and breathed into them, filling them with the very breath of Himself, the essence of Who and What He is. When we meditate, the Spirit of God is going to take everything that He breathed into human language and breathe it into our consciousness, throwing more light onto our path and illuminating the entire way we go. Notice the result of meditation:

> *This Book of the Law shall not depart from your mouth, but you shall <u>meditate</u> in it day and night, that you may observe to do according to all that is written in it. For then you will make your way <u>prosperous</u>, and then you will have <u>good success</u>.* (Joshua 1:8 NKJV)

Human Beings Think In Pictures

I want us to do a little exercise right now that will help. I realize that you are reading a book, trying to follow what I am saying. But you deserve a break. You have my permission to have a little daydream, if you will.

I want you to think of your favorite place on the earth and go there right now in your thoughts. (Preferably choose a place where you have been more than once, as it makes it easier to imagine.) For some it might be a beach, for others a mall, a horse ranch, a quiet porch at home, an amusement park. The sky is the limit.

Now, here are some instructions before you put the book down to try this exercise: Spend five minutes here. Relax and let your mind wander. Let the daydream unfold, and don't stop it (unless it's something inappropriate, of course). Ready? Go.

Welcome back. How was the trip? You didn't accidently doze off, did you? Did you take your full five minutes? I imagine you may have taken more. Be as it may, back to business. Let me ask you a couple of things about this daydream that you had. I, of course, am not going to hear your responses, so let's just say these are rhetorical questions. You may want to write them down; sometimes there is wisdom in looking over your answers.

1.) Where did you go?
2.) What did you do?
3.) Who happened to enter your daydream?
4.) Was there dialogue? Who said what to whom?
5.) The main character of your daydream: what color was their shirt?
6.) Were there any objects in your daydream? (Skateboard, boat, shopping bags, vehicles, etc.?) What did they look like? Describe them.

You may be curious why I am asking these questions. I am trying to make an important point: look at how your mind brought all of these details into your daydream without your having to do anything. We could analyze the human brain, but there is no further need to do so in order to prove what I am going to say. *Human beings think in images and pictures, not words.*

I venture that a thousand people out of a thousand who do this exercise will vary in the details of their daydream. All go to different places (with a few exceptions), and all of them have different dialogue and activities. Yet, it is a safe bet that *not one* could say that all they saw were *words*, passing through their mind. Can you imagine that? Instead of a *picture* of you lying on a black sand beach, wearing a red swim suit, next to your spouse who is reading an island living magazine, while hearing the crashing of the waves and the sound of the jet skis roaring by, you see *words*: "Jet ski. Swimsuit. Magazine. Red. Ocean. Wave. Blue. Sky. People. Fun. Thirsty. Drink from straw."

This would be preposterous. Everyone sees a picture. In fact, while you've been reading this book, your mind is busy, turning words into images. That is how the mind works.

Words Create Images: A single word contains a picture within it. The combination of words that you speak or write determines the kind of picture you convey.

God's Word is no different. The Bible is made of forty books, each of which holds an image within it. When you combine these forty books, you get the total image of everything God wants us to see and know while we are on this planet.

Meditation is about pondering the words inside of Scripture until the picture that is contained in the Word begins to develop in your inward man. Meditation is the process that causes the eyes of your *spirit man* to *see*. When we come into Christ, the Holy Spirit concerns Himself with making us *see*, above anything else.

"See what, Chris? What is it that the Spirit of God wants us to *see*?"

> ***"Put on the new man who is renewed in <u>knowledge</u> according to <u>the image of Him</u> <u>who created him</u>."***
> (Colossians 3:10 NKJV)

In case the New King James Version is a little muddy, look how the English Standard Version puts it:

> *"And have put on the new self, which is being renewed in <u>knowledge</u> after <u>the image of its creator</u>."* (Colossians 3:10 ESV)

"Well, I am still not getting it, Brother Palmer."

Notice the four integral parts in the verse: *Renewed, Knowledge, Image, Creator*. This is key as to *how* meditation works to illuminate our path. The word *"renewed"* is the Greek word, *anakainoo,* which means, "to cause to grow up, new strength and vigor, to be changed into a new kind of life." It not only means the new birth in Christ, but also the maturing that comes, faith to faith, strength to strength, and glory to glory. This maturing comes through knowledge.

Peter tells us this, ***"Grace and peace be multiplied unto you through the knowledge of God, and Jesus Christ our Lord"*** (2 Peter 1:2 KJV). This is the same kind of knowledge that comes through praying in the Holy Ghost.

> ***According as his divine power hath given unto us all things that pertain unto life and godliness, through the knowledge of him** that hath called us to glory and virtue.* (2 Peter 1:3 KJV)

This knowledge is exact and precise. Praying in the Holy Ghost starts the process of receiving this knowledge. Meditation sees to it that the knowledge is *completely* delivered, particularly the knowledge that pertains to godliness (everything in the Word of God concerning God's redemptive plan for mankind).

Notice how this exact knowledge comes: "after the image." The precise knowledge that we need is encoded in an *image*. The Greek word for *image* is *eikon.* Look at a place in Scripture how it is used:

> ***So they brought it [a coin]. And He said to them, "Whose image (eikon) and inscription is this?" They said to Him, "Caesar's."*** (Mark 12:16 NKJV)

A simple image is a semblance of what has been seen. In the above passages, Caesar himself was not on the coin. His *image* was. Think of your first car or house. Do you have it in your mind? That image is *not* your car or first house. It is a *likeness* of it. Your first house may now have chintz curtains, and a family from Terre Haute calling it "home." And your first car may be rusting away in a weedy junkyard, guarded by unhappy pit bulls. (Got *that* image?)

Eikon is an *image* that is so descriptive and detailed that it can be stamped on a gold coin. An image, however, is *not* the object itself. The process of meditation is where the Spirit of God extracts the images and similitudes in the words on the Bible pages, and floods your understanding with them. The more we meditate, the more detailed the picture becomes, and the more clearly we begin to see.

I had the opportunity of visiting Vatican City in 2006. As we walked through St. Peter's Basilica, I was eager to see the world famous Sistine Chapel. When I walked in, there it was, in all of its breathtaking glory. What I was seeing was the completed image. What I did not see were the four years (1508-1512) that it took Michelangelo to do this. Although legend says he painted it while lying on his back, it is closer to the truth that he used scaffolding that was custom designed to reach the ceiling.

Contemplating the finished work, I imagined all the tourists vanished, and only the artist and the ceiling remained, alone together. Head bent backwards, sweat dripping down his face, arms aching with pain, Michelangelo was immaculately leaving his legacy to the world, a fresco that attests to his splendid ability over five hundred years later.

When you turn your life over to the Holy Spirit, the Master Painter Himself opens the doors of your life and comes walking into your chapel. After examining the ceiling (your heart), He takes His place on the scaffolding and waits for you to give Him the paint and supplies He needs to start creating the grand image. As you pray in tongues and meditate the Word of God, the pipeline opens, and the Holy Spirit begins the Work. He takes the words that you pray and meditate, and begins to create a great picture in your spirit that will last all the way into eternity. This picture is none other than the *image* of our Creator and what we look like in Him.

> **To them God willed to <u>make known</u> what are the riches of the glory of this mystery among the Gentiles: which is <u>Christ in you</u>, the hope of glory.** (Colossians 1:27 NKJV)

I have heard people read this Scripture and say, "Oh, God! Please, please! Reveal to me who I am in Christ. I want to know. I want to know."

Sadly, they never get anywhere. It's heartbreaking, because you know they are aching to enter in. They haven't learned how the divine image works and how to fuel it with prayer and meditation. Or, perhaps they know better and got sidetracked. Their seeing may be faulty.

Or perhaps they are meditating on the secular. Once, in college, I was sitting at my desk doing homework, as usual. My roommate was lying on his bed, staring up at the ceiling, wasting time, as usual.

"Palmer," he said. "I shouldn't be a leader in my youth group."

I turned and looked at him with a grin; I thought he was joking. He continued, "If I were told to speak to my small group for an hour on anything, I would have nothing to say."

I thought, *Hmm. This guy is in Bible college, and he can't give an hour talk to a few junior high kids about something from the Bible?* I was amused, because I knew that he was perfectly capable. Frank's aptitude as a teacher and minister was not in question. It was discouragement talking. It also had something to do with what he was focused on *seeing*.

"Frank, buddy, let me ask you a question. What if the youth pastor asked you to talk to the kids for an hour about your favorite television show? Y'know, that cartoon show you watch every night at your computer, three and four episodes at a time? Do you think you would be capable of speaking about that?" He started laughing; he knew I had caught him at his own game. The only fresh images inside his head were a stockpile of cartoons.

Without a doubt Frank would have been able to stand up and talk for hours about his favorite show, probably going episode by episode, in full detail, dialogue and everything. He remembered everything, even without a replay. He had meditated it in his mind while watching it. This is what God desires us to do with His Word!

So, all the while the Holy Ghost is sitting on the scaffolding, thinking, "Sure would love to start painting this fresco. Got all the blueprints right here. Brought my lunch box and headphones. I am ready for a full day of work. Only thing I need is some paint."

As in every painting job, the owner needs to supply the paint. Take the words that are in the Bible and start meditating them. Employ the Holy Ghost.

Seeing Is Looking Inward: If for some reason your eyesight were suddenly taken away, would you *still* be able to describe your bedroom? Would it *still* be possible to explain what your son, daughter, mother, father, grandparent look like? Yes. Scientists tell us that seeing is *not* done with our eyes. Our eyes only allow light to enter so that our brains can see. Seeing is done with the mind.

If, as a preacher, I had my eyeballs poked out, I would *still* be able to preach just as effectively from the Word of God, because the image of Christ is not in front of me, requiring my eyes, it is within me, inside of my heart.

God's desire, through meditation, is to build this image into our spirit so that we can bear down on it anytime that we need to speak of Christ, put words to it, and convey it to others. He has given the Holy Spirit to us for this specific purpose, to reveal the Word of God to us in an *image* form, and to paint the picture of who Christ is in us, to us, and through us the hope of glory.

When a preacher is preaching from the image they have within, they will be convincing, exciting, and convicting. You will think, "This preacher sure does believe what he is saying. It must be something he has experienced. It must be the truth."

However, have you ever watched someone bring forth the Word of God until your eyes got weary, and forced you into battle to stay awake? I have fallen asleep in church on more occasions than I would like to admit. There have been times where I was quite absorbed in what the speaker was saying, but I was fighting physical exhaustion. That is quite different from being just plain bored. Go ahead, laugh.

I am, indeed, making an indictment on bad preaching. If you are a preacher, this will be helpful. Here is a rule of thumb: *Never, and I mean **never**, preach something that you cannot **see**.* Jesus was a master teacher and preacher because He painted pictures for those He taught. This would not have been possible if He, Himself, hadn't first seen the picture He was painting for others.

Do we really want to preach something that we haven't spent prayer time gaining understanding and insight? If I were to give a five-minute dissertation to preachers about preaching, I would spend all five valuable minutes driving home this point. The ability to convince and to articulate is wrapped in the ability to *see*. A "revelation" is nothing more than a truth revealed: It was hidden at 2 p.m. and, at 3 p.m. while in prayer, you *saw* it.

Somewhere, there is a painter sitting on scaffolding, doing some painting inside you.

The Power Of *The Word* Is In The Images It Produces: God's Word is clear about itself: ***"For the Word of God is quick, and <u>powerful</u>"*** (Hebrews 4:12 KJV).

"Well, based upon the way *my* pastor preaches, it sure isn't," you may say.

How is it that two preachers can use the same text in a sermon, and one be effective, and the other not? The answer is simple: the power in the Word of God comes from the *image* that is hidden in each word. When the images are extracted by the Spirit of God and painted onto our hearts we become equipped with power.

I have noticed that until the image comes I am dependent upon my intellect. As soon as the image comes, however, I leave intellect and come up under spiritual understanding (Colossians 1:9). God wants His preachers and ministers to operate from spiritual understanding. When you minister from spiritual understanding (the understanding that your spirit has because of the image it has seen), your whole man can then be involved. Your spirit will employ your soul for the mind, will, and emotions, and it will employ your body for the purpose of animating the image. This is what makes for "good old fashioned preaching." You will always notice the difference in a preacher who has spiritual understanding versus a windbag who is just making noise, or even an intellect who has a gift of rocking people to sleep. The key is meditation, which will always unlock the image contained in the words.

Digesting The Word Of God: My mother always complained that I never let my food digest. "Chris, before you go back outside, sit and wait a while so that your food can settle." I was such an active kid that I'd come in from playing, throw down a few bites of dinner, and be back out the door in ten minutes. No wonder I have always been so skinny.

Digestion means, *"to obtain information, ideas, or principles from."* When you digest your food, your body is breaking down the substance of what you ate and converting it into nutrients that your cells can use. *Meditation is the digestion of your spirit.* Weak or immature believers are unable to become spiritual because their spirits never digest the nutrients that wait inside the Word of God, and thus they remain carnal. It is these nutrients that build up each believer and cause a renewing to come in their mind, taking them one more step further into the knowledge of God and down the path of everything that Christ has called them to become.

Here is a fact I have known since Bible school but never paid significant attention to it until I was a little further down the road in my ministry: *no author in the Bible ever taught in verses.* Many Christians slow their growth in God because they attempt to digest their favorite verses, *leaving out everything around it.* This is like watching my little nephew eat his dinner. If it were up to him, he would head right for his dessert and leave his green vegetables, carbohydrates, and meat untouched. As a good father, my brother will say, "No, son. Eat all of your food, like a good boy." My brother wants his son to get all the nutrients from the food so that there is no deficiency in his body, giving him the ability to grow up, strong and powerful (so he can drive a NASCAR).

If we really want the Holy Spirit to paint the image of Christ on our hearts, we are going to have to be good boys or girls and not just look at the portions of the Scripture that we find "encouraging" or "motivating." *Here is an original thought: the Scripture wasn't given by God to motivate you. It was given to paint within you the image of the Godhead bodily and create within you the picture of who you have become in Him.* For this to happen, you have to start meditating the *whole thing* if you want the *whole picture.*

"Yes, but I don't like the book of Romans. It is confusing." Well, I am not a fan of the color brown either, but my favorite picture has brown in it. Sure, I like red better. But you can't paint mountains with red. Mountains are brown or green, not red.

The Holy Ghost wants to use every book, every chapter, every verse to paint this masterpiece. Don't limit Him. Aren't you thankful Michelangelo used more than just red when he painted the Sistine Chapel?

The Importance of Context

"Jesus' teachings are just so random," say some people.

When we delve into the teachings of Jesus, it is very important to understand that Christ was not a disorganized, shoot-from-the-hip kind of teacher. He wasn't random. If He appears to be random, it is because we are missing the context. The context gives us the inflow (what is going into the verse) and outflow (what is coming out of the verse). If you decide to pursue the pictures and images that can be built inside of you from the Gospels, locate where a new thought of story begins and find out where it ends.

Here is an example:

Jesus has just resurrected Jairus' daughter from the dead, with many scorners and mockers nearby. Peter, James, and John, as well as Jairus and his wife, were in the room to witness this miracle, as He had put everyone else, including the other disciples, out of the room. Here is where the verse picks up:

> *⁵⁵And her spirit returned, and she arose immediately. And He commanded that she be given something to eat.*
> *⁵⁶Then her parents were astonished, but He charged them to tell no one what had happened.* (Luke 8:55-56 NKJV)

These are the last verses of Luke, chapter 8. A great percentage of people would stop meditating here. But doing so would be like throwing half of your steak in the trash while you are still hungry. The steak isn't finished. There is more to digest.

Look at how chapter nine begins: *"Then." Then* implies *right then,* just after He resurrected the girl. Inside of Jairus' home, after He performed such a great miracle, came a proof of His power.

"Then he called his disciples together." Why would Jesus need to call them together? Because He had put them out of the room. He broke the huddle before the miracle, and called the huddle together afterwards. The story is still going.

> ¹*Then he called his disciples together, and gave them power and authority over all devils, and to cure diseases.*
> ²*And he sent them to preach the kingdom of God and to heal the sick.* (Luke 9:1-2 KJV)

What a difference Luke 9:1-2 makes when we find out that it happened in Jairus' home. So much revelation awaits an exploration of this; it is phenomenal. The key to shucking it out is paying attention to the context.

The images that we need to capture from the Gospels are divided into whole stories, not always indicated by chapter divisions. When I meditate the stories of Jesus I look for where the divisions begin and end, and I deal with them from there. Don't be duped by the chapters and verses.

The Apostles Taught In Whole Letters

Exiting the book of Acts, you arrive in the Epistles, starting with Romans. Romans through Jude are letters that were written by different apostles, and they constitute a series of thoughts.

When I was in the sixth grade, a girl named Tiffany handed me a letter and told me to read it when I was by myself. The writing was definitely that of a girl. As any sixth grade boy would do, I headed to the restroom with the letter wadded in my pocket, barricaded myself into a stall, and started reading. My heart began to race. If the flowers on the front weren't enough to clue me in, the content sure enough was. "Chris, you are just so cute. I like you. Do you like me?"

This was my first love letter, an unprecedented event in my life. Should I be happy? Should I keep it a secret? Do I tell my friends? All I knew was one thing: it was exciting reading it. I read the whole page of mush over and over again, reminding myself how cute I was. This letter contained words that were meticulously placed next to each other in an assortment of sentences and paragraphs in order to do one thing: communicate, to me, the image of me inside of her.

And, boy, did she succeed. My head was enormous for days, both in school and out. Everywhere I walked, I had a new stride in my step. All that was missing was the Bee Gee's "Staying Alive" playing in the air around my head. Though Tiffany and I never married, she taught me what letters have the ability to do.

When Tiffany gave me her love letter, I didn't read twenty-five percent of it, then fold it up and stuff it back into my pocket. I eagerly read the whole thing, understanding that every word was a stroke of the brush, painting a larger image: her true feelings toward me.

Similarly, each verse in an Epistle is a brush stroke that goes toward painting the grand image contained within the letter itself. Beginning from 1:1 and going all the way to the end, each letter paints a picture of everything that the Spirit of God has painted inside of the writer through revelation knowledge, and inspired him to write it at that very moment. As with the Gospels, it is easy to make the same mistake and divide the epistles into chapters and verses. But every Epistle is one complete image and thought within itself.

Our understanding is now formed to see every epistle as a full and complete picture. Our goal, therefore, is to see the image that the writer sought to convey to the Church or churches to which he was writing. Sadly, it is often never realized because we get carried away with our affection for one particular stroke of the brush (one verse), and never see how it fits in with the rest of the brush strokes.

When I noticed that each letter sought to paint a picture within me, I stopped my *regular* reading of a chapter in one book, and skipping to a chapter in another book. People regularly do that. On Monday, they read 2 Peter 2. Tuesday, it is Revelation 13. Wednesday, they are somehow in Hebrews 8. On Thursday, they are in Luke.

Of course, if the individual is studying a topic, that is one thing. But I am not referring to topical study. I rather refer to random Bible excavation that has no rhyme or reason.

"Well, I still get something out of it." Yes, I am sure you do. It is the Word of God after all. But whatever you get, it is highly limited and incomplete, because you are not connecting to the image.

Producing the Image

In the digital age, darkrooms have almost become extinct. For you who have never seen a photo developed outside of your camera phone, there was a day when film had to be brought to a darkroom so that the actinic rays of light could be excluded from the photograph, making the picture visible on paper. Darkrooms don't capture the image. That is the camera's job. Darkrooms merely bring forth the image that was placed on the paper by the camera.

Similarly, meditation is not responsible for putting the image into the Scripture. The image was placed into the Scripture when the Holy Ghost breathed upon it, making it the inspired Word of God. Meditation, with the Help of the Spirit, enables you to develop the image that is already there.

In the summer of 2011, while at his home in Texas, a prophet of God spoke to me and said, "Young man, you are above the Law because of the spirit." I remember how hard that word hit my spirit man. I also remember how it went completely past my understanding.

Flying home, the Spirit of God called me to get into the darkroom of meditation. The Lord reminded me of what this prophet of God had said, then told me, "Son, I am going to give to you a revelation concerning this that will open up a floodgate of revelation knowledge and begin a new stream of authority in your life." I got really excited. This was when the Lord told me to begin reading the book of Romans, over and over again.

When I heard these instructions I was a bit uneasy. Romans has never been the easiest book to understand. Just about every false doctrine comes from a misunderstanding of Romans. It didn't take me long to get discouraged. I read the book of Romans sixteen times before I finally went back to God to throw in the towel.

The Lord's answer to me was to back out of Romans and park over in Galatians. I was relieved. Galatians is ten chapters shorter. I began reading the book of Galatians over and over and over again, until it started to dawn on me what it was about. Each time I sat down to meditate Galatians, I was taking it into the darkroom to develop the image in it.

If you desire to go into the darkroom to expose the image that is found inside of the epistles, remember, you have to work with the whole image.

Stop taking a verse here and a verse there and trying to make sense of it. I recommend you discipline yourself to spend time with a whole letter until you start seeing the image. This is the process of digestion. Keep running the book through your spirit until you start absorbing all the nutrients in it. Each letter is one image, and when you put them all together, you will start seeing the grand scheme of things. The revelation that comes will be endless.

My process began in the fall of 2011, but it wasn't until around Christmas, after ceaseless time with Galatians, that I began to see it as I had never seen it before. The whole book began to make sense as a whole, rather than just a few verses here and there. Correctly understanding the word, "spirit," was the trick to figuring out what Paul was talking about in Galatians. Because of flawed grade school teaching on Galatians, each time I saw the word "spirit," I automatically assumed it was talking about the Holy Spirit. As early as age eight, I was taught that the fruits of the Spirit are the fruits of the Holy Spirit. The denominational elementary school I attended gave an award to the student of the month, called "The fruitful servant." This was conferred to whichever student demonstrated the "fruit of the Holy Spirit" for that particular month. It never occurred to me that "spirit" could be referring to the spirit of man. This kept the book of Galatians in a knot to me.

Through meditating it consistently enough, all the verses around Galatians 5:22-23 began to provide me with evidence that it was not, in fact, the fruit of the *Holy* Spirit, but rather, the fruit of a *reborn* spirit, the spirit of a man or woman who has been reconciled to God. When I finally digested this, things took off.

Galatians, I finally perceived, is about our freedom from the Law because of the new nature that we have been given as a child of God. The summary of Galatians is found at the end, where Paul says, ***"For in Christ Jesus neither circumcision nor uncircumcision avails anything, but a new creation"*** (Galatians 6:15 NKJV). This one sentence summarized six chapters of revelation knowledge, and sealed the deal for me that Paul was discussing the new man and our Sonship in Christ, and negating the old man and the Law.

After reading Galatians fifty times I felt that the Holy Spirit had developed in me a phenomenal image of Galatians. I immediately took what I had learned and began preaching it without any notes whatsoever. I would say, "Open up to the book of Galatians," and take off. Those unwritten ministry notes were unneeded because of the image developed in me in the darkroom of meditation: an everlasting and eternal image that was awarded to me because of hours of meditation. To this day, preaching on Galatians gets me so excited I can scarcely contain myself.

When it was time to exit Galatians, the Lord told me to head back into a place where I had struggled before: Romans. *Romans? Please, no. Not Romans. Romans took me to task last time.* After whining, I finally yielded to Holy Ghost and went right back into it.

Only this time, I had a key that I didn't have before. The image of the new man had been painted for me. I had a new understanding of the word "spirit." My understanding was at a different level because of what the Holy Ghost had taught me from Galatians. As a jackhammer wears away concrete, the image I gained from Galatians began to wear away the mysterious parts of Romans, and it started to slip into my spiritual understanding. I eventually finished the book of Romans fifty times and came away with marvelous truths that get me excited every time I think of them.

As I said before: Stop taking a verse here and there and attempting to make sense of it. Discipline yourself to spend time with a whole book until you start seeing the image of what God has for you. If you will do this, you will be able to take that image into *worship*—the last stop before our journey comes to an end.

CHAPTER FORTY-SEVEN

The Image of God

**"This permanent fresco of Christ that He paints on
the canvas of our hearts will be with us every time we decide to
enter into worship."**

Have you ever noticed that in worship there will be people praising, jumping, shouting, running, and crying? Yet in the same service, others just stand there, watching the clock tick? It is only natural to wonder why some aren't moved. I have heard it said, "Well, some people can't get into the music they are playing." Others say, "You know, some people don't like to act that way in public." Then others will say, "I guess we all worship in our own way." While I am not trying to come up with a general solution as to why this happens for everyone, I can, at least, shed some light on this.

All worship requires an image. In the Old Testament, the Canaanites worshiped Baal (male) and Ashtaroth (female) (Jude 2:10-23). The Philistines worshiped Dagon, a half-man, half-fish god (1 Samuel 5). Molech, the national god of the Ammorites (2 Kings 23), had the head of a calf and the arms of a man. Although many other gods and pagan deities were served in Old Testament history, the common thread was that there had to be an *object* to worship. Even astrologers found an object to worship in the sun, moon, and stars (Deuteronomy 4:19).

What sanctified the children of Israel and gave them a clear distinction from all of the godless tribes was that their God did not have an idol made like Him. God expected them to refrain from this practice. Jehovah was the only true God, and would not settle to be cast as a dumb statue that could not speak. Instead, He visited His people in the tabernacle of Moses in the Holy of Holies. As God's people, Israel was privileged.

Unlike a lifeless figure made of brass or iron, God would one day cast Himself in *living human flesh*, and visit Israel *personally*. Israel finally bowed to Jesus when He came into Jerusalem during the triumphal entry, crying, "Hosanna! Blessed is the King of Israel that cometh in the name of the Lord" (John 12:13). It is that *image* that we still magnify, lift up, and worship in this dispensation of Grace.

"Brother Palmer, I like what you are saying, but I have never *seen* Him."

Christ is seated with God at His right hand, so our ability to see Him (unless He sovereignly visits us for a very special reason) now depends on the Holy Spirit (John 16:13). When the Scripture tells us that the Holy Spirit has come to glorify Christ and speak of Him, it includes His assignment of building within our spirit a perfect picture of Who Jesus is, and who we now are in Him, as joint-heirs (Romans 8:17; Colossians 1:27).

Yielding ourselves to the Spirit of God while we meditate gives the Holy Spirit what He needs to bring forth this picture. This permanent fresco of Christ that He paints on the canvas of our hearts will be with us every time we decide to enter into worship. In any moment of worship, the eyes of our spirit search for an image to surrender to. If we have been meditating with the help of the Spirit, this image will stand at the forefront, and it will not be hard to find. As we worship the image of Christ in us, the hope of glory, we will soon find ourselves in the presence of God, as our souls begin to participate with expressions of joy, happiness, humility, thankfulness, and devotion.

Maybe you have seen people encounter Jesus in such a deep way through their worship that you desire to experience what they have. If this is the case, don't pray, "Oh God, let me have that." God isn't keeping it from you. He gave you the Holy Ghost. *Instead, surrender to the Spirit and let Him help you develop the image of Christ as you pray in the Spirit and meditate His Word.* Get this in place and you will have an image in you that the world can never take away. It wouldn't matter if you were thrown into prison and locked away from the rest of society. That image will always be there to bear down on whenever you want. You will be able to initiate worship at any moment, any time, in any place. What a threat you will become to the enemy when he knows that you can release the presence of God anywhere you go because you have built an image of Christ in you, with the help of the Holy Spirit. With this in place, you will be able to initiate the presence of God, on purpose, at any point of your journey. Just worship.

CHAPTER FORTY-EIGHT

The Path Leads All the Way Home

"Even Alexander the Great, in all of his splendor and opulence, cannot compare to the least of those who sit down with Christ for all the ages to come."

There is excitement that comes at the beginning of every journey. I feel this exhilaration when I am packing to go overseas for a couple of weeks, and I know that quests and adventures await. As we head out, my assistant looks over just before our plane takes off and gives me a fist pound. This is our manly way of saying, "Let's do this."

As great as this feeling is, it is not better than the feeling I get when I am getting ready to go home. Anticipation is replaced with pride, accomplishment, and the heroic feeling that sets itself in my emotions. Often during the course of our missionary travels, the desire to come home with this sense of dignity is the only thing that pushes me to go over and beyond. I want to look back and say that, although we had obstacles and hardship, we didn't stop until we achieved greatness.

The flight home is the part I look forward to the most, believe it or not. The next official fist pound will not occur until we have landed. The meaning behind it changes to: "Mission accomplished." The second fist pound always means more than the first because there is more behind it: the reflection of the journey and all the "craziness" (as my assistant would say) that presented itself to us along the way. That fist pound is an indication that we have overcome.

As Paul takes us through the believer's journey in Romans 8, he emphasized in verse 28 that if we allow the Spirit of God to accompany our reborn spirit along the way, all things are going to work together for our good. This indicates that there *will* be "craziness" along the way.

Nevertheless, we have been called *"according to His purpose,"* and the Helper is going to see to it that we accomplish that purpose totally and completely, despite all of the madness that will cross our path as we venture to step into it.

Understanding Our Purpose

> *And we know that all things work together for good to those who love God, to those who are called according to His purpose.* (Romans 8:28 NKJV)

Romans 8:28 is another one of those Scriptures used on Christian knick-knacks and in Christian greeting cards. I once got a card for high school graduation that had $10 in it. When I lifted up the cash (two five dollar bills) I saw this Scripture on the card. I thought, *Gee, I sure am glad I have the Lord to help me in college because this $10 isn't going to get me far.* Of course, there is nothing wrong with using this verse in a greeting card. However, the purpose in Romans 8:28 has a broader meaning than graduation.

"Purpose" is the Greek word *prothesis* and means "the purposes of God." It is used in other verses in the New Testament:

> *[11]In whom also we have obtained an inheritance, being predestined according to <u>the purpose of Him</u> who works all things according to the counsel of His will,*
> *[12]that we who first trusted in Christ should be to the praise of His glory.* (Ephesians 1:11-12 NKJV)

> *According to <u>the eternal purpose</u> which he accomplished in Christ Jesus our Lord.* (Ephesians 3:11 NKJV)

> *Who has saved us and called us with a holy calling, not according to our works, but according to <u>His own purpose</u> and grace which was given us in Christ Jesus before time began.* (2 Timothy 1:9 NKJV)

From these verses we see one common purpose described as *"the purpose of Him,"* *"the eternal purpose,"* and *"His own purpose."* By now it should be clear that the *purpose* is not to be a rock star or a movie director or a shark on Wall Street. The *purpose* describes one very specific thing, seen in Ephesians 1:5 (NLT): *"God decided in advance to adopt us into his own family by bringing us to himself through Jesus Christ. This is what he wanted to do, and it gave him great pleasure."*

The total purpose that God has for humankind in this age is to adopt all back into His family, through Jesus Christ. God went through great lengths to make this possible. Now it is up to us to take the journey into this purpose.

The Hidden Path

This is *"the mystery which has been hid from ages and generations, but now is made manifest to his saints"* (Colossians 1:26 KJV).

Think back to when you began the first grade, and you endured your first social studies class. From there you went on to learn US History I, US History II, World History I to IV, and Ancient History. Then, you read about wars, politics, kings, rulers, economies, architecture, culture, and philosophies. I can't count how many civilizations my education required me to study from the time I was a boy.

In all the epic tales I read and of all the facts I studied, never did I ever see a mention of God's eternal purpose. No historian ever informed me that, through all of the clashes of civilization amidst the rise and fall of kingdoms, there was a God who was absolute and complete love, working to adopt every race and generation of people back into His family.

The path was hidden. Yet, now it is no longer a mystery to the world. God has revealed His love through Jesus Christ and makes a call for the whole world to begin its journey and take the path that ends in a glorified body, ruling with Jesus.

What can compare to such a thing? Even Alexander the Great, in all of his splendor and opulence, cannot compare to the least of those who sit down with Christ for all the ages to come. If people knew that this path existed, and knew what it leads to, they would forsake all and take the journey.

What Can Stop Us?

In light of this purpose, Paul wrote in Romans 8:31 (KJV), ***"What shall we then say to these things? If God be for us, who can be against us?"*** What is there in this life that can come between your Father and you? God so eagerly wanted you as a part of His family that He came down to suffer with you and purchase you back from the Kingdom of Darkness. There is no length that Jesus will not go to get you to take this journey, and there is no length that the Holy Ghost will not go to keep you on it.

Jesus was God's ultimate sacrifice. If He paid the price for us to enter into this newness of life, what won't He do to remove any barrier that attempts to keep us from reaching our inheritance? (Romans 8:32). All things that we need to finish our course come from the Helper. He is our best friend, and the One who walks hand in hand with us on this journey. He sees everything ahead of us and will not fail to warn. He sees everything around us and will not cease to make us aware. He is all-knowing, all-powerful, always present.

We have the whole Godhead to help us along this path of transformation. Who can stop us from getting home? Satan? Principalities? Powers? Rulers? Wicked Spirits? The Law? Men? The flesh? Persecution?

> *35 **Who shall separate us from the love of Christ? Shall tribulation, or distress, or persecution, or famine, or nakedness, or peril, or sword?***
> *36 **As it is written: "For Your sake we are killed all day long; We are accounted as sheep for the slaughter."***
> *37 **Yet in all these things we are <u>more than conquerors</u> through Him who loved us.***
> *38 **For I am persuaded that neither death nor life, nor angels nor principalities nor powers, nor things present nor things to come,***

> *39nor height nor depth, nor any other created thing,*
> *shall be able to separate us from the love of God which*
> *is in Christ Jesus our Lord.* (Romans 8:35-39 NKJV)

From the moment we take the journey, we become conquerors. This was Paul's way of saying, "No matter what you face and no matter what comes your way, nothing can get you off this path, considering all that God has provided for us to make this journey. Everything we need has been freely provided. All we have to do is go." Who would know better than this decorated veteran who, despite all that hell threw at him, finished His journey by saying:

> *7I have fought a good fight, I have finished my course,*
> *I have kept the faith;*
> *8Henceforth there is laid up for me a crown of*
> *righteousness, which the Lord, the righteous judge,*
> *shall give me at that day: <u>and not to me only, but unto</u>*
> *<u>all them also that love his appearing.</u>* (2 Timothy 4:7-8
> KJV)

Make the Journey

God, who is Love, has laid out a path for all humans to travel. On every continent, in every country, in territories and states, in cities, villages, and townships: God desires every man, woman, and child to get on this path of transformation that will lead them to Him and the inheritance that awaits the Redeemed. In a world that grows madder and madder, the path becomes brighter and brighter. The Father calls you today and says, "Will you make the journey? Will you turn yourself over to my Spirit to help you walk into everything that I have laid out for those that believe?" The path is before you, leading all the way home. The Godhead awaits you. Take up the High Calling of God in Christ Jesus and make *the Believer's Journey*.

"But the path of the just is as the shining light, that shineth more and more unto the perfect day." (Proverbs 4:18 KJV)

APPENDIX I

To Make the Journey

¹³Enter ye in at the straight gate; for wide is the gate, and broad is the way, that leadeth to destruction, and many there be which go in thereat:
¹⁴Because straight is the gate, and narrow is the way, which leadeth unto life, and few there be that find it.
(Matthew 7:13-14 KJV)

If you desire to get on the path that leads to life and make the journey into God, I would like you to pray this prayer with your mouth and mean it from your heart:

God, I come before you today and I confess that I am a sinner. I was born into sin and need to be reconciled to you. I believe that you sent your Son, Jesus Christ, into the earth to die a bloody and painful death that I may be born again. He died on the cross for my sin and rose again. I place my faith and trust in Him. Jesus, I ask you to be the Savior and Lord of my life and I surrender to you. I thank you that my old nature is gone and that I have become a new creature in You. I am born from above. Satan, I renounce you and every work that you have wrought in my life. Your plan is now void. I am walking in fellowship with God, who is now my Father, and Jesus Christ who is now my Lord and brother. Amen.

Congratulations and welcome to the family. I want to encourage you to find a local church that believes in the power of the Holy Ghost and that teaches God's Word, and join with them to help you grow on your journey.

APPENDIX II

To Receive the Guide

But ye shall receive power, after that the Holy Ghost is come upon you: and ye shall be witnesses unto me both in Jerusalem, and in all Judea, and in Samaria, and unto the uttermost part of the earth. (Acts 1:8 KJV)

Just as salvation is a free gift that is available now, so too is the Baptism in the Holy Ghost. God wants you to receive this free gift today so that you can have boldness to reconcile those around you to Him. Along with this power to be a living witness of Jesus comes your prayer language. I want you to pray and ask the Lord for this gift. Jesus said:

⁷Ask, and it will be given you; seek, and you will find; knock, and it will be opened to you.
⁸For every one who asks receives; and he who seeks finds; and to him who knocks it will be opened.
(Matthew 7:7-8 NKJV)

After you pray, you will notice an unction in your belly. Connect your words to that unction and speak them forth from your lips. Don't be concerned what to say next. You will notice that when you put sound to the unction it will open up a spring of utterance, and there will be your prayer language. It may not "feel" like much (or it may). Nevertheless, you will see supernatural results as you spend time with this prayer language, allowing the Holy Ghost to guide you along this journey. Pray this prayer with your mouth and mean it from your heart:

"Father, thank You that you have provided me with the Guide, the Holy Ghost. I want Him to be my Helper and to reveal to me more of Jesus. I believe

that this baptism is for today and that I can have it now. I ask you to fully submerge me in Your Spirit and in power. Fill me with fire. Jesus, baptize me into the fullness of Your Spirit so that I can witness that You live. I yield myself totally to the Holy Ghost. I believe I receive it now, in Jesus name."

Now go ahead and open up your lips and begin speaking forth the mysteries of God that pertain to your life and godliness.

About the Author

Chris Palmer is an international teacher and preacher of God's Word. In 2009 Chris began his organization, Chris Palmer Ministries (CPM), to teach believers worldwide how to deepen their revelation of Jesus Christ through the help of the Holy Spirit. In addition to being a minister and author, Chris hosts his regular radio program "Transforming Truth," which is heard by listeners every week. Rev. Palmer resides in his home state of Michigan.

Printed in Great Britain
by Amazon.co.uk, Ltd.,
Marston Gate.